AF587877

Rasha Dakkak

Scenes From a Classroom

With the commencement of our first semester, the Sandberg Instituut sent us an email about implementing strict corona measures. Each department could schedule eight students to be present in the department-designated space at any given time. There were particular days that we could be on campus, specific time slots, and the seventeen of us could never be present at the same time.

It was a no-brainer to look for a new spot.

Durable Discussions

Lama Aloul
Saja Amro
Julina Vanille Bezold
Rasha Dakkak
Anna Celda
Farah Fayyad
Mohamed Gaber
Ayman Hassan
Siwar Kraitem
Ott Metusala
Naira Nigrelli
Karmel Sabri
Qusai Al Saify
Sarah Saleh
Mohammed Tatour
Jara van Teeffelen
Samira Vogel

essays from the Disarming Design Department

Annelys de Vet

How Do We Learn Together?

Yesterday I had a conversation in our common space with Ayman about his work. We were sitting in the blue room, where he was slowly taking apart the walls, creating a hole revealing the outside. The portal allowed daylight to finally enter this room. Each time we talk, our conversation makes me think about what we create and how we exist, and often it unsettles me. Ayman observes, he leaves traces, and in doing so questions current conditions. He mentioned how he sees me working in the institute as someone who is always punching holes in walls to find alternatives. In this sense, I embody what I feel we have been doing as a temporary department in the last two years; we have been pushing against institutional boundaries – in school, in society, and in life.

Having been the departmental head of the Design Department for a decade, I question what a disciplinary focus brings. We tend to think in discrete fields like design, art, or architecture, and struggle in actualising positions and alternatives beyond the dominant frameworks. Yet the complexity of our time requires an engagement with different material, methodological, and theoretical frameworks. Problems are layered and contextual, and might require an unsettling of the status quo. Schools are regularly shaped by their histories, and their walls aren't always facing another future. That's why it is interesting that the Sandberg Instituut initiated its Temporary Programmes; temporary departments that exist for two years, each focusing on a specific theme or urgency. It's how this institution creates change from within, by inviting temporary initiatives to be part of the school, to create new conditions for building other tomorrows.

This is how the Disarming Design Department was founded in 2020; a programme that positioned design as a cultural tool to oppose authority and create knowledge with affection, desire, and imagination. Its aim was to foster disarming ways of knowing, starting from place-based understandings and acknowledging critical pedagogy. The curriculum responded to the research and artistic work of the students. We supported collaborative educational models like student-run initiatives and workshops, experimental publishing, hybrid platforms, live radio shows, and other joint structures.

What took place in these two years came with discomfort on many levels, the pandemic and lockdown being only one of them. What was prevailing was the amount of love that was found in all aspects of making, weaving, folding, caring, cooking, celebrating, demonstrating, translating, and juxtaposing; in short, in *doing together*. We were enacting other ways of knowing and becoming. This offered perspectives in thinking about art and design as emancipatory politics, and as a practice of hope; by making what is deemed impossible possible.

Rana Ghavami

Between Two Suns Are Words That Make Your Heart Skip a Beat

The beginning is always tricky and difficult to recall, as it just happens to you. So is the ending, even though its grip on your heart has its reach. Trickery and the heart are the two coordinates for me to approximate some of my experiences and intentions that have been part of the process of writing and conversing about these texts over the course of three months, which I can only remember with bursting laughter, joy, and a lot of heat. Dear Siwar, Rasha, Gaber, Jara, Anna, Sarah, Ott, Lama, Farah, Samira, Naira, Karmel, Saja, Siko, Qusai, Julina, and Ayman, as a thank you, this last note is for you.

Let me take us from this page to a piece of paper, crumpled up at the edge of my table where I drafted an outline for our classes at the beginning of our second year, knowing really well how and by whom this outline would be read, questioned, and forgotten.

Let me read back to you parts of the prompts I have found in the folds of this paper, even though the sentences have changed and appear to be sticky, as though they were written in ink and smudged, turned into imageries, now that I have unfolded the paper and laid it out flat in front of me. Knowing that you have heard me read out loud to you one of the more humorous and surprising texts that Sherida had selected for us in her workshop on literary devices, I hope you can recall the slight trembling and insistence in my voice as you go through this note. I want my voice to speak to the situations I am about to list, as they have been formative to determining, albeit loosely, what research, writing, making, reading, waiting, eating, and spending time together means.

I was anticipating our first class, yet it felt as though the process of admissions, especially for those coming from abroad, was prolonged. The time between the files, the emails, and finally the arrival, was extended by the pandemic and the measures we had to take. The screen, the digital boards, and the PDFs – which were once procedural, mundane, and draining – had become the means with which to keep going, and even created a setting for teaching, dancing, chatting, and working.

As much as the measures were definitive, you as a group, together with the help of the school, found an alternative space for the department in the south of Amsterdam, near the RAI Convention Centre. From then on, we would meet on the second floor at FaFu, one of the last buildings left standing amidst bleak luxury loft developments. It felt close and convenient for me to have our classes there, as I knew the river near the building from my pandemic walks.

As you were making a place there in that kitchen and the blue room with a secret door in the back, desires were forged amongst the recipes, music, discussions, texts, guests, late nights, drawings, and the radio. It was in this place where recollections of lives and fractured histories were shared, and now are traced throughout these essays. Amidst the objects, dreams, places, songs, lands, and friends – the keepers and the forgers of stories across two suns – we were living with the ongoingness of fractured histories, oppression, and resistance, which culminated around the time we marched together in the streets of Amsterdam in solidarity with Palestine in May of 2021.

Having experienced all too well how the historical present between displacement and dispossession is juxtaposed and sampled, manipulated and exploited, your impulse was to collapse the multiple coordinates and distances between past struggles and current experiences, turning political statements into everyday actions. It was between two suns that you (trans)formed your education. It was in such recollections of our experiences that I outlined the prompts for the essays to come. It is you who prompts me to ask: What emerges when we place research in the poetics of the everyday, where forms are fully lived?

Radio Diasbura in Sandberg's basement K29 was the first space we shared as a department while looking for a place to settle.

Dee-yas-bura:
Diaspora, with
an accent.

Gaber [on air]:

"Diaspora has something to do with our presence here, but I get that sensation in Cairo as well."

The water for the tea is boiling, and the coffee is on the stove. In our narrow kitchen, Qusai grabbed glasses from the top of the bar to our large oval-shaped table.

A few of us have gathered around the table, anticipating the arrival of the rest of the group. Others are on the orange sofa, waiting for a sign that we're beginning.

Naira watered the plants.

Tea and coffee are ready. Our day begins with cinnamon biscuits, zaatar, which one of us brought from home, olive oil, and bread.

Who are we missing? Jara wonders, and Julina replies while looking down at her phone, checking our "no tutors" telegram group: Lama had texted that she would be eleven minutes late.

The class starts.

Finding a space for our department may seem to put our questions to rest. Fabulous Future (FaFu) was the starting point of so many collective dialogues, meetings, controversies, and arguments about how to run such a space.

How do we maintain the order of things?

How do we operate the space?

Who facilitates the payment of the rent?

Who is there first thing in the morning to open the door for our tutors?

When something goes wrong, who shows up?

When the power goes down, who is in charge of dealing with the electrician?

Objects from the adjacent antique shop flanked the space's entrance. When you walked into the studio, you'd notice a few of these old wooden objects since the neighbour would occasionally offer us a few units to help us furnish.

What can we do to save the building?

At FaFu, we found ourselves unexpectedly advocating for a cause, as members of a community, who are threatened with eviction, as the municipality of Amsterdam is planning to demolish the building within the coming year or years.

In a pot, Anna fries onions and carrots in olive oil and possibly other veggies if we have them, such as leek or parsnip. Siwar adds garlic and seasonings when it's almost done browning. Saja adds lentils and water; enough to cover the food with two fingers. She cooks them until the lentils are tender. Anna grinds coriander and parsley, and makes a mix with some garlic, salt, and olive oil in a mortar with a pestle. Siwar removes the soup from the heat and stirs in the herb-garlic mixture and a generous glug of sherry vinegar.

She yells: The soup is ready!

We'd bring out our off-white pleated tablecloth, which Anna and Ott fashioned out of leftover fabrics for special occasions, like our feedback feast or monthly dinners. The pattern – with a layer screen-printed on the cloth each time we use it – records some of our dialogues and memories, just as the fabric bears witness to our meals together.

Karmel, Mohammed,
and Sarah took turns
playing music.

- ▸ Do You Love Me – Sufian Bouhrara, Bendalys
- ▸ Forest Nativity – Francis Bebey

▸ Batnadini بتناديني – Donia Massoud

- ▸ Ouda – Hamid Al Shaeri
- ▸ Rakeek – El Waili, Zaid Khaled
- ▸ Mtaktak – Al Nather, Shabjdeed
- ▸ La Danse De Nadia – Elias Rahbani
- ▸ Asmar – Samira Tawfik
- ▸ Didi – Live A Bercy 1, 2, 3 Soleils – Khaled, Rachid Taha, Faudel
- ▸ Bass Esmae Minni – Saria Al Sawas

▸ ياريتك – أذينة العلي ◂

▸ In Ann – Daboor, Shabjdeed

اهدى
chill

ماهو كلشي باين في المحنة
because everything shows in crisis

Since residing in Amsterdam, we constantly hear about educational institutions developing diversity and inclusion policies and how they support movements such as Black Lives Matter, climate justice, and decolonisation to confront our world's injustices.

Amid a rapidly unfolding chain of events in late April and May of 2021 – protests against Israeli plans to ethnically cleanse the Palestinian neighbourhood of Sheikh Jarrah in Jerusalem, days of violent Israeli raids and hundreds of injuries at the Al-Aqsa Mosque, and a bombing campaign on the Gaza Strip – we watched our institution remain silent.

Devastation filled our hearts day in and day out as we went unrecognised by the institute that had brought us all together.

Their silence filled us with anger and frustration.

We gathered at Ayman and Samira's apartment to draft a statement.

Dear Executive Board of the Gerrit Rietveld Academie,

In light of the current international movement for the liberation of Palestine, and the historical and monumental reclamation of established discourses and narratives, we, the students of the Disarming Design Department at Sandberg Institute, find it immoral that Sandberg and Rietveld have remained publicly silent so far. You claim to teach decolonial theory and yet have failed to take even the smallest of action in solidarity with Palestine.

This year, your lack of action is more problematic than ever, given, as you have stated officially before, our department "is derived from the long-term collaboration between the Design Department and the design platform 'Disarming Design from Palestine', which is committed to design practices that deal with conditions of conflict, oppressive forces and entangled histories."

We ask you to condemn the settler-colonial genocidal entity that is the "state of Israel", that is committing crimes against humanity, ethnic cleansing, and human rights violations as we speak. There can be no neutral position today. It is very simple. Silence aligns you with the oppressor.

We demand your immediate action through a public statement on all social media platforms and the institutions' websites at the very least. Decolonial theory is nothing without decolonial practice.

Sincerely,
The students of Disarming Design

Lama Aloul, Saja Amro, Julina Vanille Bezold, Rasha Dakkak, Farah Fayyad, Mohamed Gaber, Anna Celda, Ayman Hassan, Siwar Kraitem, Ott Metusala, Naira Nigrelli, Karmel Sabri, Qusai Al Saify, Sarah Saleh, Mohammed Tatour, Jara van Teeffelen, Samira Vogel

The statement was insufficient. To make our case more persuasive, we needed to prepare a presentation for the board of directors on the role of academic and cultural institutions in supporting their students during times of crisis, along with case studies on the involvement of Dutch educational institutions in opposing Apartheid in South Africa.

We would continue to meet at the apartment for a month, either before or after a protest, as Ayman and Samira were the ones who lived closest to Dam Square, where the demonstrations in Amsterdam would take place. We'd take turns carrying the three fabric banners we stenciled in Lifta, an open-source typeface by Palestinian designer Omaima Dajani.

"فلسطين"
"FREE PALESTINE"

Catalysed by Diwan's* invitation that Rana extended to us, we offered to hold a talk on institutional solidarity in our space.

With Agustina's soft spot for radio and connectivity, she suggested using Radio Diasbura to broadcast to a wider network of allies.

Together, Rana, Rasha, Farah, and Ayman prepared the following script for the radio show.

* A platform co-initiated by Fadwa Naamna, Hilda Moucharrafieh, Ehsan Fardjadniya, Margarita Osipian, Emirhakin, and that works in collaboration with the W139 artistic core group (2021–2023).

(10 minutes)
Introduction hosts Diwan + context of the conversation

(15 minutes) Question 1

Defining solidarity

- The meaning of Free Palestine
- Reclaiming the narrative
- Call to action and active social change

(40 minutes) Question 2

In the context of art education and institutions in the Netherlands

- Sharing our experience / conversation with the board (of the institution)
- Board's hesitations and concerns: multiplicity of voices and positions within the schools, unpacking hesitation and concerns of board and others alike.
- In parallel: values of the institution and claim to human rights
- Calling out for solidarity is not a call to polarise or dismiss

(25 minutes) Question 3

Failure of the institution

- How is the call for solidarity delayed / refused / dismissed?
- Experiences of various guests
- What has worked / has been working for us so far?
- Intersectional approach to solidarity

(15 minutes) Question 4

What's next? From institutional critique to institutional building

- Cultural boycott (examples of divestment projects)
- Beyond the statement

(10 minutes) Q&A

To disarm:
to take a weapon away
to deprive of means, reason, or disposition to be hostile
to make harmless
to win over

I still remember the moment when we were all, momentarily, aligned. We, the seventeen of us, wanted a new name.

When something is disarming, it calms hostility. Whose hostility is evoked in naming this department, Disarming Design?

The term 'disarming' was questioned in our ongoing discussions due to its misleading connotations with the Arabic-speaking world, from which eleven of us hail; it seemed to exoticise, conjuring up images of hostility, rage, and suspicion. It was hard to overlook the setting in which we operate and how the act of arming or disarming might frame us.

It was also obscure whether we were learning to unarm design. Are we disarming design broadly speaking, or just a specific design discourse and practice? Are we here to be unarmed by design? Is it the idea to be disarmed by a particular school of thought? Or should design be disarming?

We also grappled with the act of naming. The requirement for a fixed name to ensure and validate the department's uniqueness, transforming it into something verging on the monumental.

We opted for the initials DD after two years of deliberation, negotiation, and sometimes acceptance, acknowledging a lineage of lengthier conversations that emerged when naming events occurred during our time at Disarming Design, such as Diasbura Radio and Disclosing Discomfort, the title of an exhibition we held at Mediamatic in Amsterdam in November 2021.

We felt a sense in what began as a pun, where we can interpret DD according to media and outlets.

In a call with Yazan, he unveiled another facet of this naming strategy, listing corporations that have sidelined their names in favour of initials, such as BP, KFC, etc. They undergo such rebranding that is diametrically opposed to their past in an effort to conceal their histories.

Another case in point is the IDF, which has been called into question since the IOF may be a better reflection of how Israel has abandoned its ‘defensive’ military tactics in favour of an ‘offensive’ one.

The extensive list of possible DD translations accentuates this point: meanings shift, allowing each of us some leeway in reading these two years as we see fit. It permits all to input their views:

Disclosing Discomforts
Design Department
Desired Discipline
Decentralised Depictions
Developing Discrepancy
Denying Definitions
Disassembling Details
Daily Decisions
Dismantling Discourses
Doubting Data
Double Displacement
Disorganised Drama
Daring Dance
Dazzling Days
Diaspora Dialogues
Decolonising Decolonisation
Dutch Design
Dodging Dogma
Depth Dwellers
Distance Decay
Dramatic Dinosaurs
Dear Deviants
Devoted Devices
Detailed Detours
Damned Dadaism
Deployed Desires
Divine Dialects
Direct Development
Decentralising Decisions
Done Deal
Divergent Demonstration

Distorted Discourses
Demanded Discourses
Distant Departure
Dramatic Difference
Dissemination Dreams
Diving Deep
Deadly Discussions
Discursive Discourse
Disobedient Devices
Dirty Dicks
Different Disappointments
Debating Design
Distressful Disorders
Distinctive Distress
Dominant Disputes
Despite Division
Darkness Descending
Double Dilemma
Definite Demands
Debatable Discussable
Deepest Desires
Doubling Down
Dumb Deadlines
Decent Drafts
Desirable Delights
Delicious Dough
Delectable Dates
Digesting Delights
Diasbura Delights
:D:D
Durable Discussions

Mohammed Tatour

The Closest Thing to Home is the Supermarket

SEPTEMBER 2020

We arrived in Amsterdam from Jerusalem. My partner and I put the luggage in our new home and we naturally moved on to the next task; filling our empty fridge with food. In searching for a supermarket, the first place we managed to find was 'Albert Heijn'; a mainstream supermarket chain. Good lighting means a customer will stay in a shop longer and potentially purchase more – this didn't work for us! Not only that, the language barrier made us feel a bit undesirable while scanning the labels of the products through Google Translate from Dutch to Arabic to find products familiar to our taste. The minimal design and typography and the ever-present Albert Heijn logo confused me. Perhaps my eyes are used to seeing food as a form of hospitality. Or perhaps my perception of taste is informed by overly-detailed and ornate design. Am I buying a loaf of bread or an iPhone? As we proceeded to look for the most essential ingredient, olive oil, I approached a Moroccan employee and asked him for a recommendation. He smiled and candidly replied: "If you want taste, then you should go to the Turkish place in front, that's where I get my groceries… ".

The Turkish place in front is not even on Google Maps, but both of us instinctively recognised the store by how the vegetables and fruit were arranged outside. Hospitality: a watermelon with a knife next to it. A real sense of belonging.

This small lead and friendly face guided me to find the comfort I needed in a foreign context.

DECEMBER 2021

COVID-19 is here to stay; one year later I still see the same scenes. There has been no development in this regard and it feels to me like a copy-paste. A repetition of what it felt like when we first arrived; in a lockdown, with supermarkets as the only places that are still open. Loss of taste is a possible symptom of COVID-19, but this is not what my story is pushing to tell, it's the relation between us and taste, to the core.

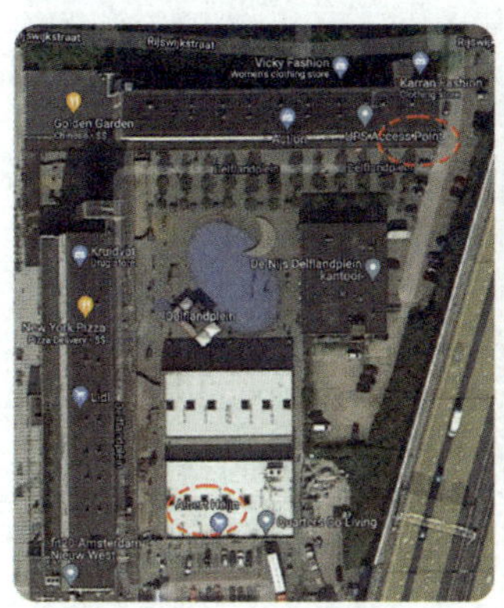

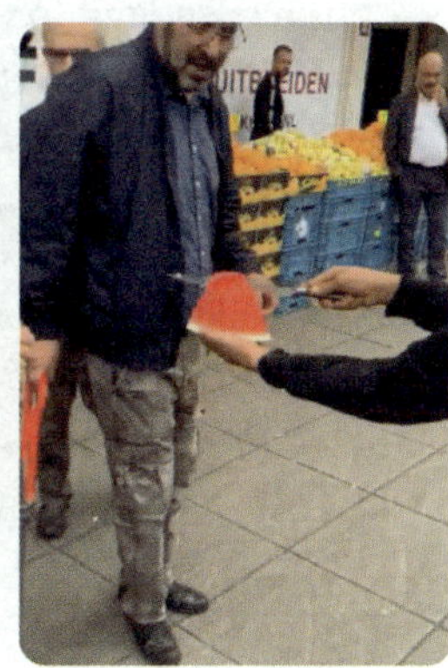

WHEN STATELESS MEETS TASTELESS

Even if you don't know how to cook, food is part of your interiority and emotional world, and a means to survive. As a Palestinian from a family of lower socio-economic privilege, born and raised in Occupied Palestine, my relation to food and identity is confronted by multi-layered conflicts, forces, and realities. Working in the kitchen of an Israeli-owned bar or restaurant is one of the more accessible ways of earning a living – even though survival in this context means making barely enough income to make it to the end of the month. Our Israeli colonisers know it is us, the Palestinians, who have good taste, and who are the most in need of income.

When your whole neighbourhood works at a restaurant, you can develop a career as a cook with little prior experience. I had to help my family take care of expenses, which was a justification for me to start working at the age of sixteen while doing my finals in high school. I started off as a dishwasher in a restaurant, earning little money – but just enough for this age. From dishwashing to line-cook, I started making small dishes that Israeli colonisers marketed as their own, preparing those dishes while laughing at our own stolen reality. The menu included Arabic cheese, which cost five Shekels at the market but was priced at thirty-five Shekels or more; Arabic Salad, which was renamed Israeli Salad; and other foods that have come to be stolen. When you are born into a working-class family there's no way back, and structurally – I mean, the Israeli colonisers have planned very well that – you remain that way until the day you die, fact. Long shifts every day, and you start becoming very professional in half a year, that's what happened to me, but also the kitchen is where our colonisers kind of trust us the most. The Palestinian-run kitchen transforms into a place of 'importance', where you are on top of the world, but the moment you step outside, you become just another Arab.

And sometimes I hate it when it feels like I'm barking up the wrong tree. Most of the time I feel that I'm all the trees when I have difficulty identifying, describing, and expressing emotions or micro-scenes. An interview with Vivien Sansour, a Palestinian artist, by Jennifer Higgie, an Australian novelist, reminded me of the complexity of sharing our relation to food in a foreign context.

It's just an article, but to me, it's also an ongoing scene happening around the world. The interview begins like this, as Jennifer asks Vivien: "What was your favourite food?"

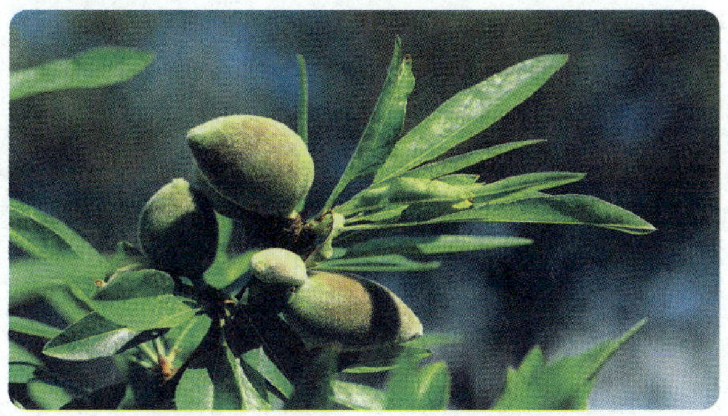

Vivien replies "Green almonds; we ate them with salt. People sold them on the street but, as kids, we were always attacking somebody's tree for them, and getting shouted at. But I also like almonds in their middle stage, when they're kind of between a nut and a fruit." Jennifer replies: "Do you know, I had no idea about the different stages of almonds. I've only ever eaten them from a packet."[1]

The house I grew up in is on El Karmel mountain (جبل الكرمل) in the small neighbourhood of Kababir. We had a balcony and under it a lot of trees. One of the trees close to the balcony was a very tall almond tree. When we were young, we used to pick green almonds effortlessly and eat them in between meals until my mother came home from work.

1 "Writer and Activist Vivien Sansour on Food, Farming, Heritage and Healing," interview by Jennifer Higgie, *Frieze*, August 19, 2019, www.frieze.com/article/writer-and-activist-vivien-sansour-food-farming-heritage-and-healing.

PACKED HOME البيت معلب

A five-minute walk from my new apartment in Amsterdam, I discover SuperMaroc, and the first Bled (Arabic بِلَاد (bilād)) on a jar of olives, which means home, city, and country. In the busy aisle of olives, the word that translates to 'home' called me; it was like being in front of a Jerusalemite supermarket.

It was not
the
thinking brain,

it was the
welcoming
words.

'Classical conditioning theory' (also known as Pavlovian or respondent conditioning), first studied by Russian physiologist Ivan Pavlov, is a behavioural procedure in which a biologically potent stimulus (e.g. food) is paired with a previously neutral stimulus. I as a consumer am subjected to packages as stimuli. Stimuli, in the case of Bled products, are heavily cultured to affect the subject's response to nostalgia and to trigger a desired behaviour. Packaging touches bodies intimately and directly. Packaging affects the emotions, sentiments, and passions of displaced communities and their basic need for familiar foods. In further investigation of this specific product and many other similar products, I discovered the manufacturers are designing products specifically for the purpose of selling to Arab consumers in the EU.

A particular smell makes us unknowingly re-enter a space completely forgotten by the retinal memory; the nostrils awaken a forgotten image, and we are tempted to enter a vivid daydream. The nose makes the eyes remember.[2]

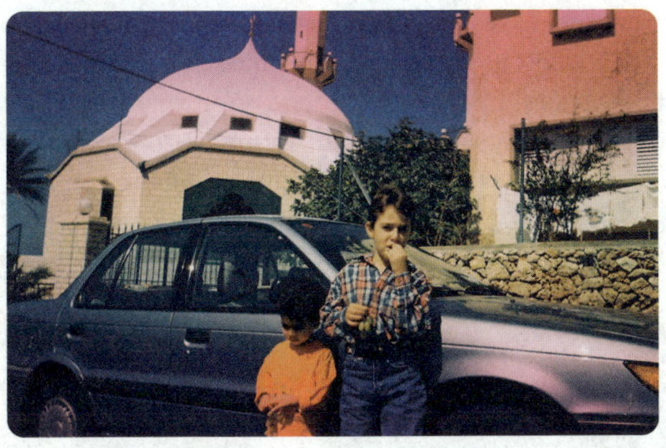

In Pavlov's theory and Juhani's quoted above, the mind connects the nose with the eyes, rebuilding displaced sentiments. It keeps the space and taste close to your heart, healing trauma through creating a remembered home, a different landscape. This constant resistance leads immigrants to a lifestyle they lived back home, just in a different geography, and keeps integration as a colonial process to 'civilise' communities.

2 Juhani Pallasmaa, *The Eyes of the Skin: Architecture and the Senses* (Chichester: John Wiley & Sons, 2005) 54.

The current industrial mass production of visual imagery tends to alienate vision from emotional involvement and identification and to turn imagery into a mesmerizing flow without focus or participation.[3]

Over the passing years, I've kept a folder on my computer called 'scanned', where I would keep references of packages that had caught my emotions. I would buy and bring these products home to study their design, for my gratification, for my soul. Amongst the many files is a scan of the packaging of Rambo chips.

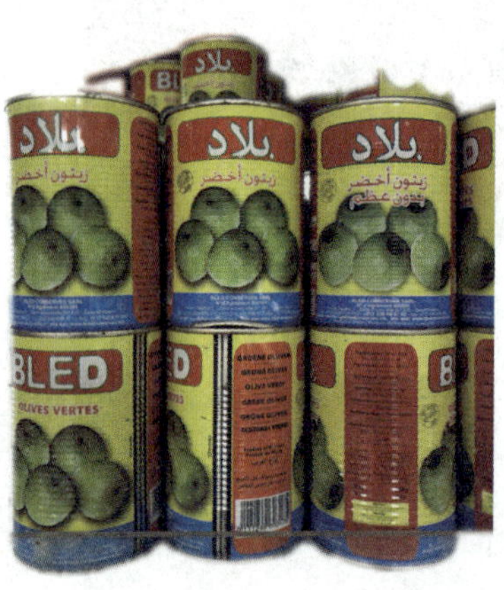

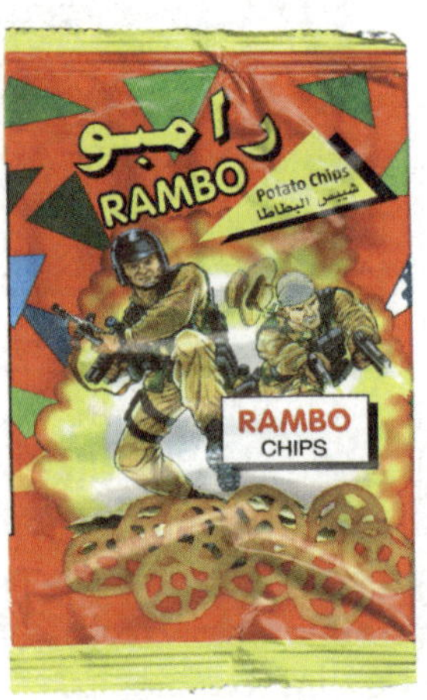

3 Pallasmaa, *The Eyes of the Skin*, 22.

CIRCLES OF COLOURS

The similarity between that scan and the graphics of the olive jar become so clear when looking at the colour combinations, which are possessed first by our landscape, our food second, our homes third. They appear in this order because it's a colour journey on the road of life. Maybe I'm not a colour specialist, but let me tell you that my mother is. Her living room environment includes a million shades of *brown;* woody brown; soil brown; earth brown; cheap brown, too; plastic brown. Some of these colours do not exist outside, but in her living room are present as aged patterns of persistence. Every object talks to the other as though all of them were made in the same factory, or by the same brand. While mesmerised looking at objects or furniture, you recognise the cheapness, a taste that you can't argue with, but live with. With time you study visuals most of the time, and you start seeing the make-up of this taste, which your mother inherited from her mother, and you, by investigating it, and without changing anything, proudly inherit too.

Reds; passion, my favourite colour. If my writing makes you somehow hungry, so does red, which is the most luxurious dish for me. Bandoura Baladeye (literally, real farm tomato), strawberries from Gaza that my sister brought with her from Jenin, or cherry and apple from El Golan, or fake Persian carpets with dominant red, but most noticed is Khat Ahmar (literally, red line), blood, or Latinised packages or billboards you will see walking in the streets.

Greens; plenty of trees (not the ones that originated in Europe). Green is where you celebrate olive trees as part of your legacy in elementary school, planning a day for it, singing for it, plenty of dishes made of it, way before hugging trees, my neighbourhood is known not only for olive trees but actually more for carob trees, and it specialises in one dessert called Qras Be Kharob, which they make from carob syrup over the whole day on firewood, and the neighbourhood comes with circle-shaped dough, and throws it inside a big metal barrel, and the taste here I can't really write about or describe; mysticism.

On the other hand, you have this, which later in my life formed me to comprehend and pay attention, but I don't want to elaborate more on it. It will ruin my whole enjoyment of writing, and our journey here. I would like to leave here quotes that conclude decades of Israeli colonisation:

> *The native olive, carob, and pistachio trees are therefore uprooted in favor of European conifers and eucalyptus.*
>
> *These trees are not adapted to the Palestinian [climate]; they are unable to absorb the sunlight and actually contribute to global warming.*[4]

Yellows; sun for everybody, except zionists;

> *How canst thou ever see red, green, and blue*
> *If thou dost not see the light before the hue?*
> *When thy mind is in all colors lost*
> *All colors veil the light from thy sight*[5]

This light, which may manifest as yellow, golden, or white, connects the heavenly world with the terrestrial. In the previously mentioned

4 Sami Erchoff, "'Green Zionism' Buries Palestinian Memory Through Forestation," Inside Arabia, October 2, 2021, insidearabia.com/green-zionism-buries-palestinian-memory-through-forestation.

5 Rumi, thirteenth-century Persian poet.

packages, the designers used yellow to connect the typography and images by using it as background. And we notice the images are not complete; it's a cut from Morocco, in the Bled olives package we can see only the olives without the rest of the landscape, as though the jar is encouraging the mind to complete the image itself.

There are circles of thoughts that I can't ignore after this chapter, and that I would like to include: circles of history, circles of confusion that will maybe take us nowhere. Most of the time, in our current capitalist world, stereotypical representations make a product expand more easily. Dubai is always linked to jewellery stores. Camels, bedouins, and palm trees are straightforward parts of Arabic food or drinks packaging. The graphics on these packages always make me think about how western aesthetics influence the graphic designers of these products, how their references come together. For instance, including colours of our landscape, an American character meets Arabic typography. The market right now is at its peak in Latinisation. Cinema, news, books, paintings of misconceptions. On the other hand, the graphics on these products (which, in design education, are dismissed as 'low graphics') appear just the way that we have been taught. Graphic design students are taught to disregard 'low graphics' as opposed to 'good' design, or what 'the foreign embassy of graphic design' would like students to carry out in the 'real' world, so the streets are Latinised and the education is too, or at least it depends where geographically we speak of.

I barely know how graphic design education goes in other Arab countries. In my case, everything is colonised, including education, and big identity crises come with it all as one package. Juhani's book also took me to the switch that happened in the last decade around us, and through our own visual making, with big credit to the internet. Juhani's book also took me to the switch that happened in the last decade around us, and through our own visual making, with big credit to the internet, which "alienate[s] vision from emotional involvement and identification ...". Identification becomes more complex with modern technology and capitalism, but by choosing emotional involvement, and nostalgia with it, 'low graphics' became 'good graphics', more welcomed. Not everything is meant for the design awards, sometimes low graphics welcome more emotional involvement and identification than the 'good graphics'. Low graphics can take the viewers to a deep emotional state and induce nostalgia. Low graphics can take us back in time and place.

SPACE MAKING = SACRED SPACE

Grocery shopping, a most mundane and taken-for-granted activity, is practised by immigrants with an awareness of socio-cultural meaning. The social use of ethnic shopping spaces indicates that immigrants are not only consumers in ethnic shopping places but co-actors in producing the unique ethnic retail environment. Culturally distinct shopping places can be easily distinguished from mainstream ones by the ethnicity of owners, employees, and consumers, as well as their signage, indoor decor, background music, product offer, and service languages used.

The feel of fitting in, when I visit *SuperMaroc*, starts already when I enter. Amsterdam becomes two volumes. The smell of the seasoning bags, all kinds and each labelled in Arabic, calls me. In the other corner I hear employees of the vegetables and fruits department chatting in Moroccan accents, with every client entering the space from outside, about the mint they succeed in importing from Morocco. They start explaining the differences, how the leaves are bigger and the taste is different, and for me it is stunning; it's only mint! The same with olives, again you have the ones that are pre-packed, but you can also choose to fill a bag with the ones homemade in Morocco.

Sometimes, I find that it's only the mingling between consumers or employees that makes you feel like you almost found something so important. Are you going to cook a three Michelin star dish? No, it's just the thrill of finding things that are going to help you re-imagine.

Wherever in the world we go, we take our food with us; through research, I found an engaging article called "Cultural and Social Influences on Food Consumption in Dutch Residents of Turkish and Moroccan Origin: A Qualitative Study".[6] Through reading, quotes taken from the groups included in the study brought to my awareness the fact that despite the growth of ethnic shopping spaces, there is still a shortage in taste; the ones that ethnic consumers can not give up on.

> *My father always brings 50–60 liters of olive oil back from Morocco each year, and sugar, onions, all the things he likes and that taste different here. He wants the authentic flavour.*

6 Mary Nicolau et al., "Cultural and social influences on food consumption in dutch residents of Turkish and Moroccan origin: a qualitative study," *Journal of Nutrition Education and Behavior* 41, no. 4 (Summer 2009): 232–241.

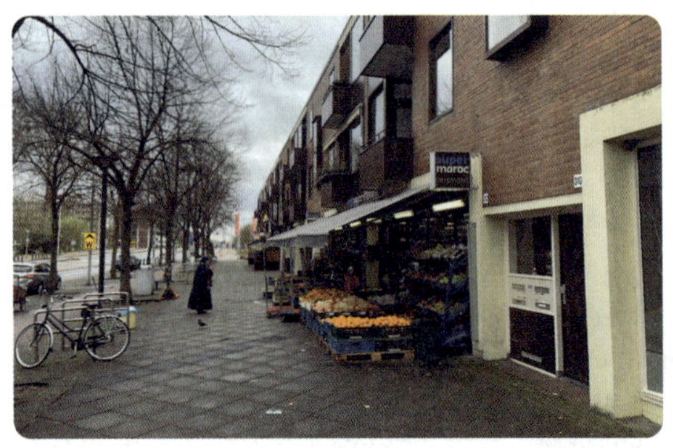

I bring olive oil with me every year. In my village, they have the most delicious olive oil.

And the search for good olive oil remains. If we can't find it we bring it with us from back home, a taste you appreciate only when it's missing, the value of which grows with relocation.

I never thought about the importance of food until I relocated, it's new to me. Via this research and experience, I tried to understand that feeling. The research above proves that more communities share the same experience.

COMPETING MAINSTREAM SUPERMARKET CHAINS

Albert Heijn comprehended and noticed the fast growth of ethnic shopping spaces, leading them to include a tiny section in their supermarkets that offers 'exotic' food: tahini, walnuts, peanuts, dried fruit, halal meat, etc.

The traditional neoclassical economic approach has not put culture into the equation of consumption.[7]

The current cultural interpretations of consumption emphasizing meanings, identity, and representations include little on the convergence of economy and culture in practice.[8]

Ethnic shopping spaces, with their particular cultural ambiance and product mix, may communicate strong and sophisticated cultural messages to individuals from (the same) ethnic communities.

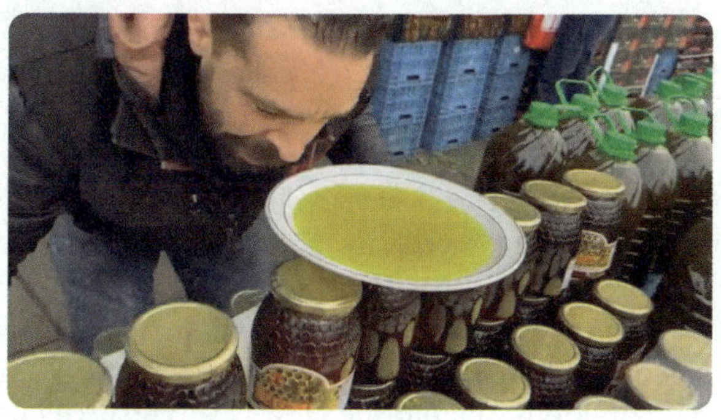

Through shopping practices, such as socialising and interacting with coethnics, minority consumers may become co-actors in producing a unique ethnic retail environment. Ethnic identity may play a

7 Trevor Barnes, "Culture: Economy," in *Spaces of Geographical Thought: Deconstructing Human Geography's Binaries*, eds. Paul Cloke and Ron Johnston (London: SAGE Publications Ltd, 2005), 61–80.

8 Peter Jackson, "Commercial Cultures: Transcending the Cultural and the Economic," *Progress in Human Geography* 26, no. 1 (February 2002): 3–18.

critical role in an immigrant's choice between ethnic shopping venues and mainstream ones. Given the different location-patterns of racial and mainstream shopping sites, any spatial choice of an immigrant consumer may be the result of an interplay between accessibility and ethnic identity.

More than five countries are mentioned while one of the employees of Supermarket Yakhlaf, in viral TikTok and YouTube videos, calls out where each fruit or vegetable is coming from: Spain, Italy, different countries in North Africa. The joy, the different calls for the skilled ability to import products, is different to me; I've never seen it before. Back home, once in a while, when local supermarkets imported some unique snack from the US or Europe, we knew about it and paid less attention to it. In Supermarket Yakhlaf chains, located in different locations around Amsterdam, it's like winning a cup performance to strong ethnic identifiers, who are more influenced by targeted media that use their language and cultural symbols, and they are more likely to consume culturally-specific products. Every product has been celebrated differently, in three different languages, too; opening a fruit or vegetable can happen in Dutch or Spanish; trying the watermelon with the rest of the pedestrians in Moroccan; sniffing the olive oil and deciding only from the smell the quality of it. It keeps on display how valuable it is to visit this sacred space.

These videos are a new level of constant resistance. It's here to stay and even to witness the growth of it, to be a part of it, even to contribute a warm beautiful colour to the grey, and to flatten the idea that all of this is contamination.

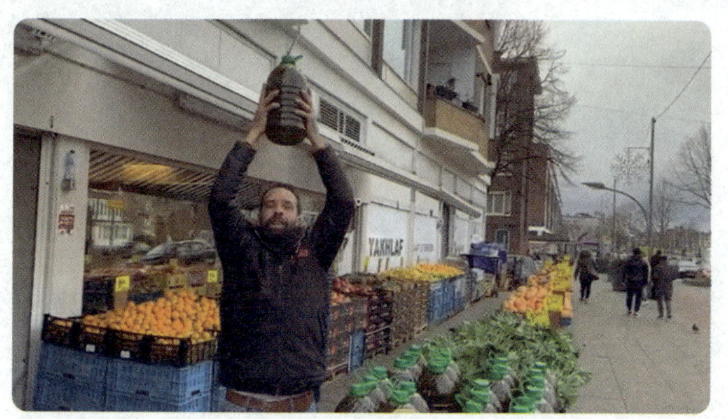
YAKHLAF

Rasha Dakkak

Sifting Through Design Memory

A word, a text,
together with two objects,
I hold them in my chest.

Impressions accumulate, and one story provokes another, feeding into each other and out again, forming a kaleidoscopic memoir of being in multiple worlds and presenting queries that alter through contemplation, finding, or perception. The text perhaps has one primary subject, yet it has a prismatic effect, introducing others; characters, influences, timelines, geographies, and systems.

لعنة جارية[1]

‹ *THE STICKER* ›

We gathered at the break of dawn. Everyone pitched in to help with preparations, as we always do, through thick and thin. Despite overwhelming sentiments, we had several tasks to complete. I took the responsibility of purchasing the Qurans and designing the sticker that goes inside to distribute them to those attending the funeral. It seemed to be the kind of task I could handle. That it was. My uncle suggested that I go to *Dar Al-Hedaya*, a street store in my aunt's neighborhood that he had learned about from a friend. They print those stickers and place them, he said.

To design the sticker, I looked around our house for examples of stickers in Qurans, as we had some from past funerals we had attended over the years. I was inspired by what was written on them but couldn't connect with their overwhelming aesthetics and visual rhetoric.

1 A curse that never ceases.

In commemoration of my grandfather, I added a Quran verse, probably the most frequently quoted one about death. Another sentence set in smaller type size stated that this is a *Sadaqa Jariyah*,[2] a perpetual charity and tribute to my grandfather that asks whoever holds this book to pray for him. Yesterday's date, the day he passed away. And lastly, a slim black frame.

My cousin drove me to the shop our uncle had recommended to us. One usually enters a store like *Dar Al-Hedaya* in search of something particular. Books and educational CDs on religious topics arranged by theme, prayer beads sorted by length and color, prayer mats piled in a corner, and a middle-aged man behind his computer.

I placed an order for 200 Qurans that included the sticker. The man shook his head left and right in slow succession as he opened the ready-to-print file I had shared. He was visibly distressed that I had used a single font for all of the body text. He sought to convince me to increase the size of the type, particularly the sentences set in 11.5 pt.

"Can we please just print this design?"
"I know very well what I'm doing," I concluded, consciously refraining from saying anything else.

I was pleased with my small contribution to my grandfather's funeral. As the printer warmed up, I strolled around the shop, waiting for my order. I pondered about the man's contribution, and the likely outcome if he were in charge.

2 *Sadaqah Jariyah* is a charity that continues to benefit people long-term and continues to earn the giver rewards, even after death.

A fondness for excess is a recurring feature of the individuals he represented to me, mashing together different visual elements. Perhaps he would have used some textured gradients in the background, or a backdrop with an opaque image of the Kaaba. And a plethora of fonts rendering each sentence distinctively, disregarding typographic standards, such as using a smaller number of fonts to convey a message. A calligraphic font to imbue the Quran verse with instant veneration. A bold font to write down the name of the deceased. Perhaps it's outlined, or it has a drop shadow. Set in burgundy, blue, black, green, gradients, all at once. And, naturally, an ornamented frame that I thought was no longer the expression of our culture to encompass all of these elements.

As I waited, I thought about this man that portrayed the 'uneducated'. Ones who lacked formal schooling and created small-scale yet widely disseminated aesthetics. I worried how those with little or no formal education affected visual literacy. The aesthetics generated by these individuals were agonizing to a so-called 'educated' person.

Although this man worked with what I recognised as elements of design, I would never have referred to him as a professional designer.

As a child of accredited universities and international design schools, I inherited my association with 'good design': the aesthetic dictatorship, the anti-ornament mentality, and the notion that there are criteria for knowing that the man at *Dar Al-Hedaya* did not meet. This man, who has most certainly learned a great deal by living and doing, is continually discredited by cultural hegemony simply because he has not adhered to the knowledge-norms taught at institutions.

Munir Fasheh also captures this in his anecdote about how, after reaching the pinnacle of his teaching career, he recognized that his uneducated mother would apply mathematics in ways he couldn't understand or perform.

> *Math was necessary for my mother in a much more profound and real sense than it was for me. Unable to read or write, my mother routinely took rectangles of fabric and, with few measurements (using chalk), cut them and turned them into beautiful, perfectly fitted clothing for people. In 1976 I realized that the math she was using was beyond my comprehension. Moreover, although math was a subject matter that I studied and taught, for her it was basic to the operation of her understanding. What she was doing was math, in the sense that it embodied order, pattern, and relations. It was math because she was breaking a whole into smaller parts and constructing a new whole out of the pieces, a new whole that had its own style, shape, and size, and that had to fit a specific person.*[3]

Our inclination for experience over abstract forms of reasoning can foster the development of more emotional and embodied forms of knowledge. Dipesh Chakrabarty refers to this as a performative understanding of citizenship. Chakrabarty argues, in an article[4] on the relationship between democracy, education, and museums,

3 Munir Fasheh, "Community Education: To Reclaim and Transform What Has Been Made Invisible," New Alphabet School, August 25, 2021, newalphabetschool.hkw.de/community-education-to-reclaim-and-transform-what-has-been-made-invisible/.

4 Dipesh Chakrabarty, "Museums in Late Democracies," *Humanities Research* 9, no.1 (January 2009), 5–12.

that having access to democracy was regarded as a pedagogical understanding of citizenship, based on the presumption that people were not born with privileges but earned them through formal education systems.

When they elevate information and analytical processes over the embodied and lived, enabling the brain to take precedence over the senses, these formal education systems cultivate individuals to compare and assess one another.

Despite the rise of a performative understanding, these retellings mirror a state of collective hypnosis, as we still associate learning with the completion of advanced formal education and the meeting of specified criteria, confining learning to the dissemination of predefined knowledge.

رحلة على بساط[5]

‹ *THE PRAYER MAT* ›

I had the idea to design a prayer mat a few years ago.

We always had several prayer mats in our house. We had more than five mats, even though we are a family of five. On their pilgrimage to Mecca, my parents would purchase new ones. We sometimes received some as a present, usually accompanied with Zamzam water, from a family member or a work colleague who had recently returned from Mecca.

I proposed a project titled *Reinterpreting Ritual Aesthetics* for my master's thesis at the Basel School of Design in Switzerland. I wanted to take the time I had in Basel to study how this object had evolved

5 A journey on a rug.

historically and to consider the formation of its aesthetics. Due to commodity culture, the prayer mat became an essential part of Salāh, but I found it hard to bond with at times. The recurring motifs gave me the sensation that we were constrained to them. I thought about how we perceive our visual inheritance and how we react to it. I thought about how maintaining consistency or adhering to a particular aesthetic has advantages. I thought about how, over time, visual reproduction, along with an excess of devotion to what we acquired over the years, turned this inheritance into lifeless cliches.

I commenced the project by traveling to Abu Dhabi for two weeks, where I photographed fifty-two prayer mats, creating a small collection of photographs that I always referred to while working. After conducting research, analyzing images, and reading about the subject, I observed that one of the most distinct visual attributes of the prayer mat is that it is unidirectional rather than symmetrical, pointing the way toward a distant sacred. The motifs that appear on it repeatedly accentuate the top and bottom of the mat. This knowledge was my starting point. The question was, what visual clues could I use to communicate this sense of direction while still relating to the object's origin and purpose?

In Basel, I presented my research and some design ideas to an audience that was mostly unfamiliar with the object. One of the proposals had a calligraphic image-text used to induce contemplation – by shifting across semiotic registers – and to challenge an old opposition to using lettering as a motif. I had chosen two verbs; the one at the bottom morphed into the one at the top. The morphing repeated five times to reflect prayer times throughout the day. While Salāh translates to prayer, Falāh is the Arabic word for success, and is defined religiously as the triumph in obtaining eternal, blissful life. To display the two verbs, I chose square Kufic, characterized by its clean, straight lines, angularity, and apparent rhythm.

As I shared this proposal during my class presentations, I was often asked how my efforts to "reduce to the essentials" represented the culture from which this object originated. It constantly felt like an implicit assumption that I was viewing this object from a western gaze or that such an object should always celebrate ornament. I recognized the casual nature with which my audience threw around some hypotheses. My proposal differed from the oriental rug they knew. It bore no resemblance to the ones they have access to in the nearest Persian store or the ones depicted in European paintings such as Hans Holbein the Younger's *The Ambassadors*, Jan van Eyck's *Lucca Madonna*, and Jean-Leon Gerome's *The Carpet Merchant*. It had nothing to do with the packaging of dates and henna goods, most likely from the same region. It felt as though particular individuals possessed particular aesthetics while others did not.

The previous designers of the mats, I believed, had provided matching principles.

The dimensions of the prayer mat were calculated with a prostrate kneeling figure in mind. The Mihrab or prayer niche is a semi-circular niche in a mosque's wall and an architectural element that is a prevalent icon on prayer mats. This form is also prevalent in various architectural traditions: the apse of churches, the ark of synagogues, and the throne niche of palaces –among others – are all possible origins of the Mihrab. When deposited within the Islamic architectural and cultural context, the form acquired new functions. During the reign of the Ummayyad caliph Al-Walid

Ibn Abd Al-Malik,[6] the Mihrab or prayer niche – either flat or concave – was first introduced as Qibla's marker or idiom, to give the illusion of directionality in mosques. When concave, it also served as an architectural acoustic device. The Mihrab supports the mat's most distinguishing feature in that it is unidirectional rather than symmetrical, with a clear top and bottom. The inclusion of it permits the object to act as a portable mosque. Once seen as a metaphor depicting a transition from the earthly to the celestial world, this aesthetic component provides an outlet for the systematic organization of sense experience, establishing its political role.

In a world where everything, even a cell, is a migrant, is there a singular home for a principle like "reducing to the essentials"? How did it become so simple to declare specific notions?

Growing up, I was captivated with ideas like repurposing objects and striving for less. Every summer when I visited Aleppo, I marveled at my grandmother's miraculous ability to change the fates of objects, granting them a second path and purpose. I don't recall her tossing anything out. And when I was fourteen, I was exposed to verses from Abu al-Atãhiyah's ascetic poetry as well as Zuhd teachings.

رغيف خبز يابس ... تأكله في زاويه
وكوز ماء بارد ... تشربهُ من صافيه
وغرفة ضيّقه ... نفسك فيها خاليه
معتبرًا بمن مضى ... من القرون الخالية
خيرٌ من الساعات في ... في القصور العاليه[7]

6 An Ummayad Caliph who ruled from 705 until 715.

7 A poem by Abu al-Atahiyah (748–828). Abu al-Atahiyah was among the principal Arab poets of the early Islamic era.

It's likely that my admiration for simplification began earlier as a reaction to the homes I grew up in, where it seemed that furniture and other objects of use and decoration didn't have to pass any criteria before being admitted into our living room. On the table in the center of the room sat a bright blue marble planter and a plant with pinkish glass petals and pebbles instead of sand. White crochet swans with red beaks danced around the artificial plant. In the corner of the room sat a Chinese four-panel black lacquer room divider depicting another 'natural' scene with trees, plants, and birds. The Chinese room divider obstructed the route between the dining table and the kitchen since it blocked the door behind it. Why did it sit there, hindering space rather than helping to create it? It has always perplexed me.

الطريق إلى بداية[8]

‹ *RHETORIC OF THE IMAGE BY ROLAND BARTHES* ›

Classroom I:
There were olive trees, citrus groves, and almond orchards. The posters depicted a land with no people, a vacant paradise with fine green hills, to entice the onlookers to emigrate. The next slide showed nicely composed black-and-white photographs of individuals in motion. Their bodies appeared exhausted, and their faces showed a range of melancholy expressions. They dragged themselves along a seemingly never-ending trail. Another slide depicted militants carrying rifles while wearing a scarf, a keffiyeh, to conceal their faces and identities, a furious Palestinian liberation movement.

8 The path to a beginning.

Then there was a portrait of the late Palestinian president Yasser Arafat, rocking his keffiyeh as he shortly became the one face that represented the Palestinian people.

As I sat in this classroom, with my eyes fixed to the flickering screen, listening to Yazan Khalili analyze a Palestinian history conveyed through imagery, I remembered the Panzani advertisement.

Classroom II, III, IV:
Packets of pasta noodles, a tin can of pasta sauce, tomatoes, peppers, a mushroom, and onions fall from a half-open string bag, indicating the return from the market. The ad's content is displayed in light yellow and green hues on a red background. "Pates – Sauce – Parmesan, A l'italienne de luxe", read the image. In his text "Rhetoric of the Image", Roland Barthes concentrated on commercials, declaring that they contain a highly condensed image that aims for maximum efficiency in transferring a definite message and an intended meaning. Through an Italian advertisement for a French audience, the author explored the overview of the different types of messages; linguistic, denoted, and connoted.

In all these classrooms, we analyzed images to extract the messages they carried. Nonetheless, due to uniformity in discourse, I had studied Roland Barthes' work multiple times in different periods and geographies. It seemed like there was only one way to conduct this lesson. It was only recently that I was in a classroom where I could explore semiotics in imagery, only this time, I could see myself reflected in the material.

In other classrooms where I had studied, there were countless cases of disembodiment. Some of my teachers focused on perceptual studies of visual form, adopted by the Basel School of Design, to develop capacities for critically analyzing situations. It was no surprise that after completing my undergraduate studies in Sharjah, I had chosen to pursue graduate studies in Basel.

In my history class I scanned through the hefty *Meggs' History of Graphic Design*. The book offered more than 1,400 images, revealing a saga of design characters and innovations that define the graphic design field. Mesopotamia, the cradle of civilization, Egyptian hieroglyphs, papyrus, illuminated manuscripts, flip, flip, flip, flip, flip, flip, flip, flip, flip, flip, endless flipping.

Is this it? This encounter always got me thinking of the saying اخترعنا الصفر ووقفنا عنده 'We invented the zero and stopped there'.

In the renovated basement of my school's building, we had access to a digital fabrication lab with laser cutters, CNC machines, a 3D printer, and two 6-axis Kuka robots programmed for one-off or repetitive tasks performed with a high degree of accuracy. Yet I graduated with no training in drawing letterforms or working with Arabic type. My school focused on making technical advancements instead of devoting resources to teaching fundamentals such as letterforms.

Going down memory lane, I recall other times when I didn't experience the same sensation of distance and exclusion. It was when I encountered my teacher Tarek Al-Ghoussein's earlier works, in which he expressed his lack of direct familiarity with Palestine. His awareness of the deprivation of his fundamental right to a home infiltrated the work. I remember him once lending me a six-part documentary film series presenting Palestinian refugees displaced in 1948 and their descendants. The first three episodes were more historical and informative, starting with Nakba, while the three other episodes dealt with identity formation and the impact of being in diaspora, looked at strategies for the right of return, and discussed ideas of representation. I reflect on how the conjunction of these experiences prompted me to develop *May you Wake Up to a Homeland*, a work in which I tried to portray my precarious status as a Palestinian refugee.

As Donna Haraway wrote, "only partial perspective promises objective vision[...]". Her text *The Persistence of Vision* illustrates how instead of investing in particularity and embodiment, humans have gone to tremendous lengths to see faraway planets in the solar system and simultaneously zoomed in to understand the mucous membrane lining the gut cavity of a marine worm.

I think about learning that integrates the domain of the embodied, taking me through the evolution of 'طاسة الرعبة,' the magical silver bowl we kept at home that was inscribed with Quranic verses and had healing powers. Or learning that gave me access to stories like Ahmed Omar's and his conception of Majid, the children's magazine I waited for at the end of every week. Or Mohie El-Deen El-Labbad's visual notes from a fast trip to Abu Dhabi and his remarks. And many, many, many others.

كلمات ليست ككلمات[9]

‹ *GRAPHIC* ›

One of my playlists, which I listen to routinely, has some Arabic classics and other tunes re-imagining folklore and traditional Shami[10] music. From this harvest, the song يما ويا يابي pops up, and as the band sings the words "يا يما اعطيني اعطيني لأبو قميصا طحيني بالليل ياعيني بالليل," I can't help but smile! They repeat two times: "Mother, I want to marry the one with the beige (tahini) shirt." The word طحيني catches my attention every single time. It is not in my dictionary, but it should be. I'm certain I listen to songs that mention other colors, but these lyrics jump out to me since طحيني means beige, and I've never learned how to call beige anything other than beige in the three languages[11] I know.

طحيني originates from طحين (flour).

My sentiment and association with the words beige and طحيني are not the same. The word طحيني conjures up a slew of alternative names in my head:

قمحي، رملي، ألخ

On my screen, in another tab, I have Engy's email from August 2020, while we were working on Bayn's inaugural issue, and I had sent her the translation of her contribution.

9 Words that are not like others.

10 Shami, also called Levantine Arabic or simply Levantine, is a subgroup of mutually intelligible vernacular Arabic varieties spoken in the Levant, in Syria, Lebanon, Jordan, and Palestine.

11 Arabic, English, and French.

All is good, just one question. Is the person working on the translation Emirati or Egyptian? We write Graphic with a ج not a غ. But if you are using standard Emirati for all translations then it's ok ...

I respond; I am working mainly with Bassem Yousri for the translation.

Bassem is of Egyptian origin. The presumption that he could be Emirati arises since I was in Abu Dhabi at the time we worked on this text and exchanged emails.

Her remark prompts me to consider the sources of the two words:

تصميم، غرافيكي/ جرافيكي

جذر الكلمة أي أصلها التي نشأت منه، وقد يكون ثلاثيًا وقد يكون رباعيًا.

The word's root, the source from whence it stemmed, can be of three letters or four.

تصميم، صمّمَ

The definition of صمّمَ is familiar; it might have different meanings depending on the context, but it hardly needs explaining.

غرافيكي/ جرافيكي

I cannot think of any Arabic roots for this word. According to most specialized dictionaries, the word comes via Latin from Greek 'graphikos'.

In her text[12] for Bayn, Engy writes about how she interprets the French and German renditions of the term 'Graphic Design', contrasting them with the English, which she considers to be too frigid a word to characterize this discipline of visual communication, sounding dry and out of date.

The English term 'Graphic Design' was opted to be translated into Arabic. This current term, which has a brief and peculiar history, coincided with the institutionalization of design education during the last century.

Through Bayn and my work on the inaugural issue, I recognized how critical the subject of language and translation is. Prior, it had been mostly theoretical. As a platform dedicated to writing, researching, and learning about design from the Arab-speaking region, it was paradoxical that the texts received were in English and then translated to Arabic with the assistance of a translator.

We had several terminologies phonetically translated.

أيديولوجية، جندر، سايكديليك، الأنثروبولوجية، التيبوغرافيا، بيداغوجيا، ألخ.

(ideology, gender, psychedelic, anthropology, typography, pedagogy, etc.)

Others appear flimsily constructed. They seem to cater to the ears but not the minds and hearts, with a tendency to decontextualize and dehistoricize the subject matter at hand. They don't light up parts of my brain. Anytime I come across such words in a text, I have the feeling that I am nailed in one place, unable to move from one notion to the next, and am instead spinning around myself.

12 Engy Aly, "Sporadic Notes On Design Education," *Bayn*, August 19, 2020.

And the void between these words and my ability to integrate them into my daily speech is wide wide wide.

Language is more than just an expression of formed ideas; it is also a crucial component of the cognitive process. Dr. Khaldoun AlNaqeeb links language underdevelopment with thought poverty, noting that educators have detected an increase in linguistic deficiency among students and a consequent imbalance in the production of meaning.

ففي الثقافة يتم انتاج المعنى ويتم توزيعه في المجتمع بواسطة لغة التواصل. وقد لاحظ المربون اتساع ظاهرة القصور اللغوي لدى طلبة العربية بشكل ملفت للنظر، وما يتبعها من اختلال في انتاج المعنى[13].

My ravenous inner dictionary wants another term to describe what I do. My eagerness for an alternative drives me to seek out vocabulary originating from the roots of the language, from collective memory, from lived experiences. Language to use in my everyday routine.

In his poem "The Dice Player", Mahmoud Darwish said it succinctly:

كان يمكن أَلاَّ أكون أَنا من أَنا
كان يمكن أَلاَّ أكون هنا
كان يمكن أَن تسقط الطائرة بي صباحاً
ومن حسن حظّيَ أَني نؤُوم الضحى
فتأخّرْتُ عن موعد الطائرة
كان يمكن أَلاَّ أرى الشام والقاهرة
ولا متحف اللوفر، والمدن الساحرة

13 Dr. Khaldoun AlNaqeeb, "المشكل التربوي والثورة آلصامتة: دراسة في سوسيولوجيا الثقافة", July 1993.

I could have not been who I am. I could have not been here.

My morning flight may have crashed with me on board. But fortunately, I am a late riser and missed the flight. I would not have been able to see Damascus and Cairo, the Louvre, and the enchanting cities.

Locales, timings, occurrences, and having witnessed or not witnessed, all contribute to his definition of who he is and how he came to be.

I compose this text with this acknowledgment. And I am asking, of myself, of a tomorrow, at which teaching embraces the lived experience as an intrinsic part of the learning process, toppling the hierarchical framework that segregates bodies and knowledges. A practice capable of reconciling with the intricacies of history that have led us here. A teaching aiding us in better situating ourselves and not wallowing in the emphasis on development as catching up. A practice that enables us to be; think, make, and articulate in our native tongues.

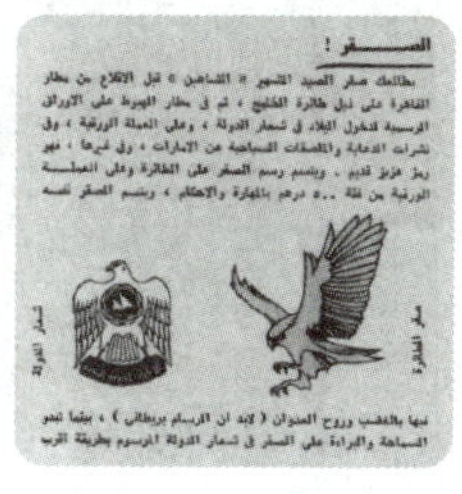

الصقر !

يطالعك صقر الصيد الشهير « الشاهين » قبل الإقلاع من مطار القاهرة على ذيل طائرة الخليج ، ثم في مطار الهبوط على الأوراق الرسمية لدخول البلاد في شعار الدولة ، وعلى العملة الورقية ، وفي نشرات الدعاية والملصقات السياحية عن الإمارات ، وفي غيرها ، فهو رمز عزيز قديم . ويتسم رسم الصقر على الطائرة وعلى العملة الورقية من فئة ٥٠٠ درهم بالمهارة والإحكام ، ويتسم الصقر نفسه

صقر الطائرة

شعار الدولة

فيها بالغضب وروح العدوان (لابد أن الرسام بريطاني) ، بينما تبدو السماحة والبراءة على الصقر في شعار الدولة المرسوم بطريقة العرب

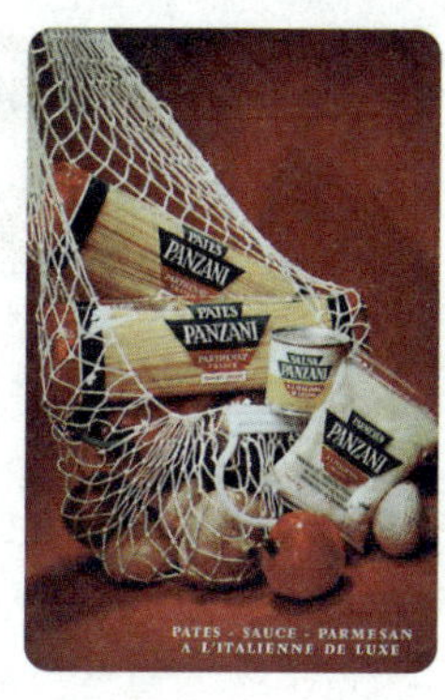

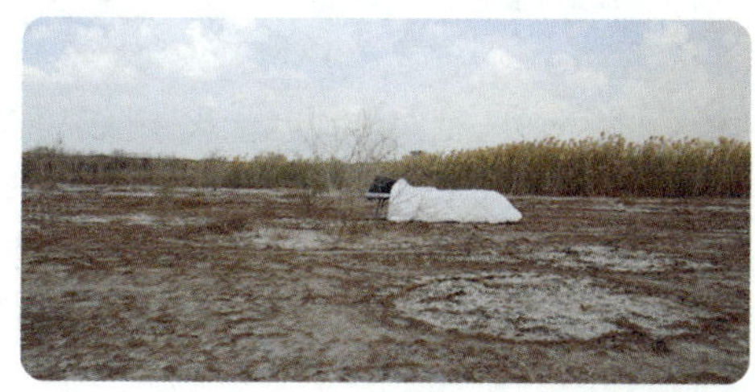

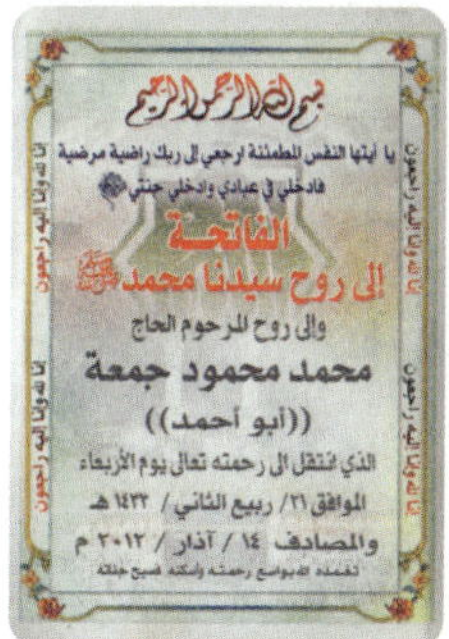

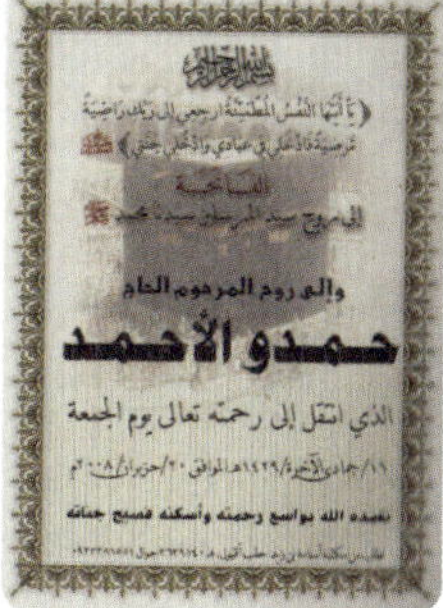

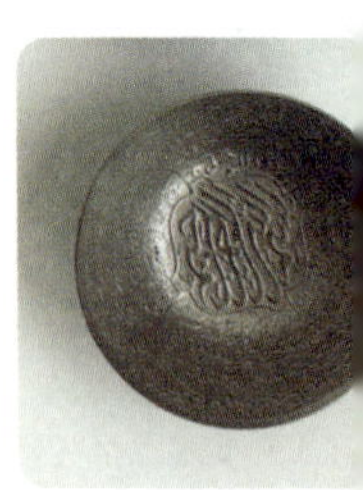

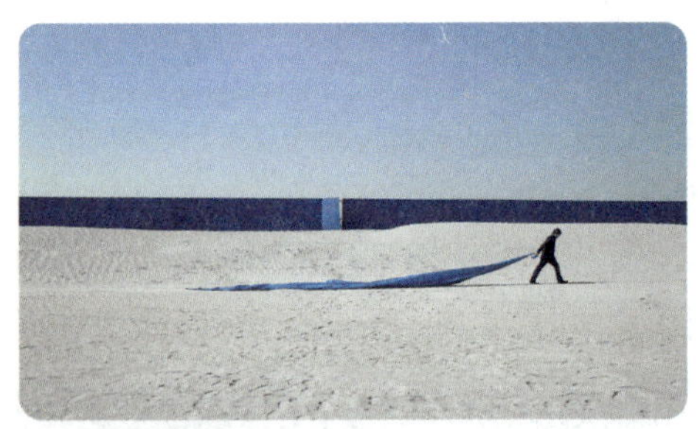

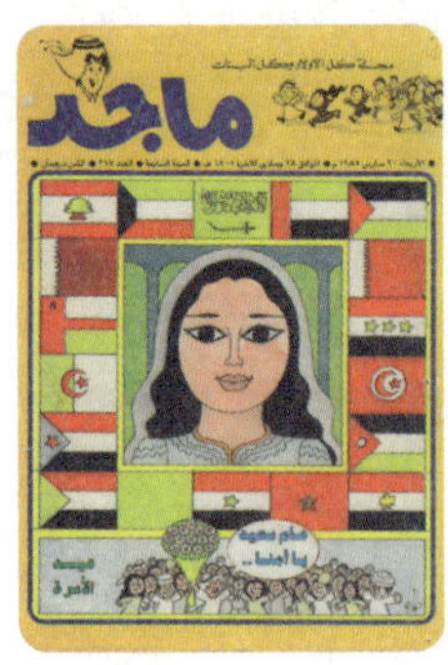

مجلة كل الأولاد وكل البنات
ماجد

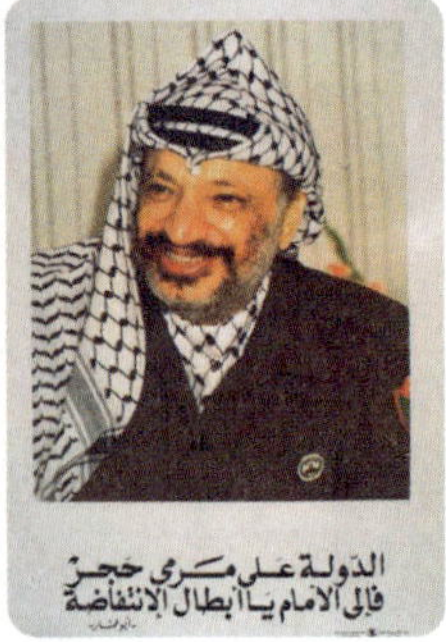

الدولة على مرمى حجر
فإلى الامام يا أبطال الإنتفاضة

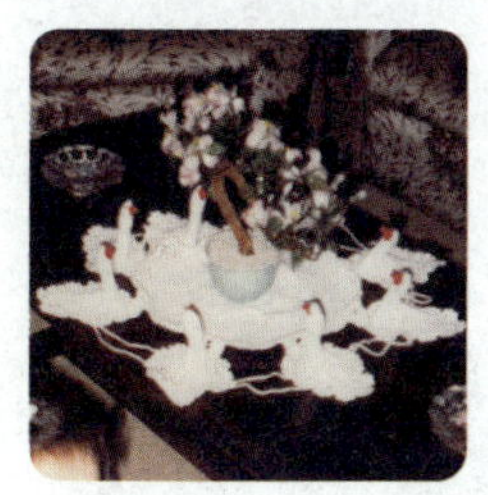

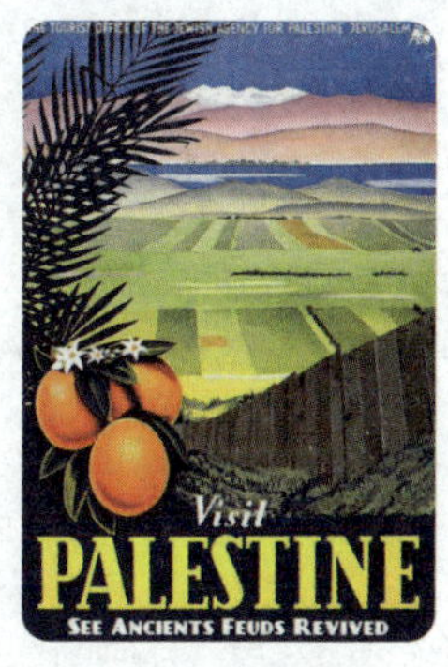
Visit
PALESTINE
SEE ANCIENTS FEUDS REVIVED

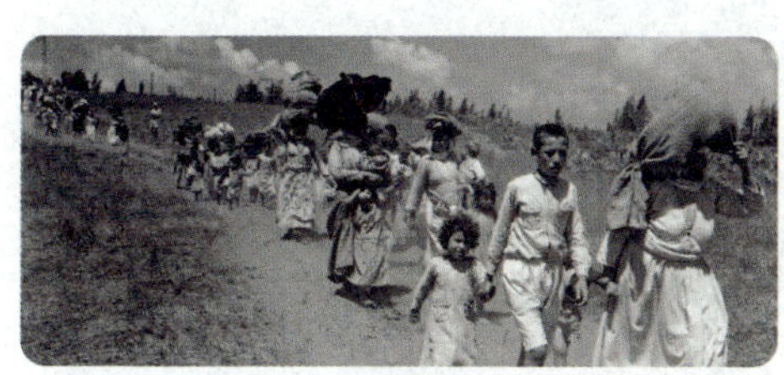

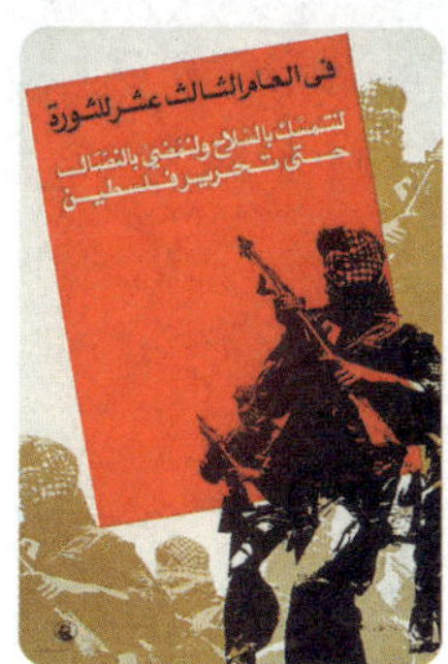
فى العام الثالث عشر للثورة
لنتمسك بالسلاح ولنمضي بالنضال
حتى تحرير فلسطين

Jara van Teeffelen

How to Regain Freedom

INTRODUCTION

My father and I imagined a school in our neighbour's garden. As though we were kids of a similar age, we jointly took breakfast, then I went running towards the school. "Quick, quick, the soldiers do pow-pow," I pointed my fingers towards my father to come and hide with me in the school. While running, I chanted, "Wein, wein, wein, Al Shaa'b al Arabi wein?" ("Where, where, where is the Arab people?"), a well-known song often played on local TV. After we did our counting exercises at school, I opened the imaginary door of the garden house and put my hand on my mouth, seemingly in shock. "Look! Everything is broken. The sleeping room, the dining room, even the kitchen."

"She apparently remembered the images of Jarjou'eh's damaged house that we visited a few days before. I asked her to tell the journalists what happened," commented my father. "Yes, yes, all the journalists should know," I replied. Afterwards, we played shopping; we went to the shopping section of the garden and bought a new TV and couches. "At least she learned to understand that you can do something to change a situation. Helplessness is the worst. I hope we can avoid it," my father wrote at the end of that diary entry.[1]

During the second Intifada (2000–2004), my father wrote a diary documenting our family's everyday life through the eyes of his five-year-old daughter, which was later published as a small book under the title *Only in Heaven Are There No Checkpoints*. Re-experiencing the war and curfews, I was able to realise how fairy

1 Toine van Teeffelen, *Only in Heaven Are There No Checkpoints: The Retold Diary of Yara, a Child from Bethlehem* (Bethlehem, Palestine: Arab Education Institute (AEI-Open Windows), 2011).

tales and imagination helped me to deal with the reality of being brought up under unusual circumstances.

Throughout my upbringing in the West Bank, I was exposed early on to shootings and bombardments, which mostly occurred during the beginning of the second Intifada, right around the time that my younger brother was born. My father used to explain that these loud noises were caused by St George, a local patron saint, thundering on his horse and cleaving the skies of Bethlehem. Feeding oneself and others with imagination was a way to cope with the reality of living there and then. Soon enough, I was creating imaginary and absurd scenarios and solutions to the oppressive reality, and slowly this became my way of revolting against political rhetoric.

Humour became part of the Palestinian resistance as an indirect outcome of the Israeli occupation, the absurdities of oppression, and the failure of the so-called peace process. Mockery and ridicule have to some extent contributed to Palestinian awareness-raising and cultural resistance. Certain genres such as fairy tales have helped to create a broader sense of imagination and humour in order to open up to various comparisons and metaphors to make it possible for a child to bear and cope with certain violent events. Children, but also adults, can apply the existing 'light' genres of imagination to their situation in daily life.

The function of imagination and humour actually goes beyond coping. After many decades of occupation – young people in Bethlehem and the West Bank don't know any other reality – the capacity of Palestinians living under occupation to see different or alternative futures, or to ask 'what if' questions and to 'dream', has become very limited. Palestinians are, at present, rather depoliticised, resigned to staying in an 'open-air prison', apathetic, consumption-oriented, or primarily interested in the survival of the family or in emigration as an escape option.[2] Many are in fact unable to experience a sense of contrasting worlds, and may be completely closed up in a world of suffering because of the experience of trauma. Or they might share a cynical belief that the world is manipulated by conspiratorial forces. Within such an (inter-)subjective, closed world, one cannot easily recognise the possibility of a different, desirable world, nor does one open up to a form of hope for change.

Back in 2008, a collective from Belgium visited the Arab Educational Institute, founded by a group of Palestinian educators in 1986 in Bethlehem, which later became an NGO affiliated to the international peace movement 'Pax Christi'. The collective came to organise a summer school programme in which I took part, together with eleven other children from the Bethlehem area between the ages of nine and twelve years. The purpose was the development of a stop motion video produced for Plural +, a youth video festival on migration, diversity, and social inclusion. We were tasked to write down a story that included a struggle in Palestinian daily life, a couple of characters, a plot, and a resolution, showcasing the perception of a Palestinian child living under Intifada circumstances.

Visualise this:

You are a child.

You are living in the city of Bethlehem
in occupied Palestine.

2 Yaser Alashqar, "The Politics of Social Structures in the Palestinian Case: From National Resistance to Depoliticization and Liberalization," *Social Sciences* 7, no. 4 (April 2018): 69, www.mdpi.com/2076-0760/7/4/69.

You have a loving and caring mother who prepares food every single day and asks you to bring some to your grandmother.

Your grandmother lives on the other side of the city. You put on your coat and head towards your grandmother's house.

You are not able to reach your grandmother's house because a four-metre wall has been built between your house and your grandmother's.

What are the next steps you take in order to reach your grandma to deliver her your mother's delicious home cooked Mulukhiyah?[3]

The story the children and I developed at the time was about a young girl named Warda who used to bring her mother's home-cooked food to her grandmother's house every single day. One day, Warda's daily path to that house is interrupted by the building of a four-metre high barrier, symbolising the apartheid wall located in the West Bank. The young girl feels devastated, sits in front of the wall, and starts crying. A small boy approaches Warda and suggests that she throws stones against the wall to knock it down. Warda appreciates the boy's help and decides to accept his advice but fails to break down the barrier. A carpenter is on his way to work and notices Warda throwing stones. He proposes to cut down a tree and use it as a ladder. The carpenter uses his saw to chop the tree, and proceeds to place it against the wall. Warda climbs it but then

3 Warda - PLURAL+ 2009. YouTube. Belgium / Palestine: PLURAL UNAOC-IOM, 2009. www.youtube.com/watch?v=qcW3LMhLYX0.

realises that there's no way to descend the wall on the other side. She decides to go back and meet a wizard. He is saddened by Warda's situation and hands her a pencil: "This pencil is very special. Draw your dream, and you'll see what happens." Warda decides to draw a huge bird, which turns into a real one. She jumps onto the bird and is finally able to cross the wall and reach her grandma's house.[4]

This is a magical story that took place in a realistic setting and convinced us to think the impossible. The story happens in a place where birds fly us around the city, and wizards hand us special pencils that turn everything we draw into something tangible. A magical world that becomes the norm, at least for a moment.

The story was a collaborative effort between the participating Palestinian children. The Belgian team gave us a set of workshops in which we learned how to come up with a plot, draw some characters, and make a stop motion video. Since all of us were brought up with lots of fairy tales, we decided to implement them in crossing the apartheid wall, which at the time was observing its four-year anniversary. The wall played a big part in our childhoods, especially after we were forced to accept, from one day to the next, that it wasn't possible anymore to reach a neighbouring city or village in the Jerusalem area. Applying magic to the plot allowed us to re-imagine our daily life as children. It also allowed us to envision a more hopeful future.

4 PLURAL UNAOC–IOM, "Warda."

BACKGROUND

After graduating from high school in Bethlehem, I decided to go and study abroad. The Netherlands was my number one option, since I am half Dutch, and I could more or less speak the language. In 2015 I took a gap year, travelled to the Netherlands, and lived with a guest family in the city of Amersfoort to strengthen my Dutch language and get accustomed to the country. The year after, I applied to the Royal Academy of Art (KABK) in The Hague, and graduated after four years from the Interactive Media Design department.

Following up on previous projects I had worked on during the preceding couple of years, I realised how imagination and humour played a big role in conceptualising most of my work. I addressed the ongoing situation in Palestine in a playful way as my own way of dealing with the harsh reality of the West Bank. Focusing on getting my ideas across, I used fairy tales, memes, and popular culture as sources of inspiration.

During my bachelor's research at the KABK, I developed a method that helped me come up with ideas for some of my projects. I used Google Images as a main source of inspiration, and allowed myself to use whatever I stumbled upon as elements for an upcoming project. I closed my eyes and selected three images by pinpointing my finger towards the screen and choosing whatever image my finger landed on. If I had chosen a dumpling, a flying cat, and a bridge, I would write down a story that combined these three elements in order to overcome a part of the everyday challenges of a Palestinian. Forcing objects onto a challenge no matter their size, function, or impact, slowly developed into the already existing method of

Forced Analogy, which I later came across while Googling how an ordinary object, that is usually not used as a tool, can overcome a certain challenge and in fact 'solve it conceptually', by either using it as a complete whole or by dismantling it and defining its properties. The aim is to create a world where unrealistic 'solutions' to the situation in Palestine can be proposed, and new possibilities foreseen. An imaginary reality where hamburgers can be used in order to cross the apartheid wall.

Our Palestinian history does not only consist of conflict and suffering but in fact also of attempts to overcome them, as seen during the first Intifada (1987–91), when many acted out of the belief that a new, transformative world was possible. Recognising the absurdities in a specific situation enables Palestinians to distinguish between both the real-life world of suffering, and the absent world of what is universally considered an 'ordinary life'. And seeing this new world is a form of consolation. Acknowledging both worlds makes it possible to compare and contrast, to detect the incompatibilities and incongruities, and to keep the tension between them. Imagination and humour are essential for bringing different existing or possible worlds into conflict with each other. Therefore, the perception of incompatibilities is necessary for establishing a sense of absurdity. Understanding a situation or event as absurd requires one to make explicit the fundamental conflicts between the ordinary world of suffering and the desirable world of a normal life. Tensions can be brought out and new creative possibilities imagined in order to keep up a hopeful spirit, necessary for staying sane and, ultimately, for survival.

In other words, the tension between both worlds creates a hope based upon the recognition of the existence of a different, more desirable world in contrast to the existing suffering world. The struggle against despair is an agent in itself. In its turn, hope can open up a horizon of new possibilities in situations of deep oppression, such as in refugee camps where a history of continuous child arrests exists, and where power inequality is so great that it is difficult to imagine any possibility of change.

FORCED ANALOGY: WHAT IS IT?

A Forced Analogy as it is known in design practices can be used to encourage you to think of a mobile phone as a boat, and then as a tree. The purpose of the method for a phone manufacturer, such as the company Nokia, would be to draw commercially interesting ideas from such unexpected analogies.[5] Forced Analogy as a creative tool can also, however, be used for different non-commercial purposes, such as to generate political humour by reframing a given reality and seeking to destroy habitual patterns of thinking in order to establish new relationships.[6] It encourages people to see a problem in a completely different way. It is a creative technique that helps to break out of accustomed patterns of thought,[7] and makes use of the findings that we grasp our environment by, bringing things

5 Geoff Higgins, "The Forced Analogy Method," How to Be a Facilitator, accessed December 2021, howtobeafacilitator.blogspot.com/2011/08/forced-analogy-method.html.

6 Allen D. Spiegel and Herbert H. Hyman, *Strategic Health Planning: Methods and Techniques Applied to Marketing and Management* (Norwood, NJ: Ablex Publishing Corp., 1993): 173.

7 "Forced Analogy," Flip, accessed November 2021, www.ask-flip.com/method/396.

that are dissimilar into the same category, in order to generate and develop new perspectives around a certain issue.[8]

When comparing two seemingly unrelated things in order to imagine a kind of imaginary solution or overcome a challenge, our mental perspective on a problem or challenge can be adjusted. In their memory, people dispose of an enormously wide range of narratives that allow us to bring up different understandings of our daily life.

The purpose of Forced Analogy is, in my case, not so much the creation of a new world of real solutions, but one in which imaginative solutions help Palestinians to cope with some of the challenges they face in their daily lives. In other words, constructing a reality that is based upon one's imaginative and creative abilities. In many real life situations, imagination has only limited relevance. For instance, playful imagination cannot solve the real-life problem of the lack of resources in an area like Gaza. However, even in situations of dire material need, survival is never only a matter of material supplies.

Hope is relevant to any situation of need, and thus imagination is also relevant to any situation of need. What comes first, the chicken or the egg – the hopeful spirit or the material circumstances of life? Well, in my opinion, there's much to say for the statement that people without hope have severe difficulty in facing the material circumstances of life.

8 John Dabell, "Forced Association," John Dabell: Every Day is a School Day, January 14, 2020, johndabell.com/2020/01/14/forced-association/.

The Israeli occupation of the Palestinian lands can be reframed using the creative technique of Forced Analogy. The idea here is to show how, when 'forcing' an object onto a challenge, limitations can be liberating, as they evoke ideas that can be used to deal with or overcome an obstacle.

Forced Analogy can be seen as a practical approach for dealing with a certain difficulty, suggesting that Palestinians have some way of dealing with an obstacle. This is unlike dealing with the feeling of a deeply oppressive reality, which appears to allow for very few clear counter-strategies, let alone overcoming challenges in a short period of time.

The Apartheid Wall radiates a deep sense that the situation is desperate, as it emphasises the oppressive inequality of power that exists, and makes reality seemingly unchangeable. It is also a tangible everyday challenge for Palestinians. Ever since it was constructed between 2003 and 2005, Palestinians have fought their way through it in order to reclaim their lands and gain some freedom of movement. A Forced Analogy applied to the Wall brings out the elements of irony and absurdity as a dimension of brainstorming. An object can be used as part of a challenge to overcome a potential disaster. An object can be dismantled, added onto another object, or used as a whole in order for it to act as a tool with which to survive, and to open Palestinians up to a sense of hope.

Katniss Everdeen

Katniss is like an arrow.

She's a valuable weapon and tool in a battle,
and she doesn't break easily.

Katniss is as straight as an arrow;
She's brutally honest and she says exactly what she means.

She makes impossible choices as quickly
as an arrow zips through the air,
and her words are as piercing as an arrow's tip.

Katniss has a softer side like an arrow has feathers.

Much like the arrow's feathers
keep it on track and on balance,

Katniss's love for her friends
and family keeps her on course.[9]

9 Going the Distance, "Forced Analogy Poetry- Characterization and Critical Thinking- Any Story," Teachers Pay Teachers, accessed December 2021, www.teacherspayteachers.com/Product/Forced-Analogy-POETRY-Characterization-and-Critical-Thinking-Any-Story-3356552.

QUESTIONS ON FORCED ANALOGY

The process of playfully opening up the imagination, and in doing so using political humour to good effect, is not for each and everybody the same. Reality can be very differently perceived depending on the position one has in the political setting. In one of Banksy's paintings, on display in the Walled Off Hotel in Bethlehem, an Israeli soldier and a Palestinian are having a pillow fight. Banksy shows here the political conflict as a symmetry. In doing so, he enlarges the playing field for cultural resistance and makes it relatable to other cultures, as well as to his worldwide audience. Everybody is familiar with pillow fights. His visual joke is therefore effective in reaching out to the world. But this example is also ambiguous and difficult to classify. It is not clear whether the pillow fight perpetuates or challenges oppression. This work can be seen as falsely stabilising the situation, since it papers over the real inequality between the soldier and the Palestinian. However it can also be seen as challenging the relationship, as it places soldiers at the same level as children. In Israel, this example would perhaps be seen as challenging power relations, but it can be perceived by Palestinians as a way of hiding the political system of occupation and oppression, by making the relationship between the Israelis and the Palestinians appear symmetrical.

Is it possible to develop 'design tools' from and for everyday life that bring back the playful and humorous capacity to dream and to see alternative realities, despite the power relations that suggest reality to be unchangeable? Is it possible to encourage people to develop their own real-life tools that do not reinforce the existing situation but that help to think through broader problems in a critical way?

OBJECTIVES:

When answering these questions in an educational context, different goals and intentions can be envisioned. Here are some of the most important objectives that arise when Forced Analogy is used in a creative Palestinian educational setting.

- Promoting critical and creative thinking
- Introducing new forms of arts education among Palestinians
- Enhancing users' creativity
- Creating awareness about the impact of the Separation/ Apartheid wall and land confiscation in Palestine

HOW IT WORKS:

Imagination and absurdity often work well alongside humour. They often show that people have a sense that different worlds are possible, and that at least the longing for a different, more ordinary, or desirable world cannot be suppressed.

In following the step-by-step overview, the participant is invited to work through the various steps needed in order to overcome a certain challenge, chosen by them, using one object, in order to regain a certain value that went missing.

Steps:

1. Choose a concrete scenario related to Palestine that you want to investigate.
2. Select a value that is at stake or that is clearly relevant to the scenario, such as the negation of love, generosity, or solidarity.

3. Define, in a series of brief sentences, the ways in which this scenario can be broken down into: (1) a setting, (2) a character, (3) a challenge or complication, (4) any actions for dealing with or overcoming complication, (5) results, (6) the value-message of the narrative.
4. Choose an object from this second, desirable world of normal daily life. Note: an object can be either dismantled, or used as a whole.
5. Come up with a story using the object in order to repair the scenario in line with the value selected. Write down the story.
6. Evaluate the story: does the repair story give you new insights into how the present, hopeless state of affairs in Palestine can be tackled?

EXAMPLE:

When applied to education and awareness-raising, Forced Analogy can be profitably seen as a narrative journey, where one journeys from point A (the problem setting) to point B (a great crisis) to point C (the possible solution to the problem), making little steps in between.

Let's take the example of the Apartheid Wall. Almost everybody in the occupied West Bank is able to narrate various stories that demonstrate its destructive power: no access to one's lands and properties, humiliation by soldiers at checkpoints, a feeling that one is living in an open-air prison.

The main values that are affected by the Wall include freedom and human connection. The Wall exists in a setting of desolated, wounded lands and houses. Characters include Palestinians with permits and soldiers at checkpoints and in watchtowers; complications can involve people who are not allowed to pass.

Now, the point of this educational exercise is to challenge the players to introduce a Forced Analogy by choosing an object in order to help them overcome this challenge, and help them bring back that value of freedom. A walking stick and a sun screen or parasol could be used as objects here in order to fix the issue. How can a walking stick and a parasol support the value of freedom? Perhaps the stick is able to poke holes every time it touches the Wall. The parasol could act as protection against the sun – used to screen oneself from any soldier's investigation at a checkpoint.

Do such playful, humorous analogies help in creating a new, possibly more hopeful vision of a different world? One can imagine a play in which Palestinians are equipped with walking sticks and umbrellas to walk their journey of life, passing from point A to B to C, managing all the threats to their freedom of movement using their two hands and arms. The Palestinian becomes the centre of a fairy tale in which great obstacles are cleverly overcome. A protest march of Palestinians in real life who carry walking sticks and umbrellas can be viewed as a demonstration for freedom, and old Palestinian refugees with walking sticks can symbolise the longing of returning to old ancestral lands.

SUMMARY

- Humour, imagination, and a sense of the absurdity of reality can help Palestinians to cope, but also aid in seeing new, hopeful possibilities.
- Forced Analogy is a method that can help to generate imagination by following a series of educational steps.
- A seemingly unrelated object from the daily environment can be used to create an imaginative story of overcoming obstacles that brings the desirable world of ordinary life into a constructive tension with the suffering world faced by Palestinians.

Farah Fayyad

Who or What Taught You to Imagine

Trauma produces a memory in fragments.[1]
My memory is not so good.
Most of my friends know this about me.
In fact I'm called Dory[2] *on my best friend's phone,*
like from Finding Nemo.
Mostly it feels like fog, punctured by tall,
violently magnetic landmarks.

This essay explores these landmarks.

And the title of this essay is the question from my tutor, Rana Ghavami, that made me start writing it.

1 In *In the Dream House* by Carmen Maria Muchado, the author writes the history of an abusive relationship through a set of stylistically varying vignettes. Shocking but also inevitable, each fragment of pain is in its place, and cannot possibly be anywhere else or for anyone else.

2 A blue tang fish who suffers short-term memory loss.

MOKHTAR

You know when you know you kind of disappointed someone and even though you haven't seen them in years it still crosses your mind at least once a week that you need to make some reparations? Mokhtar knew there was a big possibility of him being forgotten. In fact he quite clearly and eloquently asked me to try not to forget him. He said something along the lines of "All my students take what they came for and go without a trace." Unlike him and his own teacher, we only spent around a year or so together.

I want to not fuck up. This was the intention driving me. I told him this, but with nicer language and in Arabic of course, because he's an older gentleman and demands a lot of respect. When he floats into a room you can feel the weight of everything he knows. How he carries his body and how he sits and breathes in a certain way before drawing letters. Another calligrapher writes, "When I direct the brush, I stop breathing. This also limits the size of the calligraphy; a brush stroke cannot last longer than it takes my heart to beat."[3]

The body decides. The size of the paper decides.
The angle of the tip of the pen decides. You don't decide.
You trust your eye and your breath and your teacher and you try to relax while still being completely alert and serious.

I want to not fuck up. It was that simple for me. Not wanting to make a wrong connection between two characters that would lock them into a toxic relationship until the end of time, I wanted

3 Hassan Massoudi, "Two Daughters of the Same Parents," in *Arabic Graffiti*, eds. P. Zoghbi and D. Karl (Berlin: From Here to Fame, 2011), 31.

to know exactly how many times a 'ه'[4] could shapeshift and still be itself at the end of the day. I didn't want anybody reading me incorrectly, because of a neck that was too long or a bowl too narrow. Or because of clumsiness and distraction. Because of sitting and breathing strangely or because of over-confidence.

Mokhtar knew he would be forgotten. Maybe to him it seems that I took whatever I needed and left. If education is a form of transference, I would rather not imagine the completion of learning. He's in every letter I draw, every negative space, and every eye and arm. Every word I write and every short or long connection I make. Whenever my fingers fumble with a new pen. I really should give him a call. I was his last student. In his late seventies, he could no longer hold the pen steady so well, but the structures of his letters and words were flawless, perfect math, perfect proportions. He had been taught by his father who was taught by his own father. A lineage of real calligraphers.

He would come over every Friday and we would sit together at my dining table. There's nothing quite like a master-apprentice relationship. With craft there is really no better way. There is time that needs to be spent together. I spent time with him so I could spend time with the form, structure, and logic of the Arabic script.

Mokhtar El-Baba had been a calligrapher since he could write. His father had trained him for a decade, six days a week and eight hours a day for ten years, before he gave him an actual client. He said he would only take a break on Sundays. And whenever he reviewed his

4 Sketch of how many forms of ه I can write with one pen, one stroke, and in my basic handwriting.

work, he could tell exactly which pieces were made on a Monday, because that one day of rest and no practice showed.

I loved to watch him teach. As much as I enjoyed the practice itself, I could argue that his company had been even more valuable.[5] His feedback was pure comedic genius. One letter looked like it just tripped in front of everyone it knew and was very embarrassed. One was enraged and taking it out on its friend by doubling in size. One looked like it needed a death bed, urgently. Things like that. The letters were actual characters. They had personalities and we could talk about their behaviour. Like us, they had the ability to respond to external and internal circumstances. They had a private life and a public life. What appears on the entrance of a mosque, for example? Massive, ornamented words, exuding confidence and intellect, expensive, rich with history and ornament. And in contrast, what appears in a small poem, or a little talisman? Words that are more like birds, big empty spaces and fleeting moments where characters appear and disappear into each other, an intention whispered in the morning.

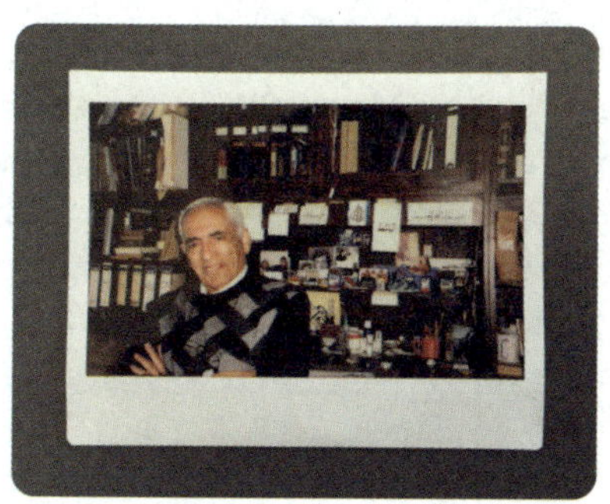

5 Also, look how cute he is.

For me what is most fascinating is how letters can respond to each other. Unlike Latin scripts, Arabic characters are all connected, so each letter can embody various forms depending on a precise context. There are four basic states: isolated, initial, medial, and final. We also need to take into account certain combinations within a word. Some letters cause whoever comes before them to invert. Imagine that. Making the one standing next to you flip because of your presence. And ligatures in Arabic are intimate relationships. Sometimes you need to compromise your shape to suit whoever is holding your hand so that you look better together. Sometimes, no matter how hard you try, there are gaps that you can only fill with ornaments rather than core forms. Sometimes two characters disappear in the appearance of a third shape composed of their strange combination. Chemistry. Magic.

I never wanted to become a calligrapher. I just wanted to understand how to play with characters correctly.

If I understand you then I can play with you.
I will not try to recreate you or perfect you or reinvent you.
I just want to know who you are and how I can dress you.

There was a time when hand-made Arabic characters seemed to be taking over the entire city. During the 2019 uprising in Lebanon, Arabic was everywhere, inside our lungs and through our mouths, on our bodies, our clothes, written, drawn, painted, sprayed. Sometimes fast and urgent, and other times slow and with a planned composition. I made a sign with my friend featuring a line from one of our favourite pop songs. Proper lettering. A lot of people took photos of it.

Those days I thought a lot about the role of these characters and this script. The shift between them being on the small, quiet practice sheets between Mokhtar and myself, and how they got bigger and louder and much more reactive and urgent during the protests. It became apparent to a lot of people living in Lebanon during that time that the uprising triggered what some called a "return" to Arabic.
Arabic in public space.
But Arabic is public space.
We gather in it, we form small intimate bonds in it.
We are held together by it.

Mokhar had been inside longer than I had, and when I arrived he was so very welcoming. He showed me around with warmth and generosity.

Mokhtar would come over once a week. I looked forward to those Fridays with him. He always refused to eat or drink anything at our house, even though my mother insisted every time. He would always say the same thing. I already had everything I needed before coming here. He was a disciplined man to say the least. Discipline. It's a good word.

Mokhtar conjures letters into being.
A sentence is a landscape complete with families, friends, histories.

Mokhtar also brought about a reality where he was alone, again.
Or did I do that?
Did I fulfil his prophecy?
If I could just remember where his house is I would pop by next time I'm in Beirut, then all of this would be okay.

Mokhtar left me with a vague panic that might stay forever it seems.
The inevitable and final annihilation of the craft.
Maybe this is what he knew was coming.

All tools are now buttons.
All liquid is now math.
All paper is now light.

Some days I miss the severity and comfort
of my heart in its broken state.
It's the only place I could still go to spend time with you.
You didn't smell like garbage and burnt tires there
and I could still lie to myself.

And some days I want to rip all my skin off
because you touched it.

BEIRUT

The damage is comprehensive. This is a letter.
By all means this is a letter. By both means.
I to you.
And the form of language.

If you were a letter you would be a 'ر'. Your tongue has to roll a bit and your mouth stays open. *Ra.*

Soft. Curved. Seemingly welcoming from afar. But whenever someone gets close to you there's this negative space that cannot be resolved no matter how hard I try, and then your leg intrudes on the teeth of those that are close to you and it's just not a good sight. Living with you is complicated and terrifying.

So I spit myself out.[6]

With what agency and what level of control over my choice I am still not sure. Most days there's no ground under my feet and also the world is constantly becoming this strange simulation where people don't stare or yell and there's no rage in every corner and in every face.

I miss your warmth, there's nothing like it. Every day I work on breaking the illusion I built for you. I had a beautiful photo of you framed and hung on a wall very high up, definitely out of reach. I could never allow a single speck of dust to settle anywhere near your edges, let alone across your face. I protected you at all costs. Especially from my own feelings towards you. These days I'm comfortable using the word ugly. Deceptive. Toxic.

6 Julia Kristeva, *Powers of Horror: An Essay on Abjection* (New York: Columbia University Press, 1982).

In *Purity and Danger*, Mary Douglas defines dirt as "matter out of place".[7] My memory takes a quiet stroll to that text whenever I think of you. She tries to say that all the dirt is simply misplaced objects. It's when an object steps outside of whatever boundary we think we're comfortable putting it in. Maybe this is the feeling I constantly have when I'm here. A liminal state. On the margin between multiple positions.

No access to your space and even less access to your time. This a letter to you as in the you that I lost and the us that you destroyed.

I have a fear of irrelevance. If you're not my audience then there's nothing I want to say.

There's this shitty motivational Instagram thing that I saw once and never forgot. It said something like "you can never swim in the same river twice".[8] One because the water has moved and two because you are different. But then why do I and so many people I know have this kind of cyclical relationship with you? Love at first sight, devaluation, intermittent positive reinforcement, humiliation, pleasure, self-dismissal, paralysing fear at the thought of leaving, and knowing that there is nothing to do but leave.

Even though I don't want to,
I always want to go back.
Makes a great pattern.

7 Mary Douglas, *Purity and Danger* (London and New York: Routledge, 1966).

8 Re-written by some random motivational influencer but based on the original text by Greek philosopher Heraclitus.

I'm becoming friends with loss. Even the things that I thought I could never accept. The fact that Mokhtar never picked up and maybe he passed away quietly on his own and maybe he's the last real calligrapher and then that's it. It's just memories and nostalgia scattered across the earth.

I envy those who have never met you. You know this feeling I get that if I can't enjoy you then nobody else should be able to. You've made me strangely selfish and I hate the idea that you can survive without me. I totally fell for your aesthetics and the wild nights. An intimacy I never had with anybody else. The unpredictability. The feeling that each time could easily be the last. You made me friends with loss. How you made me resilient and how much I fucking hate that word. You also gave me this false hero complex because it seems I survived something.

Especially these last two years. You made me guilty for leaving you and an idiot for not really wanting to. You made me nostalgic and selfish and sad and now I also have trust issues.

Hyper-independence is a trauma response, apparently.
It's the kind of post-trauma that makes one vulnerable all the time, crying in public. That's easy to romanticise. But also maybe that's the internalised patriarchy talking.

How many times do you think your heart can break?
Mine feels like ground meat. Paste.
At least you can argue that it's back together, more or less.
And now it's spreadable.

My father called me by my cousin's name
once when I was a kid.
One of the reasons why my eyes watered today.

In a distant future I'm sobbing I'm sure,
and remembering you.

THE JOKE

You know that evil frog under the fig tree in *Pan's Labyrinth*? In our case, it's a bundle of old men that refuse to budge. They only lie. And make money. Our uprising was supposed to be those three stones. But the frog didn't explode. We did.

A tipping point where it wasn't funny anymore to talk about how corrupt our country is. Chuckling at stories like this had been common practice for years.

Haha I just paid someone and got my
driving licence without ever touching a car.
Haha I don't pay taxes.
Haha I paid some guy and he did
all my paperwork for a visa.
Haha did you hear that at LAU you can just pay
and get your diploma without having to do shit.
Haha I paid and got out of jail so easily.
Haha I made a phone call to some asshole
and got a job I'm not qualified for.
Haha haha haha.

We were done laughing, so we took to the streets. The star slogan: Killon yaani killon.[9] All of them means all of them, or all means all. All means no exceptions. All is absolute. All cannot mean some. All cannot mean all but one. All means all. You can't half agree. You're in or out.

9 In Arabic. كلن يعني كلن

The uprising was a disaster. And I hate myself for saying that. It was exciting in the beginning, between October and December 2019. We would gather and just wait to be attacked. We lifted words above our heads; drawn by many hands and screamed through many lungs.

The most difficult protest was the one a few days after the explosion in Beirut's port. We had spent the days after the blast sweeping glass and blood and carnage and rubble and opening the streets and helping grandmas pack their houses and handing out food and water and trying not to break the fuck down. Our government had done this. We knew it. It wasn't an external attack. It was the result of

Haha I confiscated and improperly stored
tonnes of ammonium nitrate and I'm gonna
sell them for a million dollars.
Haha I got a million dollars for free.
Haha it's a miracle only 218 people died.

It could have been a bigger massacre had it not been for Covid and the timing. 6:09 pm on August 4. It was a Tuesday.
The following Saturday our rage was spilling out of every pore in our bodies. Not only did our government cause an explosion that destroyed the city, it also took away whatever tiny sense of safety one could feel inside their home. Danger is usually more probable outside the walls of your own house. The tear gas started relatively early that day, around 4pm. I was home by 10pm. That rarely happens. The protests are usually the most fun and action-packed at night. Funny how our definition of fun is constantly shifting. We shared the violence. We shared the care that comes after the violence. We bonded. I never thought I'd be able to smoke a cigarette under the tear gas.

I went with my toxic ex that day on his motorcycle (of course he has a motorcycle because he's a fucking asshole, and he always used to drive it drunk). Anyway we had parked the motorcycle in a small street across the highway that led to all the action. After inhaling a sufficient amount of tear gas and being chased through the tiny alleyways of Gemmayze like a Pacman game in the pitch dark because the explosion took out all the electricity cables, we got to the bike which was now surrounded by at least six men in uniforms. Mostly army, but some riot police. There was a line of around seven or eight guys with their heads down getting arrested. Being a damsel in distress can get you out of almost anything in Lebanon (thank you, patriarchy). Toxic ex was hesitant (he always seemed manly, brooding, full of wisdom and courage, but really a scared small cowardly child underneath) and said, "Let's just leave it there." I said "No way, that's your bike (and in my head, mine, what an idiot I was), we're not going home walking after all this shit," I approached the first uniform without saying anything and he responded, "Please leave or get in line with them," pointing at the sad and defeated guys waiting to be taken to the police station for the night. Fuck. I backed off but I was not satisfied. I saw an older man, army uniform, just next to the bike, almost leaning on it.

I was wearing short shorts and spoke gently.

F: Hi sorry this is our motorcycle
we really just want to go home.
[His eyes softened.
He moved slightly to the right,
shifting his weight off the motorcycle.]

Man: Yes, please go ahead. Why do you seem so afraid?
F: Well you're supposed to protect us but now we need protection from you.
I made him sad. We drove away quickly.

In those earlier days between October and December 2019, if I had to explain it socially, the setting was like an American high-school movie cafeteria, only during the darkest of times in our little city. I was excitedly sharing with toxic ex that we took the printing machine to Riad al Solh, and that's where we staged this public intervention where we printed for free on the clothes of protestors. "At the heart of the protest," I said, with pride. He responded with a subtle eye roll. He had this way of looking up with his eyes rather than his whole head. "It was the heart of the 'festival'," he said, and that he would never go there. It was where the cute designers and food truck people would gather. It was the place where you could take your kids and get them corn and beans with lemon and cumin and sandwiches and candies and hear some nice revolutionary songs. There was no fire and no fear.

One street down was where the real men were, if we are to adhere to the macho scenography of it all. That's where you'd go if you were serious. If tear gas doesn't bother you and if you know how to fight and if you have an escape route and if you're ready to die maybe. If you're ready to break into government buildings and risk being arrested. If the swarms of Hezbollah motorcycles don't scare the shit out of you.

A little further up on the Ring[10] was where the intellectuals usually gathered. These are people that work with NGOs and come up with

10 A major highway in Beirut that links the east side to the west side.

the best slogans. The people that work in culture. It was also where you'd go with a bottle of whisky some nights and share it with your friends. A place where you can walk around and be social. It's also easy to run. Maybe that's what differentiated all these areas; how easily you could get the fuck away from there. Crowds from similar social scenes anyway gravitate towards each other. I remember I would call my friends and see where they were, kind of like on a Friday night when you want to grab a drink and you're scouting to see who is where. That's how it was.

Until it wasn't. Until it became bones breaking and eyeballs falling out of place just four days after the entire city exploded. As if there wasn't enough carnage. What a slap in the face that day was.

Fuck resilience.
Resilience ignores the conditions of its unwanted presence. Resilience is a flag I never wanted lifted so high above my head. Generational, in our case, and though it seems to recede sometimes, it never really leaves. It is what I'm expected to pack into my suitcase, wherever I go.

When you close your eyes, do you see
every home as the ruin it will become?
The remembering starts in the centre.
An obliteration of measure in the nuclear gut.
And then quick invading light
Moments of annihilating density;
collapsed into darkness reconciled as
decayed thunder.
The malignant formation of a pink cloud.
Did the mountains tremble?
Of course, they did. But to no great import.

– My friend, Sara Huneidi

THE EXPLOSION

It happened exactly one month and sixteen days before my move to Amsterdam.
August 4, 2020. 6:09 pm.

It started with a fire at the port. I was on my balcony with my best friend planning where to go out for a drink that night. There was a fire but there's always a fire or if it's not a fire it's something else. When you live in Beirut you get used to catastrophes. In fact you might even find some unsettling comfort in them.

The fire became fireworks.

It was only a few minutes and then the air got completely sucked away from our lungs and then a roaring scream seemingly endless sound and glass flying absolutely everywhere, stabbing and penetrating sandstone walls, and the building was shaking and nothing was in its place anymore.

I felt it inside. In all my organs.
You can imagine the carnage.
You've probably also seen the carnage.
It wasn't quiet for a while after that.

That night there was a lot of screaming. The next morning there was only the sound of glass being swept up across the entire city and neighbours thanking God for each other's safety.

Beirut exploded right above our heads and under our feet and in our organs. Everyone now has a story. Salim was sitting on his sofa and ran inside just in time before the massive window right behind his head exploded out of the old sandstone walls. I don't know where Mokhtar was, but I hope he's safe now.

Our government did this. If we needed fuel to continue protesting, this could be considered a gift. But you know by now that that's not how things work in Beirut.

For a few years before 2019, time used to be easier, contained in its own peculiar way. A witness one could reason with to a certain extent. You knew when it was moving fast or slow, when it was making you anxious, when you didn't want it to ever end. You could talk to it, and it would respond. More or less kindly, it used to be more gentle with its rhythms. Or at least if there were moments of resentment, time responded with possible plotlines that we could understand. We knew that some events would dull down in hours, days, weeks. We could digest the momentum.

The malignant pink cloud broke time. Jaded, it transformed it into a monster. Still not sure who it's seeking revenge on. It now moves, stops, disappears with a vengeance. There is no grace left in time after the explosion. No kindness. No container that can hold it and no language, spoken or otherwise, that can facilitate an understanding. I answer most questions with "I really don't know". Plans make me anxious. I can't imagine the future. I can't even imagine this weekend to be honest.

With most broken relationships, time heals. What happens now that the healer has turned violent? We seek refuge mostly in each other. In quiet moments, over a glass of vodka soda with lemon juice, under a scaffolding.

A massive wheat silo protected the western part of the city from the damage.

Beirut's pigeons are the only clear winners now.
Tonnes of wheat now abundantly available to them, they are ecstatic.

When I was a child the idea of infinity terrified me.
The fact that between 1 and 1.01
there's an infinite number of numbers.
The fact that there will always be
more music
more recipes
more colours
Fomo.
Knowing for sure that I could never know everything.

SALIM

Salim Samara grew up in the suburb of the suburb of a very broken city during its worst time. He has killed people. Literal death. He has been to jail. One time he told me only two things can make a boy a man: marriage and jail.

You know when two people are completely in love with the same thing it's almost as though they could be in love with each other. Salim taught me how to screen print. Properly print. He makes magic with mesh and ink. Nothing is impossible and if it is, then you must be in the wrong place but that's also very rare. There's an expression in Arabic that translates to 'breaking your head'.[11] Salim loves to break his head. This is done mostly in order to find solutions.

Salim is direct. Wise. Transparent. Loyal. Beyond perceptive. Imagine growing up around guns and extreme right-wing politics and swastika tattoos in Beirut, and so much whisky and cocaine, but then choosing ink instead. Salim makes dreams happen.

You want to print a CMYK photograph on the stacked edges of a thousand sheets of paper? Done. You need to break up with your toxic boyfriend? "God gives meat to those without teeth."[12] I asked him if I was the meat or the toothless person in this scenario and he just smiled.

Imagine someone who sees everything in you. All the trust and all the hope and all the potential and you're the most capable person in the world.

11 In Arabic. تكسير راس

12 In Arabic. ربنا بيعطي لحمة ليلي ما عنده سنان

"You pull out the thorns with your own hands."[13] This one is about karma and how you're responsible for your own actions and that you need to deal with consequences yourself. Salim always knows exactly what to say.

It's a dead-end street, so park outside and then it's the last building on the right in the basement, under a grocery delivery shop called NokNok. The stairs are kind of chipped here and there, and I've witnessed many people trip. A treacherous path on the way down to the kingdom. If you make it down the stairs you reach a thick black metal gate with mesh inserts. The smell of the paint thinner is thick in the air, along with a low-frequency buzzing that you'll get used to soon enough. Sometimes I like to wait a little bit before I announce my arrival. The amount of profanity that comes from this tiny, brightly lit space is incredible. If it's your first time you must establish a relationship of mutual respect with the king, Salim. He can smell entitlement even before your foot narrowly misses that chipped step.

He works fast but absolutely hates when anybody tries to rush him. Give him all the time in the world and he'll do the thing right now. The first time I met Salim was through a phone call. I was working with NT on setting up a printing station at one of her book launches. She had kicked me off the project months earlier because she was certain I stole her ideas but then she needed me so there I was. I was having trouble finding printing ink. I was also such an amateur, I really didn't know shit. Anyway, I called and asked if he would sell me ink. He said he doesn't do that but if I wanted to print I was welcome to pass by the studio. He was clearly

13 In Arabic. كل واحد يقلع شوكه بإيديه

frustrated with me and this silly little request. Did I not know who I was talking to? I didn't.

The second encounter was much worse. I was working at Studio Safar (where I allegedly stole and implemented NT's ideas and dreams, of course, in order for me to get ahead with my career on her back), and we had a client who was the daughter of an insanely rich man who was so fucked up that he was wanted in Japan and had to flee back to Lebanon inside a cello case. That's the story at least. Anyway, daddy's girl here had her father's eyebrows and was a jewellery designer. Paper was not good enough for her. She wanted business cards made of pure brass. Not wanting to engrave it, we had to screen print. I went with a colleague so we could face Salim together. I was a bit scared of him in those days. We walked in and presented this nasty little brass sample we had and he literally laughed and said: "This is garbage." It was garbage, but eventually he printed the cards and everyone was happy.

The third encounter was the charm. I wanted to print one hundred little cards and there was no proper space at my studio to do this. I came to him. Damsel in distress, with the shittiest screen you can imagine. Tiny, maybe 25 x 15 cm. Wobbly, loose, horrible. He had zero patience. But he said: "You know what?", to the guy who works there with him, "Set her up on this old machine and let her do what she wants, this won't work anyway." He gave me a squeegee and some ink and I started printing. He would look over his shoulder every now and then. Not a drop of ink out of place, all the prints were sharp. At some point I could physically feel the ice melting, and that's when he understood that I was as in love with this process as he was.

He's so graceful when he works. He can smoke a cigarette while using both his hands and one of his legs for other things. There's cigarette ash all over the place. He says he doesn't like attention but I think he absolutely loves it. People come in and see him in ripped dirty jeans and a t-shirt as old as he is and assume he's the lowest in the chain of command. Why would a king look like that? He could be in a suit smoking a cigar inside a small office where only he has air conditioning, but that's not who he is. And that's not what screen printing is. Your hands and your feet have to be in it. Nothing can be done from a distance.

Whenever anybody dares to announce the end of print,
I think of Salim.
No, there is no end to print.
There is no end to spending time learning
at the hands of a master
like Mokhtar.
There is no end to loss and there is no end to how many
times an Arabic letter could shapeshift.

BIBLIOGRAPHY:

Mamdani, Mahmod. Neither Settler nor Native: The Making and Unmaking of Permanent Minorities. *London: Harvard University Press, 2020.*

Lugones, Maria. "The Coloniality of Gender." Worlds & Knowledges Otherwise, *2 (Spring 2008): 1–17.*

Muchado, Carmen Maria. In the Dream House. *Minneapolis: Graywolf Press, 2019.*

Massoudi, Hassan. "Two Daughters of the Same Parents." In Arabic Graffiti, *edited by P. Zoghbi and D. Karl, 31–32. Berlin: From Here to Fame, 2011.*

Kristeva, Julia. Powers of Horror: An Essay on Abjection. *New York: Columbia University Press, 1982.*

Douglas, Mary. Purity and Danger. *London and New York: Routledge, 1966.*

Carstens, Delphi. "Hyperstition: An Introduction." Interview with Nick Land. Orphan Drift Archive, 2009. Accessed: www.orphandriftarchive.com/articles/hyperstition-an-introduction/.

Berlant, Lauren. "Intimacy: A Special Issue." Critical Inquiry *24, no. 2 (1998): 281–288.*

Berlant, Lauren. "Without Exception: On the Ordinariness of Violence." Interviewed by Brad Evans. Los Angeles Review of Books, *July 30, 2018. Accessed: lareviewofbooks.org/article/without-exception-on-the-ordinariness-of-violence/.*

Ott Metusala

How Do We Live?

In 1988 I was born in Tallinn, when the country was still referred to as the Estonian Soviet Socialist Republic. The restoration of the independence of The Republic of Estonia came almost three and a half years later. Officially, the occupation of the territory by Soviet Russia ended on August 31, 1994, when the last (then already Russian Federation) troops left the former Estonian SSR.

To this day you can still find leftovers of the Soviet occupation in Estonia. The Stalinist houses reached Estonia when the new regime wanted to show its greatness and power. After the death of Stalin, the modernist ideas in architecture and design supported the notion of a better socialist world, where supposedly everyone had a good life.[1] While the home was a personal space not dictated by the political scene, its individual elements were still submitted to a grid that enforced a uniform appearance.[2] This is because during this period there was only a limited number of producers of interior design objects.

On a regular basis I scroll on local Estonian online marketplaces through the category '*nõukogudeaegne*', containing objects from the Soviet era. I can easily spend hours looking at old furniture, books, appliances, or other household items produced in the USSR. There is one group of objects particularly familiar to me, as my grandmother used to work as a lamp designer. From 1965 to 1992, she worked as an artist-constructor in Estoplast, a factory producing lighting fixtures for the modern Soviet Estonian household. Through my

1 Ester Vaitmaa, "Stalinistlik maja," Delfi, November 18, 2016, longread.delfi.ee/forte/stalinistlik-maja?id=76115407.

2 Yulia Karpova, *Comradely Objects: Design and Material Culture in Soviet Russia, 1960s–80s* (Manchester: Manchester University Press, 2020), doi.org/10.7765/9781526139863.

grandparents' house and my grandmother's job I will explore the Soviet household as an artificial scene. Reflecting upon their daily environment has helped me to learn about the technological and aesthetic issues of Estonian homes today.

THE APARTMENT

My grandparents' apartment in Tallinn is situated in a Soviet housing block. On the property, located at 23 Võistluse Street, there were a number of smaller wooden houses before the Second World War. In June 1973, a nine-storey panel house with seventy-two apartments was completed according to the standardised designs. The apartments are about sixty square metres, each with three rooms; a kitchen, bathroom, and toilet.

Once you enter one of the taupe coloured concrete buildings you can already imagine how the others look. There is a spacious yard in front, where parking for residents is organised.[3] The entrance has a single concrete step in front and it brings you to a glass door with an intercom beside it. The sound of the door being opened is quite distinctive and it keeps beeping until you have closed the door.

A door on the left takes you to the basement. The staircase in front of you takes you to the elevated ground floor (first floor in Estonia) above the half-submerged extra storage spaces. The mailboxes are on the ground floor, on the wall opposite the entrance. Right in front of the mailboxes are the doors to the elevator. Each hallway leads to four apartments and they look almost the same. The original doors have been replaced by metal ones, or they have been covered in leather.

3 "Võistluse tn 23, KÜ Aafrika," Juhkentali ja Keldrimäe, www.juhkentali-keldrimae.eu/kogukond/voistluse-tn-23-ku-aafrika.

When you share a third of each hallway you can choose to build an extra wall in front of this common space, therefore the hallways keep getting smaller and smaller. Demand for more private space and interior design additions in the hallways have slowly transformed these spaces into different characters over the years.

My grandparents had the luxury to be the first to choose an apartment in the building. They chose the last one, number seventy-two. We begin on their green balcony, on the north side of the building. On a sunny day the view over the city towards the sea is beautiful. On the left you can see the newer skyscrapers. Their glass facades reflect the mediaeval old town, and the brick and concrete both within and surrounding the historic centre. The reflective architecture no longer attempts to insert a different and new utopian language into the restless sign-system of the surrounding city. It rather seeks to reflect that very language.

When walking back into the apartment, you enter the living room. On the left there is a small cupboard that is made out of heavily varnished wood. When these surfaces get old, the wood pattern starts to peel off revealing a sawdust plate that is underneath. It's cheaper to use leftovers from the wood production to make the boards. Covering them with a thin layer of real wood creates an illusion of material.

From the living room you can enter the second bedroom towards the other side of the apartment, and the hallway towards the bathroom, kitchen, and smaller bedroom. The small room is wall-to-wall covered in books. A particularly desirable piece of furniture is a sectional cabinet sunk under a thick layer of lacquer, which was a mandatory element and a symbol of status in the modern home of that time.[4] The bed and the worktable are wrapped between two full walls of shelves and low cabinets with doors.

The rooms themselves could look very dark if you do not put any thought into the colours of the spaces or their lighting. In the bigger bedroom the wall used to be painted a dark turquoise blue. I always thought the colour combined with the air bubbles beneath made it look like an aquarium. However, most of the walls of their apartment are white and it makes the spaces look rather calm.

THE COUCH

In the middle of the living room sits a sectional couch. It consists of square pieces made out of wood that are mostly hidden by the fabric cover. These sections can be combined into the desired shape in many different configurations. In my grandparents' living room their couch forms an 'L' shape and runs across the wall. It ends at the low cupboard next to the balcony and stretches left towards the centre of the room. The cushions on the couch are loosely resting on top of the wooden frame. If the couch is reassembled it could also be used for sleeping. The textile is printed in a heavy floral pattern that feels out of place with its almost baroque look. I wonder if the fabric was changed at some point, as I only remember it in simple colour schemes – brown, red, and other darker colours. It also used to be cheaper to change the fabric on the couch rather than ordering a new one.

4 "Meenutame nõukogudeaegsest mööblidisaini — tikkjalgadest sektsioonkapini," Moodnekodu, November 8, 2016, moodnekodu.delfi.ee/artikkel/76188921/meenutame-noukogudeaegsest-mooblidisaini-tikkjalgadest-sektsioonkapini.

The new apartment buildings needed furniture to fit the spaces. Modularity offered a possibility to combine smaller parts together into desired shapes and sizes. Apartments were often small. Modular solutions used in the production of furniture were economical and fitting for a multitude of possibilities, but in general resulted in the new houses all looking very similar. When you lift up the loose cushions on top of my grandparents' couch you find small storage compartments underneath. Each compartment is about thirty centimetres deep, and with five to six of them you have almost a whole cupboard full of hidden storage.

LAMPS

In one of these compartments, my grandmother had kept some of her sketches from the time she worked at Estoplast. There are small models of furniture for children's rooms, drawings of animals, and a lot of lighting fixtures. Most of the sketches are original designs for lamps made in Estoplast, both for mass production and for custom orders.

Most of the lamps in their house were produced in Estoplast. The one attached to the wall above the corner of the couch was designed by my grandmother. It's a simple cylinder-shaped black base with a short and wide diffuser for the light. It's all made out of metal. The base is painted black and the diffuser covered in a shiny nickel coating. Originally it was made for an exhibition of Estoplast's products, and has never been produced on a mass scale. Next to the blueprints that were hidden in the couch, this lamp is the only existing copy. It's labelled as "Lamp design for director's office" (dated October 28, 1987).

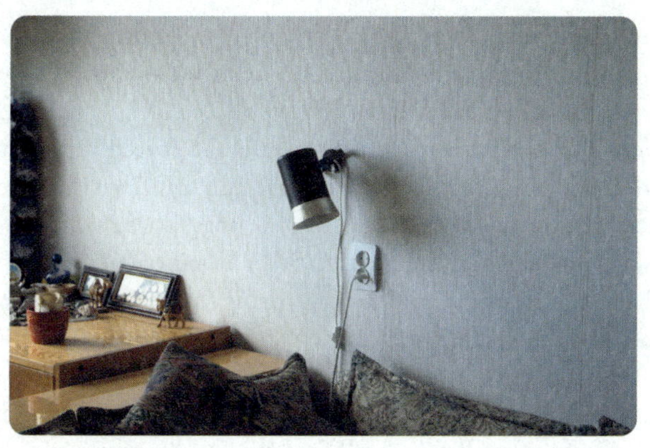

Another series of sketches depict the five-pointed (red) star as a clear association to the communist regime. Only governmental institutions could use aesthetics and materials that didn't reflect the living standards set for the working population. It turns out they are part of a series of models made together with her colleague Lilian Linnaks for the high-ranking ministers' offices in the Kremlin. This series of lamps required materials that were reflective of the status of their environment – green marble and gold details. In contrast to the modernist mass-produced products, these designs feel old fashioned but also more elaborate. My grandmother was unsure which one was the chosen one for the Kremlin, and where it was eventually situated in the complex. "In an office of a secretary of certain affairs," she replied when I asked, and many familiar names were mentioned in the process of trying to remember the moment.

My grandmother used to have a newspaper displaying an image of their lamps in the Kremlin in Moscow. The image apparently appeared in *Rahva Hääl* ('The People's Voice'), the official daily newspaper of the Communist Party of Estonia during the Soviet occupation. It was founded shortly after the first Soviet takeover in 1940, based on the offices and resources of *Uus Eesti* ('New Estonia'), an earlier Estonian newspaper. In search of the image, I ended up going to the National Library and looking through the archive of *Rahva Hääl* during the years these sketches were drawn. The images of the politicians and their offices were always on the first page of the newspaper. During the period when Leonid Brezhnev (1964–1982) was in power I could not find the lamp. The call to get the lamp must have come from people under the Andropov rule (November 10, 1982 – February 9, 1984). His former KGB office looked like it could fit with the sketches. In an article appearing in October 1984, there was suddenly a lamp on the table of Konstantin Chernenko's office. He was a Soviet politician and General Secretary of the Communist Party of the Soviet Union at that time. His reign was brief – from February 13, 1984 until his death on March 10, 1985. I showed the image to my grandmother and she said it was not it.

WORKSHOP

It's no secret anymore that my big source of inspiration is my grandmother Kirsti and her work at Estoplast, also known as Estoplast Experimental Plant.[5] Estoplast was founded in 1959, when the factories Presto and Elektrometall were merged and received a new name. It was literally a synthesis of plastics and metal.

5 '*katsetehas*' in Estonian. Nowadays this term is most close to a pilot plant: a pilot plant is a pre-commercial production system that employs new production technology and/or produces small volumes of new technology-based products, mainly for the purpose of learning about the new technology.

Plastic was a relatively new and revolutionary material at that time. Before polypropylene plastic came to be in use, the factory used bakelite compounds that were rougher and not so clear in colour. This had a depressing look to it and, with everything else also being produced in dark colours, it wasn't aesthetically appealing. Plastic and polypropylene plastic[6] allowed for easier casting of different shapes and a brighter palette.

By the 1970s, Estoplast was the leading factory in the Soviet Union for designing and producing lamps. Their catalogue was well-known in the Soviet Union. Every luminary or switch made at Estoplast had gone through all the stages of processing at the factory; only the production of glass and textile was outsourced. After expanding the technology of plastic production, the designers had the freedom to think of new, interesting ways to deal with the shapes of the lighting. New technology broadened the range of possibilities. Instead of what was formerly a circular lamp stand, the designers could come up with new shapes, like triangles. Before, the design was determined by the limitations of the metal milling machines.

Other limitations, however, remained. Even though the general population was in constant need of new products, it was more convenient and economical to keep on reproducing the same designs that were already in production. Nobody higher up in the company was interested in changing the system. It was easy to multiply the

6 Polypropylene (PP), also known as polypropene, is a thermoplastic polymer used in a wide variety of applications. Its properties are similar to polyethylene – the most common plastic today, primarily used for packaging (plastic bags, plastic films, geomembranes, and containers such as bottles). Polypropylene is slightly harder and more heat resistant, which makes it perfect for heat-pressing lighting fixtures.

lampshade count on a lighting fixture, one, two, three, four, five times. Often elements like wall mounts were used over long periods of time and never re-designed to fit the new means of production. By producing the same elements in bulk, they saved costs.

The word 'designer' was not in use throughout the Soviet Union. My grandmother's job, an artist-constructor, would now be called a designer. The designers worked closely with constructors during the experimental part of the production process. They knew how to make the preliminary design ideas into real handmade models. Through them, the designers could learn how to divert the problems in production and come up with new, reproducible designs. Experimentation was a huge and most desired part of the work in the factory among the artist-constructors. The eyes of the board and the Art Council in Moscow were steadily watching over the production numbers, which made the director's board less appreciative of the constant urge for change. Some of the new experiments were conducted in secret, in order to escape from the possible rage of the director's board after potential failure. Western magazines brought back from travels, or looked at in the local libraries, were a good source of inspiration for new and exciting ideas. Only a few lucky ones could travel outside of the Soviet Union during the period. Once given the opportunity, the designers brought back home the aesthetics from behind the iron curtain. Experimentation and mimicking western designs were ways for the artists to escape and resist the rigid system focused on building a perfect communist society.

CONCLUSION

The Soviet home is characterised by homogeneity, which starts already at the front door of the apartment building. The interior design of people's homes contain objects that are simple, modular, and mass produced. Due to a limited number of factories producing products, people often owned similar items. There is a big contrast between the Soviet home and the office of a politician. The latter's interiors and objects are made of luxurious and scarce materials with elaborately articulated design.

The designer's position at a Soviet factory could affect the feeling of the living situation of a generation. Even though the items for people's homes were simple, they were also modern, mimicking designs from so-called western countries. At Estoplast, their modern-looking (at the time) and clean design slowly overtook the golden-coated, rustic, and heavy visual language. This language remained, however, in the working spaces of the people in power. The political power imagined people would feel more equal and united by offering modernist interiors as a solution for better living. Little did they know this was also the result of experimentation of the workers in the factories looking at western interiors.

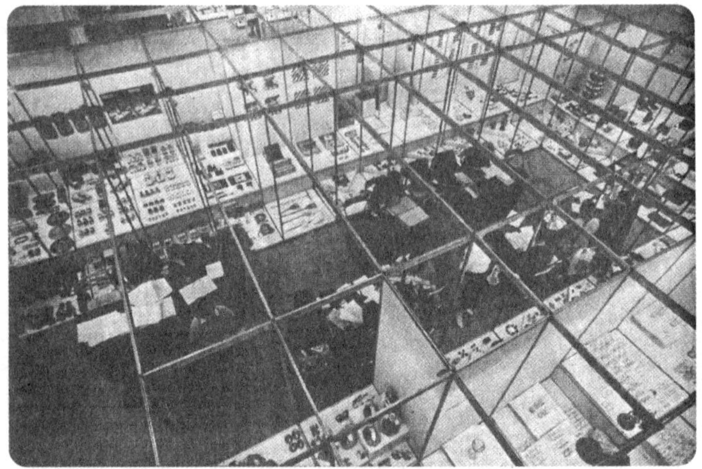

This picture combines creation, production, and trade – in the middle of the exhibition Tarbekaup 88,[7] *there is a national wholesale fair. Are these beautifully designed practical items still available to anyone who wants them? Photo: Vambola Salupuu.*

FORMERS OF OUR LIVING ENVIRONMENT

Published May 5, 1987, The People's Voice

Mediated by Hallar Lind

On the first weekend of April, a new all-Union creative association was born — the Union of Designers of the USSR. A ten-member representation of Estonian designers also participated in its founding congress in Moscow. Professor Bruno Tomberg, Head of the Design Department of the ESSR State Art Institute, comments on the story of the acquisition of the Creative Association of Industrial Artists:

> "Object culture is a natural part of everyday life. One of the central problems of the XXVII Congress of the CPSU was that the industrial products of the Soviet country must incorporate the latest achievements of scientific thought, satisfy the highest technical-economic, aesthetic and other consumer needs, and be competitive on the world market.

7 English: *Consumer Goods 88.*

In industrial art, the creation of an object is a collective activity. Until now, there has been the artist on one side and the engineers, designers, technicians, craftsmen on the other. When designing a specific object, the artist must take into account the peculiarities of technology in many ways. At the same time, technology is obsolete in many areas of production. Until now, the industrial artists of every field, each company, fought for the aesthetic values of production on their own. They did not have their own organisational connection. Some designers worked in the designers section of the Artists' Union, others in the applied arts section, etc. However, there are branches in the industry, such as appliance/widget construction, whose designers feel like a foreigner in the framework of the Artists' Union.

Of course, the core of the new union is the designers who have so far been members of the Artists' Union. Clothing artists, for example, took a very active part in creating the new union. However, there is no contradiction even if a versatile artist is a member of two creative unions at the same time.

So far, the Art Foundation and, to a certain extent, the Industrial Arts Council of the USSR Council of Ministers have contributed a lot to the joint activities of designers in our republic. We were one of the few federal republics where there was no branch of the All-Union Institute for Scientific Research in Technical Aesthetics. The experience of Lithuanians showed that the efficiency of the republican branches of the institute was relatively low."

The congress of 600 delegates approved the statutes of the Designers' Union and elected the all-union governing bodies. When can we talk about the birth of the Estonian SSR Designers' Union?

"By the decision of the Congress, all the delegates of the Congress were admitted to the union. Thus, there are currently ten members of the Designers' Union in Estonia. Four of them – the chief artist of the Art Foundation Ando Keskküla, the chief artist of "Standard" Teno Velbri, the artist Ivika Kärmik and Bruno Tomberg – were elected to the 92-member all-union board. Ilme Neemre, Secretary of the Arts Council of our Ministry of Light Industry, is a member of the All-Union Audit Committee.

By the way, in the corridors of the Moscow Congress, one wondered why a fairly prestigious Estonian design has such a small representation in the All-Union Forum. A surprising paradox became clear — the data of the Central Government of Statistics were used to establish the norms of representation, according to which there are 80 designers in Estonia (!). Namely, statisticians register as industrial artists only those people who work as artists. The job description of most designers is different from what is written on their paycheck. In some places the artist's job is not prescribed at all, in others the artist's salary is very low compared to what is done, and it is more useful to work with the constructor's job title, etc. It shows the current attitude towards industrial art. An artist is considered to be a secondary or tertiary worker, reporting to either the chief engineer, the chief technologist, or even the trade union committee. For comparison, in the Latvian SSR, the chief artist in industrial enterprises is subordinate to the director general, acting as his deputy. So the statute of a production designer is still to be developed.

We estimate the number of Estonian designers at 400. There should be at least 20 members to form a republican creative union. Ten more members need to be recruited through a Union-wide organisation. Then the association of our designers would have the rights to operate on a social basis. To form its own governing body, membership must grow to 100. I think that the organisational work in this direction will last until autumn."

Through industrial mass production, the designer's artwork reaches very large crowds, and the design of any consumer product, garment, or tool affects the aesthetic perceptions of many. What will be the role of the Designers' Union in this socially important process?

"Our first task is to make the industry more interested in supporting design and introducing the ideas of industrial artists into production. An all-Union design centre will be organised on the basis of the above-mentioned Institute of Technical Aesthetics. We also want to create a national design centre in Estonia to mediate the relationship between the creator and the manufacturer.

There are several trends in design. We have also created many outstanding unique specimens in Estonia. But this is the so-called elitist level that satisfies the few. The other direction is the transfer of design creation from industry to mass commodity. But let's monitor the reactions of the visitors of the exhibition *Tarbekaup 88* in the Blue Pavilion – a kind of a concentrate of the creations of local industrial artists. But let's follow the reactions of the visitors of the exhibition – the exhibits are world-class, but when will such beautifully designed things reach the Tallinn Department Store in sufficient quantities? In the current system of creation, production, and trade, the gap between design creation and mass production remains large. This is an issue that the Designers' Union will certainly address in order not to be ashamed of its name.

And only then is it appropriate to think about developing a unique design. At the moment, we admire the brilliant peaks of unique creation, which, however, do not have a wide support. Our level of culture is still determined by the whole.

The conversion of the magazine *Tehnitšeskaja Estetika*[8] into a publication of the Designers' Union should also contribute to the faster connection of the activities of the Creative Union with practice."

8 English: *Technical Aesthetics.*

Siwar Kraitem

The Onion, and Other Language Stories

IT BEGAN WITH A NAME

WHERE Beirut, early 1990s
ACTORS my mother, my father

I. When my parents knew they were pregnant with a girl, back in early 1991, they couldn't agree on a name.

My mother had some ideas and so did my father. But there were many issues they could not agree on, and naming their first child was one of them. Negotiations ◎ تشاور with family members only brought in more suggestions, but nothing seemed right.

My father always had one in mind, an old Arabic name, quite uncommon at the time. It was the name of an older family member that always resonated with him; a gut feeling told him it would become the name of his daughter one day. My mother, on the other hand, preferred a more modern name like Karma or Sarah. As my mom would later do, and advise me to do in situations of indecisiveness, she would perform a particular prayer ◎ استخارة (istikhara) that is meant to help decide which of the choices will eventually be the best for you.

اللَّهُمَّ إِنِّي أَستَخِيرُكَ بِعِلْمِكَ، وَأَستَقْدِرُكَ بِقُدْرَتِكَ، وَأَسأَلُكَ مِنْ فَضْلِكَ الْعَظِيمِ فَإِنَّكَ تَقْدِرُ وَلا»
أَقْدِرُ، وَتَعْلَمُ وَلا أَعْلَمُ، وَأَنْتَ عَلامُ الْغُيُوبِ..

اللَّهُمَّ إِنْ كُنتَ تَعْلَمُ أَنَّ هَذَا الأَمْرَ (هنا تسمي حاجتك) خَيْرٌ لِي فِي دِينِي وَمَعَاشِي وَعَاقِبَةِ أَمْرِي
فَاقْدُرْهُ لِي وَيَسِّرْهُ لِي ثُمَّ بَارِكْ لِي فِيهِ..

اللَّهُمَّ وَإِنْ كُنتَ تَعْلَمُ أَنَّ هَذَا الأَمْرَ (هنا تسمي حاجتك) شَرٌّ لِي فِي دِينِي وَمَعَاشِي وَعَاقِبَةِ أَمْرِي
فَاصْرِفْهُ عَنِّي وَاصْرِفْنِي عَنْهُ وَاقْدُرْ لِي الْخَيْرَ حَيْثُ كَانَ ثُمَّ ارْضِنِي بِهِ. (وَيُسَمِّي حَاجَتَهُ)

وَفِي رواية « ثُمَّ رَضِّنِي بِهِ» رَوَاهُ الْبُخَارِيُّ 1166.

In Islam in general and with my family in particular, names carry a lot of significance. A child has the right to be 'well-named' ◎ حسن

التسمية by their parents, as this will be the carrier of their personality. In Islam, it is believed that choosing a righteous name will bestow blessings onto the bearer.

While my mother was in labour at the hospital, the quarrel was still continuing to no avail. My dad paced in the waiting room outside, and most of our close relatives were impatiently awaiting my parents' first child. It was quite significant for my father's family as he was the only man among six sisters, making yours truly, the first long-awaited child that will carry my father's family name.

Finally, a solution was proposed: a draw. My dad passed along small papers to everyone present. Each wrote a desired name, folded it twice, and placed it in his hat.

Siwar سوار was picked, the old Arabic name he had always wanted.

II. So what's in a name? Why is naming such a daunting process?

Why was my father, who lived a huge part of his life abroad, more attached to this very old Arabic name, while my mother, who lived all her life in Beirut, was pulled to the other, more modern side? Perhaps she thought of me leaving the country one day, as all parents in Lebanon do, and that I would need a name that would prove easy to pronounce or remember among non-Arab speakers.

Artist and writer Marwan Moujaes[1], in his essay "The Uprooted Molar, How to Fall in Love With a Dead Animal", speaks about the struggle of the pronunciation of his name on the European border, and how this struggle follows him across the border.

1 Marwan Moujaes is a Lebanese artist and writer. In the reader: '*What Has Left Since We Left: Six Takes on Europe* ', is included an essay that he wrote entitled: The Uprooted Molar, How to Fall in Love with a Dead Animal?'

I think also of how mispronouncing names becomes an act of disrespect. I think of the effect it has. What happens when names are mispronounced or misspelled by non-speakers of a language? How does this carry an insulting weight, even when not deliberate?

In thinking about what a 'name' does to acts of protest, Etel Adnan,[2] a Lebanese writer and poet who was born in the 1920s, writes in her essay, "To Write in a Foreign Language", about how growing up in Beirut, she always heard her father say she will travel to Germany one day to be a chemist: an excuse she gave to her missionary nun-run French school in Beirut as a way to skip Arabic class. It was an excuse the school immediately welcomed, having only enforced two hours per week of Arabic classes two years prior. It was only enforced after a lot of pressure from the country's government. Before that, Arabic had been taboo at school, the 'sisters' even had 'spies' amongst some students that would record who spoke Arabic outside of class time. These students were then punished for speaking their mother tongue. This phenomenon made their relationship with Arabic sour. Even though most of them spoke Arabic in their childhood homes, they ended up speaking French or a mixture of French and Arabic in their own future homes.

In October 2019, the process of 'naming' preoccupied my thoughts again, this time in a more explicitly political fashion when it came to 'the 'protests' in Beirut. It is something I still have no conviction of a name for. We all named it 'revolution' ◎ ثورة in Arabic, the first few weeks when hope and momentum overfilled our cups. The politicians named it حراك 'harak' or 'movement', which seemed to

2 Etel Adnan was a Lebanese-American poet, essayist, and visual artist. She was born in 1925, Beirut, Lebanon and lived between Beirut, Paris, and the USA.

undermine what it actually was and make of it just another 'political movement' or voice rather than a collective uprising of a people. Others called it 'uprising' or intifada انتفاضة in Arabic, also to some in solidarity or nostalgia to the Palestinian انتفاضة.

Was it better to name it the 'October Revolution'? Although eminently, 'the October Revolution' is a popular nomination for the 'Great October Socialist Revolution', also known as 'The Bolshevik Coup', 'Bolshevik Revolution', 'Bolshevik Uprising', or 'Red October'.

Ghassan Kanafani[3], in his famous interview with Richard Carleton, engages in a 'vocabulary battle' as Carleton attempts to find 'politically correct' terms to describe the situation in between Palestine and Israel. He first calls it 'war', followed by 'civil war', then 'conflict'. As Kanafani argues with Carleton's reductive choice of words, he in turn tries to offer a more descriptive and comprehensive account. He interjects between Carleton's attempts: "It's "a people fighting for their rights", "a liberation movement fighting for justice". And after Carleton finally stumbles on his words and calls it 'whatever it best be called', Kanafani replies: 'It's not 'whatever', because this is where the problem starts.' What Kanafani meant was to highlight the weight that the choice of terminology carries. He also brings to light how vocabularies affect the way a people view their own fight, how it is perceived by others, and the imminent power structure that lies therein. It is that which determines and justifies acts of violence, disobedience, and war.

3 Ghassan Kanafani was an author and a leading member of the Palestine Liberation Front (PLO). Kanafani is also my mother's name, and so he is related to the family. Richard George Carleton was a multi-Logie Award winning Australian television journalist who interviewed Kanafani.

So as some of the previous examples suggest, naming such a sensitive political event was not a new struggle, but a historical one.

And yet, how did this language propaganda stunt also downplay the impact, discredit it, but also slowly eat away the 'belief', 'conviction', and 'trust' of the people who poured down to the streets to protest, or expose the differences rather than the similarities?

I watched as thousands flocked to the street, renewing the struggle every week with yet another issue that needed to be addressed, all relevant, all a reason to refuel a revolution. And so as 'I struggled to name it, I reconciled my dilemma by not naming it.

A fill-in-the-blanks revolution unfolds as a mapping dossier on the following spread. It is a playful personal analogy, oscillating between our instinct to conform to 'faithful ideologies' when it comes to naming, as well as maintaining a clear compass in an act of revolution. The format suggests a structure, and yet lends itself to being a diary that anyone call fill in. This dichotomy allows us to omit the rigidity, add or remove from it, replace terminologies as we see fit, and personalise our reading experience of an act of 'revolution'. It insists that all accounts are valid and that naming can be malleable rather than indoctrinating.

ENGLISH AND THE PRESENT

You are my onion peel,
the shallowest of them all,
and yet the one I use the most.

You were my first 'guest' ضيف, as Abdellatif Kilito[4] mentions in his book لن تتكلم لغتي *Thou Shalt Not Speak my Language*.

With you, I first learned to count, learned my sciences at school, but I still write with you in hesitation, wishing I wrote this with another.

Not so secretly, أتمنى لو كنت اكتب هذه في اللغة العربية

It is with you that I write these stories, partly personal, about a notion that has captured me, that of language and its lyricism, but also that of language as witness to our entangled social and geopolitical histories. I am definitely most accustomed to writing with you and yet, there are still a lot of notions you cannot help me express, especially when I think of memory and the spiritual dimension.

So I have decided to contest my own use of you in writing this essay collection, keeping my words in the tongues where they belong, mostly with my mother: Arabic. Because as Walter Benjamin[5] would say:

"Translation which intends to perform a transmitting function, cannot transmit anything but information – hence something inessential."

4 Abdelfattah Kilito is a scholar, critic, and author of a number of books on Arabic literature. His work elides the distinction between literary criticism and storytelling, analysis and fabulation. He has written many books in Arabic and French.

5 Walter Benjamin was a German Jewish philosopher, cultural critic, and essayist. His major work as a literary critic included essays on Baudelaire, Goethe, Kafka, Kraus, Leskov, Proust, Walser, and translation theory.

WEEK 1 / A WHATSAPP revolution

People first took to the streets after the threat of a tax on WhatsApp, making it a 'paid' or taxed app, in a country that is notorious for having one of the most expensive telecoms in the world. And so, WhatsApp was the first instigator of this revolution. WhatsApp also holds possibly the largest archive of the several revolution-related organisational groups. A new WhatsApp language was also coined through an explosion of context-specific stickers and gifs.

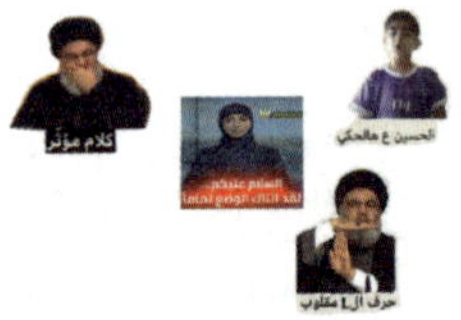

What's Up With Lebanon's WhatsApp Revolution?

NOVEMBER 8, 2019 GUEST CONTRIBUTOR

WEEK 2 / A PUBLIC SPACE revolution

Another crucial layer to the revolution was the reclaiming of abandoned, public, and private spaces. This began with the public squares in the city but even extended to highways, roads, etc, where many roadblocks took place. People renewed their understanding of spaces that were raped by the government, and of the dire need for public spaces. The most prominent example is the 'egg'; an icon of Lebanese modern architecture. It is an abandoned cinema in the central district of Beirut. Its construction had started in 1965, only to be later discontinued during the Lebanese civil war and had been closed off to the public until the night of October 17th, 2019, the night the revolution broke. It has since become a reclaimed public space that held screenings and gatherings during the protests.

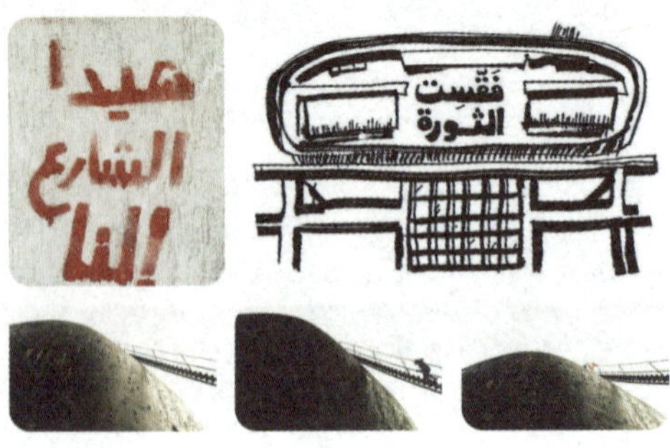

WEEK 3 / A FEMINIST revolution

Feminists took the streets, claiming feminist rights such as 'the right of a Lebanese woman to pass on the nationality to her husband and children', which is still dismissed due to political reasons. They came up with scout-like chants that addressed men in power and fought misogynistic language. Some revised curse words, eliminating and replacing misogynistic language within the vernacular language.

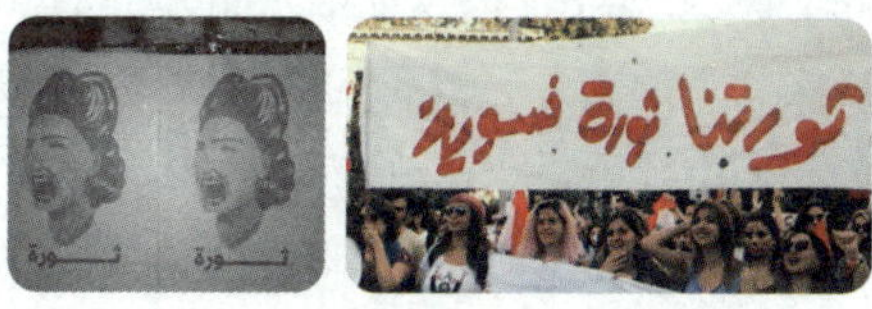

WEEK 4 / A LINGUISTIC revolution

The transformative aspect linguistically was present on many fronts, not only in relation to naming but also in observing people's own relationship to the language they use to protest, the shift to Arabic on social media. It fuelled a newfound sense of 'belonging' to an almost forfeited Arabic in people's quotidian experience. To some, who probably used Arabic only when talking to the grocer or electrician, this was quite transformative.

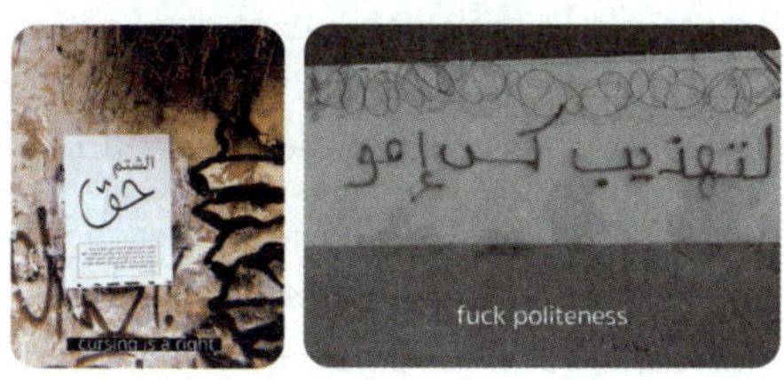

WEEK 5 / An IMPOLITE revolution

Protesters began to furiously curse politicians openly in the streets. Finally, this holiness that politicians in Lebanon paint themselves with is gone. Everyone from all ages uniting in cursing this or that minister, ridiculing the whole system of authority and insiting on our freedm of speech. This was of course attacked, especially by religious/ political leaders, such as Hezbollah who condemned the 'impolitness' of the revolution in an effort to undermine and delegitmize it. This was met by campaigns from lawyer coalitions that deemed cursing 'a right'.

THE ONION

Saturday mornings were the worst.

Every Saturday morning was cleanup day. My mother was a teacher during the week, so it was on that day off when mom planned to clean the house, cook for the week ahead, and do laundry.

7:30 am, the bell would ring, Oum Mohamad would be there first thing to help us with the tasks for the morning.

Often for lunch, we would have Mujaddara مجدرة, a dish that needs a loooot of onion and is something you cook in bulk. Flavours are often sharpened the next day, making it a good dish to be cooked on Saturday, and consumed throughout the week. And yet, onions were my worst enemy. I hated them.

> "Onions have made you such a sloooooooooooooooow eater," my mom would say.

The whole family would finish the meal, my mom would finish doing the dishes, and I would still be chewing on my last bite. She even had to buy me a timer to train me to eat faster.

I couldn't tolerate the smell around the house whenever my mom cooked, almost anything. 'Mujaddara' مجدرة and 'Mudardara' مدردرة were two of the major culprits as they ate up so many onions.

MUJADDARA مجدرة

Ingredients:

2 large onions
1 carrot
2 cups of lentils
1 cup of rice

MUDARDARA مدردرة

Ingredients:

3 large onions
1/2 cup of lentils
1 cup of rice

Even when my mom cooked stews, I would pick out the tiny, colorless pieces of onion and keep them aside.

Whenever we had hummus or foul on Sunday mornings, my brother would ask my mom for raw onions on the side. I almost puked as I saw them floating impatiently in a bowl of water, every single time.

But I loved cooking, and was determined not to allow onions to deter me from this love. It was definitely a slow process for me to begin making peace with cutting them, tearing up, pausing for a moment as the dark thoughts of skipping onions in the meal seduced my brain, before I heard my mother's voice in my head again, insisting on the absolute need to add onions when cooking.

WHERE Beirut, protest square, December 30, 2019
ACTORS me

On Monday December 30, protesting in Martyr's square, a protest that began quite peacefully, turned violent after the ISF cracked down on us with an incredible amount of tear gas. Although it was in the Western part of the open square by the Nahar newspaper building, the gas filled the air with such intensity that I just didn't know where to run to, eventually running east towards Saifi. There, by the headquarters of the 'Kataeb party' – which claimed some sort of despicable support for the protesters, attempting to wipe off their repulsive history of اغتيالات عالهوية during the civil war – is quite a large and dangerous intersection that greets all the cars driving from the North. Cars would be driving at highway speed just before the road gets slightly tighter and they arrive at this intersection. Traffic lights would occasionally be on – only useful if there would be a will to respect them on a whim.

I couldn't see. I just couldn't bring myself to open my eyes, but the smoke was getting more intense, and I had to run away from the open square and head to gemmayze, where the buildings could block or slow down the spread of the smoke.

Knowing I wasn't the only one running, I held my hand up and ran across the street to the other side, half-choking, eyes almost closed.

As I made it across, someone noticed my very obvious discomfort and passed me an onion.

I held it to my eyes, cried the toxins away.
And so the unthinkable happened: I had 'embraced' onions.
They became the weapon with which I became invincible in the face of tear gas.

Upon delving into the social penetration theory[6], I propose that when it comes to language, an onion is an anaolgy for the different languages we speak and the different layers within: sometimes weapons, and other times, aspects we embrace.

Contrary to how the existing 'Onion Analogy' looks at personality like a multilayered onion, having the public self (height, weight, gender) on the outer and the private self (values, self-concept, deep emotions) in the core, I wonder how we carry different onions, the most shallow layer outside being the one we use daily when it comes to the languages we use.

6 'The social penetration Theory' was originally created by Irwin Altman and Dalmas Taylor. It proposes that relationships get more intimate over time when people disclose more information about themselves. The Onion Analogy is used to explain the 'social penetration theory'.

Although they might appear linear, the layers reveal geo-political struggle, family history, spiritual background, to name a few, in a constant play between the personal and all other parallel layers.

An onion weeps, allowing the more hidden personal layers to surface. It exposes the vulnerabilities in the relationships with each of these languages. This act of vulnerability, allows for a metaphorical transformation and enables the possibility of reconciliation within these relationships.

It could allow us to transform the guilt or frustration of carrying certain languages (the ones mostly linked to a colonialism or imperialism), into the wealth that multilingualism brings forth through its exposure to different voices and knowledges.

ARABIC AND THE MOTHER

I wasn't very attached to you growing up. Getting to know you, and your harsh vocabulary felt more like a duty than anything else. I still spoke you every day though.

I. You are my MOTHER's mother tongue. Even though, she, too, studied in English and became an English teacher, you were her vessel of advice, care, but also scold.

II. My FATHER has a strong Beiruti accent, which I often jokingly criticised, sometimes answering him with an accent even though he knew I didn't generally speak like that. It is probably where I developed an ear for accents. It made space for inside jokes between us, adding a lightness to his mostly quiet presence at the food table.

III. I also learned you at SCHOOL, a more literary and poetic version of you, from the golden ages of Arab poetry. The only time I might have enjoyed writing in you was when I took philosophy class and had to write papers through you. This is when I saw your potential in expressing complex thoughts. You were given a less important status within my educational institution, which made it more difficult to connect with you. I still enjoyed poems of ابن الرومي and المتنبي

IV. I got to know a different aspect of you, poetic yet formal, by going deeper into RELIGION and studying the Koran. I often recited you loudly in prayer with my mother and in some classes about religion where my brother and I would go to on Saturday afternoons. You have a special place within Islam, and honouring you was something my mother wanted for us, especially because we were going to an Orthodox Christian school.

V. My GRANDMOTHER always began her letters with بسم الله الرحمن الرحيم. She would often write with you for special occasions like my birthday or Eid. I carry a very explicit memory of her handwriting and the way she always wrote recipes and letters alike with this opener.

VI. My BROTHER taught me that language is power. He taught me that there are different versions of you. He might not like to hear it as such, but using you to curse was a powerful weapon for me and one of my first lessons of empowerment.

THE WITNESS

"When I speak to you in your language, what happens to mine? Does my language continue to speak, but in silence?"

– KHATIBI, Love In Two Languages

I. My language is the epitome of the personal and yet the witness of the social, the political, and the economic. In countries crippled by mandate and colonial history, what have we that carries the scars of the past, but language?

Have we become more 'French', more 'European', more 'white', Fanon[7] would ask when speaking of how learning French in the Martinique made one more 'white', allowing 'blacks' to rise in class, through multilingualism. Similarly, in Lebanon, language(s) are a mirror of social class.

If you speak like an American, you're a spoiled rich kid who went to an American school. If you speak French at home, then an intellectual bourgeois. To make things more complicated, this is also attached to religion to a certain extent. When the French came to Lebanon in the 1920s, they also came through religious

7 Franz Omar Fanon, also known as Ibrahim Frantz Fanon, was a French West Indian psychiatrist and political philosopher from the French colony of Martinique. His works have become influential in the fields of post-colonial studies, critical theory, and Marxism. He also wrote on language.

missionaries, setting up Christian schools and congregations that taught everything in French. Other anglophone protestant missionaries also opened schools that mainly taught in English. In all of these setups, Arabic was disregarded and treated like a tertiary, almost foreign language.

II. Is it that multilingualism breeds a richness of positionalities, in reference to Sara Ahmed[8]? Does it yield a trust in those languages, and in turn create a distrust in Arabic? Does it cripple me when I think I want to write in my mother tongue, and yet, I can't?

Years and years have trained me to write in imperial and colonial languages.

So, my own language is one of distrust, one of suspicion.

In all the accounts and stories of grief towards this linguistic reality, there is linguistic oppression, but also a sense of freedom into opening up to all these worlds and gaining insight into what a multi- lingual world provides. With the multilingualism that some of these oppressive systems have enabled comes a wealth and multitude of 'orientations', as Sarah Ahmed would put it, which allows for several positions and ways of looking at the 'table'. Although realities of borders and limitations are still in place and cannot be imagined to disappear any time soon, this multitude of positionalities within the connaissance of 'colonial languages' allows for a more empathetic positioning and for room to speak, and alter, from a different position. It allows us to 'hack' this position of power and record different voices. To add to this,

8 Sara Ahmed is a British-Australian scholar whose area of study includes the intersection of feminist theory, lesbian feminism, queer theory, critical race theory, and postcolonialism.

since most of the knowledge production– or more blatantly, the recording of knowledge production– happens in the lands of the ex-colonisers, whenever we are given access to these spaces of knowledge production, we must make full use and enable these different voices. To think of more emancipating capacities, if we consider that the domination of French in the francophone world, from Africa to Eastern Europe, oppresses and subdues existing languages, it also creates liberatory movements in the more dominant language of the oppressor, creating more reach and exposure. It can also enable a multitude of voices to exist and be heard within that same language. So, for example, the fact that Fanon or Khatibi[9] wrote in French, enabled them to reach different audiences, and allowed for their voices to resonate more widely. It is a powerful stance to perfect the language of the coloniser to a point where you become able to contest their use of it and gain real significance in that realm.

III. In 'Neither Settler nor Native', Mahmood Mamdani[10] traces the concept of the nation state to 1492 in Iberia, where the idea was to 'homogenise a nation' by creating a 'homogeneous' national homeland for the Christians of Spain. Effectively, it was two things: 'ethnic cleansing' through expelling Moors and Jews, and 'colonisation' and the expansion of the monarchy overseas, which in turn also meant 'ethnic cleansing'. He quotes Thomas Babington Macaulay, a member of the Supreme Council for India in the 1830s,

9 Abdelkebir Khatibi was a prolific Moroccan literary critic, novelist, philosopher, playwright, poet, and sociologist. Affected in his late twenties by the rebellious spirit of 1960s counterculture, he challenged in his writings the social and political norms upon which the countries of the Maghreb region were constructed. He wrote several works on bi-lingualism including his novel: 'Amour Bilingue' or 'Love in Two Languages'.

10 Mahmood Mamdani, is a Ugandan academic, author, and political commentator. He currently serves as the Chancellor of Kampala International University, Uganda.

in his 'Minute on Education': "I am quite ready to take the Oriental learning at the valuation of the Orientalists themselves. I have never found one among them who could deny that a single shelf of a good European library was worth the whole native literature of India and Arabia ... We have to educate a people who cannot at present be educated by means of their mother-tongue ... We must at present do our best to form a class who may be interpreters between us and the millions whom we govern; a class of persons, Indian in blood and colour, but English in taste, in opinions, in morals, and in intellect."

This gives us some insight also into the effect this certainly had on language as well with the creation of the nationstate and this ship of 'homogenisation', which managed not only to force people to convert their beliefs and religions, but also their languages, accents, and expressions of love and dignity. I think of how many have lost their accents, their languages, disappearing under layers of new ones that bulldozed away sounds, words, terminologies, scripts, notions, memories, expressions of grief ...

As Deleuze and Guattari[11] would say: "there is no mother tongue, only a power takeover by a dominant language".Such is the political power of language, it has the capability to erase a mother tongue.

And so, similarly, it must also have the power to empower one.

11 Gilles Deleuze, a French philosopher, and Félix Guattari, a French psychoanalyst and political activist, wrote a number of works together.

THE IMPOLITE

My younger brother was always quite easily provoked.

I. It is something I figured out quite early on as his older sister, and a skill I mastered and prided myself on whenever he annoyed or bored me.

His easy irritability gave me a lot of enjoyment.

Whenever I provoked him, he would get agitated, sometimes giving me a little slap, like young siblings often do.

Once, he broke my thick, round 6-year-old glasses.

'They were starting to get too small on my face anyway', I thought.

It didn't take me long to figure out my revenge. I knew I couldn't win in a fist fight, but I could definitely win with words.

And yet, it never came without punishment.

I'd hear my father blurt out foul language every now and then, getting worked up while watching a football match, or sometimes just pouring his annoyance over the remote control that wouldn't work when switching channels from Al Jazeera to Al Arabiyya.

So whenever I got a brotherly slap, I would blurt out a '7mar' حمار or 'kol khara' كول خرا. They were seemingly 'big' words for my age, especially for a young sweet girl like myself, as my mother would say. When it got serious enough that one of us went to snitch to my mom, or if she overheard us, he for one, would get a soft slap back, sometimes with my mom's leather flip flop, and I would get few drops of chili pepper paste – Dolly's, a locally produced version of Tabasco – and a brief time-out in the toilet for my 'inappropriate' use of language.

Our mothers brought us up thinking cursing is naughty, a notion I always ignored, feeling as though it was a strong weapon, a few letters pronounced, but enough to send me away for punishment.

II. <u>WHERE</u> Beirut, October 2019

Tires burning here, tear gas filling the air, people chanting, arms raised high, carrying banners, Facebook posts suddenly in the language that had become so obliterated from my quotidian.
A banner reads بكفّي شحن طائفي

Another Facebook post :xxxxxxxxxxxxxxxxx
Are these the same people? Why are we suddenly using big words like: ‘تمويل’ ‘فراغ’?

In Arabic, of course, I tell myself.
Why shouldn’t it be in Arabic, we are after all an Arab country, it is supposedly the language that ties us all.

How can I trust the revolution if I cannot trust my mother tongue, how can I trust this ‘society’ when it cannot speak the same language?

But we curse in the same language, I tell myself.

Driving around in a little Toyota, my neighbour in a Porsche, we still shout ‘wlik kiss ikhtak iza bta3rif tsou2, leik hal 7ayawen leik’ كس اختك ازا بتعرف تسوق، ليك هالحيوان ليك، ... whenever someone made an unsignalled turn.

It is often a misogynistic cursing language. But it doesn’t matter, I tell myself.

We still use the same cursing vocabulary, so maybe that’s enough. October 2019, Beirut was another personal affirmation of this.

هيلا، هيلا، هيلا هيلا هو جبران باسيل كس امو

'Hela hela, hela hela hoooo, Gebran Bassil kiss emmo' permeating the streets gave me a sense of overjoy and filled me with a sense of community. Observing the crowd beside me shouting these rather misogynistic words towards the minister of power at the time (and his mother): women the age of my mother, teenagers, 70-year-old mustached men, all chanting in sync. How was this not the embodiment of community, an awakening of collective expression?

Did it in that moment matter what words these were? Probably not.

Could they have been replaced by any other less insulting phrase? Maybe yes, maybe no.

Did they have to go after the man's mother?

What it was, though, was common ground; a common ground that Arabic and darija Lebanese was not able to provide in that moment in time, except through curse words.

So big was the fear these echoing words planted in the political class, that days later, Hassan Nasrallah, the main figure of the Hezbollah party – putting his religious mask on – came forth to address this in his speech, stating and reminding that cursing was a SIN.

يا عرصات

Days later, the lawyer coalition, whose main purpose was to support activists that were detained left and right during the protests, published a statement, deeming cursing a 'legal right' as graffiti with messages like 'fuck politeness' and 'dick government' دولة الإير popped up everywhere around the city.

How to love in a country that teaches surrender,
says Jihyun Yun[12]*.*

Can revolution be possible without love?
So what does revolution mean in a country like Lebanon where trust and love are decaying between people? In a country so sectarian among the multitude of religious sects and social classes, cursing language was becoming the long-lost thread that began to stitch the wounds of disconnection through language.

وإير

Here it was again, impoliteness almost won us a revolution.

FRENCH AND THE HISTORY

For quite a period of time, I wished my parents had en
rolled me in a school where you were the primary focus.

I looked for opportunities to get to know you in more casual
settings. I took summer classes and
watched cooking shows to strengthen our bond.

In my anglophone school,
you were in third place.

Many rejected you and used time with you to harrass, sleep, or work on unfinished homework.

Even though you were disregarded by many others, I realised I cared for you.

You were the reason I discovered my love for learning languages.
You felt like the window to get to know other Latin neighbours.

And yet, I also hate you.
I hate that you forced yourself on me, that the geo-political landscape stood between me getting to you know your poetics.

Not one tainted by the history of things.

12 Jihyun Yun is a Korean-American poet and freelancer writer.

THE MISSPELLED

West Beirut, by Ziad Doueiri, is a film about two teenagers, Tarek and Omar, living on the streets of Beirut, their families, their struggles. It takes place in the 70s, at the onset of the civil war that erupted in 1975. Recently, one specific scene keeps replaying in my head.

1975, Beirut. Tarek, the main character, lives in the Western part of Beirut, but goes to school, a French missionary school in the eastern part of the city. He is a troublemaker, as many are in their teens, especially when he gangs up with Omar, his neighbour and partner in crime.

Every Monday morning, children in Lebanese schools sing the national anthem in a general assembly of all students. In my anglophone* Orthodox school in the 1990s, we always sang both the Lebanese and school anthems. In Tarek's case, it was the French anthem.

Lebanon was under the French mandate for a little over two decades between the years 1923 and 1946. It had a large effect on religion and education, where French religious missionary schools were set up, by priests and nuns.

Etel Adnan, acclaimed poet, painter, and writer* speaks of her time going to a French convent school, and how French education was soon attributed to power. At these schools, the history taught was that of the French, with which they passed on a hatred of the Germans of course. The customs and ideas were also all in French.

She says: "Somehow we breathed an air where it seemed that being French was superior to anyone, and as we were obviously not French, the best thing was at least to speak French. Little by little, a whole generation of educated boys and girls felt superior to the poorer kids who did not go to school and spoke only Arabic. Arabic was equated with backwardness and shame. Years later I learned that the same thing was happening all over the French empire, in Morocco, Algeria, Tunisia, Black Africa and Indochina."

You must also understand that this 'colonial' education, went far further than just exposing children to the language and history; it was quite consciously erasing any space left for Arabic at the same time. It also came in a certain double-form of power, which is still very much in place in Lebanon even half a century later; the double authority of a religious and educating figure, which produced absolutely unquestionable immunity.

Franz Fanon uses the example of the "Negro," in Antilles as an example of challenges that colonized people face regarding language. Blacks in Antilles, specifically Martinique, were pressured to speak French as opposed to Creole. By speaking French, Fanon explained that Blacks could become more "white;" achieve higher social status and think of themselves as being equal to whites in society, as can be seen in his personal example: "To speak a language is to take on a world, a culture."

Fanon addresses this issue of the 'hierarchisation' of language, which is present to a large extent in Lebanon. It unfolds this dimension that enables queering and othering, however subtle or outspoken.

To put it plainly, French speakers in Lebanon are mostly the bourgeoisie. English speakers are less sophisticated. If they spoke a more American English, they might be upper class and went to expensive private American schools, and if they spoke no languages they probably went to public schools. Public schools remain the lowest down on the pecking order in Lebanon. And even though that might be beginning to change with the collapsing economy as nobody can afford private school tuitions anymore, it is still a school many prefer to avoid.

It is with this same sneaky yet sleek sense of authority that hundreds of Catholic priests were able to systematically abuse children over decades, in most Catholic denominations around the world. It is also with this same sense of authority that Nasrallah, the general director of the Hezbollah party in Lebanon 'legitimises' his actions and intentions. It is a very common mechanism in Lebanon where religion, power, and politics often fuse into one.

Going back to the story, Tarek found himself on yet another Monday morning faycing the fact of needing to sing the French anthem. Tarek was feeling especially rebellious that morning, so he picked up a megaphone and ran to the top floor of the school building, overlooking the school's playground where the students assembled. Into the megaphone, he loudly chanted the Lebanese anthem. The rest of the students, paused for a moment, but very soon after, followed suit.

Was this a patriotic moment for him? I don't think so, it was more of a moment of 'community', a moment of realisation that the French colonial langwage was never going to provide this sense of community to him and his fellow students. It is a role that Arabic, the supposed mother tongue, should lead.

Was this a patriotic moment for him? I don't think so, it was more of a moment of 'community', a moment of realisation that the French colonial langwage was never going to provide this sense of community to him and his fellow students. It is a role that Arabic, the supposed mother tongue, should lead.

Tarek was most certainly punished for his actions. He had to be lectured on the favours France had done for Lebanon over the years and was instructed to rite the great achievements of the French mandate on the board, in French, where he deliberately misspelled the obvious word 'Monsieur'.

MESYEUX

MEUCIEUX

This eloquent act of defyance staid with me as I kept thinking of how a small act of intentional misspelling could prove so potent a reminder.[13]

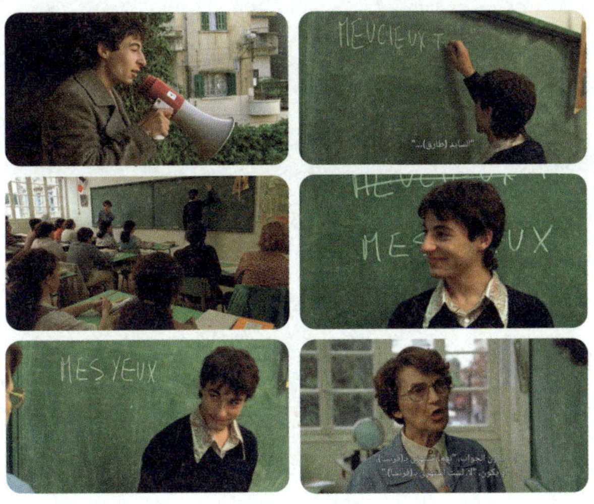

13 N.B. Words in this section have been deliberately misspelled.

ITALIAN AND MY FATHER

I got to know you to be closer to my father.

My father lived in Italy for most of his young adult years. He studied to be an Orthopedic doctor and along with his long years of studying, he did all kinds of student side-jobs. Of all the jobs he tried, cooking stuck. At home, my parents had a cooking arrangement. My mom cooked all week, my dad cooked on Sundays. He often made Italian dishes, from his famous vegetarian lasagna – that was literally on the menu whenever we hosted any family lunch – to more elaborate home-made gnocchi where we spent hours in the kitchen, boiling potatoes and modelling the gnocchis.

Cooking together was mostly how I connected and chatted with him. He would often tell me stories of his years in Italy, like this time he saved his Egyptian friend Samir who attempted a swim in the Lago Maggiore to try to impress a girl, when he couldn't actually swim, or how he became the chef of the hotel in Stresa after he began by only washing dishes there two summers earlier.

In the summer of 2006, Israel attacked Lebanon. I found myself stuck at home in very, very warm Beirut. During those ambiguous and long days at home, I needed a new hobby, something to give some sense of purpose and sanity to my summer. On yet another afternoon when my dad was glued to the TV screen watching the news, I came to him with a notebook and said: you will teach me Italian.

Buongiorno cara, come stai oggi?
Tutto apposto? Sei a casa stamattina?
Fatti sentire quando avrai tempo parleremo.

To this day, we make all sorts of deals to keep a thread of this alive. Leaving Lebanon helped, as we began texting more often, and the rule now is: we only text in Italian. You became the thread of our communication.

THE HAUNTED

"When I see people speake a foreign language that I do not understand; perplexed for a moment, I almost come to think that they are lost in their language, unable to escape from its clutches, that their condition has no remedy."

– KILITO, Thou Shalt Not Speak My Language

He speaks Arabic, she smiled to herself.
Undeniably, his broken Arabic handwriting wooed her.
She often felt a sense of fulfillment and pride whenever she heard

a European speaking Arabic, it was impressive. He a German, was flirting in her own language.

As things developed, she also learned German, mainly because of that relationship and the prospect of moving to Germany.

After moving to Europe, (not Germany), she became even more sensitive to this power dynamic. The flaunting of notions like 'decolonisation' in classes as part of the master's program under the name 'Disarming Design', and other discussions happening across different institutions in the continent, morphed this once prideful and fulfilled feeling in hearing her language being spoken by non-Arabs, into disgust, sometimes offense.

It has made me question the intentions, the motives behind non-Arabs familiarizing themselves with a language like Arabic. When Arabs growing up in the third world learned 'colonial' or 'imperial' languages, there was a clear purposeful conditioning, as part of a primary education in a country that was under mandate, but how is it when the reverse happens?

Abdellatif Kilito in his book Thou Shalt not Speak my Language speaks of this notion very literally, and describes this same feeling. He speaks of the notion of 'protectiveness of a language,' which resonates a lot, especially the farther away one gets from home. So, there is an openness to colonial languages that spreads much through our upbringing, and yet a protectiveness of the mother tongue.

Is it a feeling that this, too, is being robbed from us? Or is it, as Kilito would say, ◎ تطاول على اللغة which literally means 'stretching' the language in an act to insult or offend, in this case, offending or insulting the language itself.

In short, Kilito presumes that when an individual from a colonizer country perfects the language of the colonized, in this case, Arabic, they become not only colonizers of the land, but colonizers of the language as well.

Kilito is also considering a different form of colonialism, one that aims at not only expanding one's power but also at extinguishing its language as a form of erasure.

When Kilito talks about a language that 'inhabits', we can also probably talk about who 'haunts'. So how do unfamiliar bodies 'inhabit' 'lower' languages and, in a way, 'haunt' those languages?

At times, it triggers a certain feeling of: now that we have learned your language, we understand your culture.

Kilito offers the example of the French scholar Charles Pellat, who perfected his Arabic language, but degraded the Arabic literature as he translated it. In the introduction to his translation of works by Aljahiz, he writes, "In general Arabic books produce a sense of boredom, whatever their topic, and however attractive their titles." (1953, Viii, qtd. by Kilito, 2008, p. 11).

In this case, by perfecting the language, Charles Pellat gave himself the carte blanche to 'label' that language, to categorize it, and to insult it.

Another notion I must bring up is that in Lebanon, perfecting Arabic as a non-Arab was associated with being a 'spy' عميل as well. We even often joke about it behind closed doors, but this only implies the element of suspicion related to learning Arabic as a non-Arab.

There lies again another link between 'spying' and 'haunting', where the language is haunted for the sake of covering up a different intention, thus turning the language against its own people. Spying also often becomes a tool of 'haunting' popular movements that are given weight through language.

GERMAN AND THE POSSIBILITY

I became more nerdy about sentence structure.

I looked for linguistic links and compared you with others.
In you, I discovered 'getting to know a new language' as an adult.

I found and refound the challenge of 'picking up on an
accent', as you were far from sounds that were familiar,
I wanted to get the sounds right.

You were also attached to a certain prospect that didn't materialize.
(sigh of relief)

Everyone tells me you are a good base for the next language I will learn.

But,
I think I am starting to get a bit old,

Or,
maybe my curiosities have turned more within.

And the sense of excitement that once engulfed me at the idea of learning a new language is slowly beginning to fade.

I feel the need to go deeper into that which I already know.

I do not want to be a knower of many, but a proficient
knower of a few.

THE PERFORMATIVE

"So then if performativity was considered linguistic, how do bodily acts become performative?"

– BUTLER[14]

For some years in my teens, my mother and grandmother took me along to درس دين or a religious meeting on late Friday afternoons. They were sessions that began with a spiritual twenty minutes of ذكر or chanting together followed by a discussion or explanation of a verse from the Quran.

اللهم صلي وسلّم وبارك على سيدنا محمد عدد كمال الله وكما يليق بكماله

It was of the first times I encountered chanting loudly in a group. Although there was sometimes a discomfort associated with it, especially that I was naturally requestioning my relationship to religion at that age and battling timidness among a group of older women, there was something utterly moving, a powerful sense of overwhelming embodiment through the resonating words, and bodies swaying lightly in a circle.

Other days were the first day of Eid where I would be woken up by the sounds of تكبيرات العيد that echo throughout the city. They are also often repeated for around fifteen minutes before the call to prayer during Eid days, in celebration of the festive days.

الله أكبر الله أكبر الله أكبر.. لا إله إلا الله.. الله أكبر الله أكبر.. ولله الحمد، الله أكبر كبيرا والحمد
لله كثيرا وسبحان الله بكرة وأصيلا، لا إله إلا الله وحده، صدق وعده ونصر عبده وأعز جنده

14 Judith Butler is an American philosopher and gender theorist whose work has influenced political philosophy, ethics, and the fields of third-wave feminism, queer theory, and literary theory.

وهزم الأحزاب وحده، لا إله إلا الله ولا نعبد إلا إياه، مخلصين له الدين ولو كره الكافرون، اللهم صل على سيدنا محمد، وعلى آل سيدنا محمد، وعلى أصحاب سيدنا محمد، وعلى أنصار سيدنا محمد، وعلى أزواج سيدنا محمد، وعلى ذرية سيدنا محمد وسلم تسليما كثيرا»

In Islam, repetition is quite common. It is blessed to repeat every prayer or action three times. There is a certain value to insistence and repetition that reacts with the brain, allowing it to register information more readily.

فإن مع العسر يسرا
إن مع العسر يسرا

The way in which words and sounds create an interaction with the body, evoking an element of performativity to language, an embodiment.

It always fascinated me to see bodies praying or rotating around the kaa'bah. In Islam, there is value in collectivity, not only in sets of repeated words and phrases, but also in the congregation of bodies. Bodies in unison 'perform' prayer, they 'perform' language. In the case of religion, this repetition is often an affirmation of belief and belonging, one of 'obedience'.

Alternatively, bodies in protest seem to perform the opposite, they perform an affirmation of 'disobedience', and yet insist on the value of this 'belief' in change.

الشعب يريد اسقاط النظام

الشعب يريد اسقاط النظام
الشعب يريد اسقاط النظام

Butler speaks of performativity as part of the practice of 'protest'. She writes:

> *"Time and again, mass demonstrations take place on the street, in the square, and though these are very often motivated by different political purposes, something similar nevertheless happens: bodies congregate, they move and speak together..."*

In this case, the 'secularized' have found their spiritual, through the symbolism of protest, an almost religious act where, the '99%' are symbolically represented by the masses on the street.

The congregation of the bodies, with language as their vessel, become an enactment of the 'utopian' society they aim to build, setting up groups, lawyer-coalitions, and news platforms.

Bodies gain power when together, they echo words when spoken communally, enabling a sense of collective reassurance. Performativity, through repetition enables us to embody and inhabit language, creating relatabilities with ourselves and others.

POST-SCRIPTUM TO ARABIC

You are my language of love.

You are the language in which I was first loved, as a child, by my parents and grandparents, you are the vessel through which more complex notions of love such as religion also came to me, the love for a creator.

Undeniably, after years of confrontation and encounters with others, you are the language I decide to love in, and that which I choose to love any future generation with.

You are the home, the home I know and the home I want to build.

And yet, you remain at times quite unknown to me.

I want to get to know you deeper, all your accents and faces, your rules and mishaps.

I want to get initiated into expressing myself deeper and deeper in you.

I want to swim in your vast sea بحور العروض and allow it to transport me.

So whenever other languages come my way, I will know how to welcome them, as 'guests', borrowing from Kilito's description. I will pamper them, I will give them time and generosity, but I will know to set boundaries, I will know to set priorities, so that they do not 'inhabit' me. This will be my so-called personal contractual 'language policy', in which my loyalty remains, only to you .

CLOSING WORDS

Reflecting on my personal experience, I explored multi-lingualism, allowing my language(s) to challenge the notion that not only is the home political, so are educational and social circles that expose us to languages.

The written reflections behind this essay collection have also allowed me to think through notions such as linguistic precarity and intimacy. The fact that I contest my own use of English for writing these essays exposes me to my mother tongue's precarity, that even though my memories seem to all live in Arabic, I am using English to write about them. I notice how, except for my mother tongue, the only languages I learned or came across were European or imperial ones. This brings forward the in-betweenness that multi-lingualism and our complex linguistic upbringings exposes, swaying between the different languages and the spaces they inhabit. I question: how does that live on in our personal lives? To not to be too binary, does it manifest in continuity, erasure, or the in-between gaps? What is 'native'? How do languages create identity? Identity, seems at first quite a rigid concept. But it is then revealed to me as a malleable and nuanced notion. In rethinking our linguistic histories we can reimagine personal and collective identity, claiming agency over our linguistic futures and canons of knowledge production.

Is it our role to nurture our 'exposure' to other undermined or undetermined languages, by striving for it to become part of educational infrastructures that aim to highlight or consider knowledges created by non-Europe?

Can this be a step we take ownership of, that does not get shrugged off and discussed only in 'decolonial' Euopean spaces? Could we reclaim it rather than allow or wait for the west to 'reclaim' and 'acclaim' parts of our cultures and spiritual habits as they see fit?

By reflecting on language through different lenses, the performative, the haunted, the witness, I questioned the different roles language plays, acknowledging its active role, criticizing, yet celebrating the multi-lingual reality.

Saja Amro

The Arming Act

Reflections on Cultures of Popular Education

INTRODUCTION

Education should encourage and support you to be yourself, to have enough confidence to try and fail, to live, to experience, to love, to enjoy, to listen to the inner voice, to resonate, to initiate, to liberate, to take your time to reflect and make up your mind, to form an original opinion, to think outside of the mainstream, to help, to feel, to dance, to sing, to connect, to choose to stay or walk away, to trust, to speak, to articulate, to appreciate little things, to underrate big things, to celebrate, to mourn, to express, to ask for help, to reach out, to plan, to contextualise, to transfer knowledge through stories, to physically and emotionally engage, to learn from the lived experiences of others.

However, what institutionalised education actually prepares you for is how to perform for a deadline, to study for a test, to quantify, to measure the value of a person with grades, to think through the alphabet, to speak through academic language, to explain through theory, to disconnect from sensed reality, to withdraw from nature, to restrict learning to limited tools and methods, to legitimise the dignity of humans by their education and certificates, to claim absolute knowledge of the truth, to claim that there is only one truth, to perceive the world through reading and seeing while ignoring other senses, to encourage discipline over-excitement, to situate the teacher and the book as the only sources of knowledge.

FROM WHERE I STAND

I am a product of the institution; I'm guilty of wanting to excel in the system, of thinking it defines my self-worth. I derived my self-confidence from my social status provided by my engineering degree. Every time I was described as intelligent by a teacher, mentor, or peer, I felt flattered and confident. I felt validated for having attained straight A's my whole life, for being top in class, for being popular, for being a favourite student of my teachers, for winning local and regional math competitions for my school, for leading many initiatives and being involved in extracurricular activities every year at school, for being the students' representative. I received approval from my parents when I was ahead of my peers when compared to them on the metric scale. The feeling extends to pride when answering "both engineers" when asked what my parents do for a living. I felt blessed for getting the dream job in an elitist institution, for being paid well. When I introduced myself I threw around the names of the places I had worked for or the institutions I went to, and the names of intellectual people I know. I cared about my CV, I only did things that would look good on my CV. I wrote it on my bio on social media. I became friends with people just because they were intellectuals, I felt inspired by their status. I wanted to be an intellectual. I'm writing this essay and I want my sentences and ideas to seem smart. I came to this masters hoping this certificate would guarantee me a higher level of credibility and would lead to more job opportunities and social respect for me.

I'm also a human, a daughter of rich culture and a warm household of stories and love. I'm part of a society deeply rooted in the land and connected by its long history of neighbouring and collaboration. I obtained my harmony by walking in a beautiful green and brown mountainous landscape where hikes are mesmerising. I enjoyed eating the olive oil and Zaa'tar every morning picked from my grandfather's generous land. I regularly sat at a table full of traditional recipes passed on from my grandmother to my mother to me with my extended family. I learned from the love, sacrifice, and humorous stories of my witty grandmother. I sang along with my friends and family while picking olives, every November I've lived in my life. I sat down in the courtyard under the lemon tree to drink mint tea and gossip all summer. I celebrated in an endless number of wedding ceremonies, dressing up and dancing in a joyful atmosphere, gathering the old and the young. My skin got tanned every year in the long hot summers and regained its original colour in the winters. I spoke in a language where there are twelve words to express every level of love, a name for every hour of the day, and an endless amount of proverbs. I lived by a collective hope of a free Land where no soldiers or checkpoints exist. I shared the inevitable belief of freedom and peace with every single one of my people for the land that never saw peace. I lived and experienced all of that and more, but never learned it at any educational institution.

The gap I witnessed between my embodied experience of living and seventeen years of institutional education, the pure distinction between life and school, the bold barrier between the process of learning and the process of living, led me to question traditional education; what does it mean and where does it actually come from?

WORDS WERE NO LONGER MY ALLIES

As a child, I enjoyed using words to express myself when asked to prepare something to read on the morning school broadcast. I remember thinking how enjoyable it was to write a song or a poem; to create a body of text to argue an idea or tell a story. I lost that gift growing up. My vocabulary shrunk and my poetic ability to express myself faded away. I started to speak in equations instead of full expressive sentences; words were no longer my allies.

At home, my family called me "the philosopher" as mockery, referring to my non-stop attempts to articulate and explain my thoughts. I spoke a lot, I annoyed my mother and my teachers a lot, I was silenced most of the time (being told frequently: *Speak a lot, make a lot of mistakes, brevity is the soul of wit, no man will tolerate how much you speak, you'll get a divorce for sure)*. As a fast learner, I learned to be silent, until today I'm silent.

TABULA RASA

Tabula rasa[1] is a theory of Latin origin. It implies that individuals are born without built-in mental content, and therefore that all knowledge comes from experience or perception. This theory was developed and debated from multiple perspectives by many scholars over time. However, in the schooling system, the six-year-old student entering elementary education is considered to be a tabula rasa. They are seen as empty vessels to be filled with curricula. Although students perceive knowledge and respond to it differently, the problematic part is that the previously curated and standardised set of knowledge funnelled by the teacher is considered the only knowledge worthy of learning. That the focus of education is on what will be taught and what can be known, instead of showing *how* one can know, is, in my opinion, oppressive. By not taking into consideration the personal life experiences and the uniqueness of each and every individual, or the social and cultural richness that already started forming their personalities, the systematic act of ignoring the packages that these individuals hold while walking into a classroom is violent. It forces everyone to submit to the same set

1 Aristotle's *De Anima (On the Soul)*, 4th century BCE.

of knowledge without giving them a chance to explain their desires and aspirations. It's an act of neglect and humiliation, which starts at a young age and grows to shape an unconfident human, always waiting for an authority to steer their life and make decisions.

I do not understand where the word education comes from, or why there is a single word to describe something very essential and innate to the human that does not describe it properly. Education is a limiting word. As humans we are born with a genetic code and instincts, we come to life and start to adapt to the nature and society around us, and we learn to do that through our senses, cognition, and emotions; we are learners by nature. None of that is judged or measured on a scale by nature. The institutionalisation of education limits the learning experience to a singular format and defines its means, tools, and goals. It restricts the endless potentials of human geniality and tends to create copies of the same model. It puts humans in competition with each other and gives the trophy to one or two people, leaving the rest rethinking their self-worth. It's oppressive and traumatising for many. For those who realise it, it takes years to heal from the stains left on the body and the soul. For those who don't realise it, the institution wins the battle of blinding the senses from seeing what could be beyond the norm and the mainstream. To me, it became more and more apparent how mainstream education is a product in line with the colonial project that exists in a capitalist system, and that this is how both are reserved and regenerated. What a waste.

THE ACT OF ARMING

Since I started researching the dynamics of institutionalised education, many people directed me to use the First Intifada as an example of de-institutionalisation. We Palestinians glorify the First Intifada,[2] but what has survived time only shows little of what actually happened. The archives only show iconic pictures of people throwing rocks and confronting war machines. When searching for it, I could hardly find pictures or written testimonies of the popular education model that was developed in response to urgencies during that period.

According to my mother, who lived through that Intifada and was teaching in one of the Palestinian universities at the time, institutions were locked down and people were bound to get creative. As a form of resistance, people declared civil disobedience and initiated organisational committees to operate life. My mother says that the barbershop next door turned into a classroom and welcomed pupils inside. The women in the neighbourhood started teaching crafts and culinary art, the farmers taught farming, and the whole neighbourhood became a melting pot of knowledge-exchange. Palestinians were not helpless.

2 The First Intifada: Intifada is an Arabic word that literally means 'shaking off', and in the Palestinian context, it is understood to mean a civil uprising. The First Palestinian Intifada erupted in Gaza in December 1987, after four Palestinians were killed when an Israeli truck collided with two vans carrying Palestinian workers. Ensuing clashes spread rapidly to the rest of the Occupied Palestinian Territories. The Intifada was primarily carried out by youth, and was directed by the Unified National Leadership of the Uprising, a coalition of Palestinian political factions committed to ending the Israeli occupation and establishing Palestinian independence. Israel's heavy-handed response included closing universities, deporting activists, and destroying homes.

My mother, who worked for the Palestine Polytechnic University, recalls how the university was closed for three years. However, the lectures were held in multiple empty rooms and spaces around Hebron. Hebron is an industrial city with a lot of trading, and therefore a lot of storage spaces. She says the students would finish their classes and start organising protests and clashes. Some would be busy making posters and flyers. Others would be preparing Molotov cocktails to harass the occupation army patrols.

This situation wasn't unique to Hebron alone. One of the most famous stories was about the town of Beit Sahour, which I heard from the Palestinian educator Munir Fasheh:

> *Beit Sahour has also become an inspiration, a place of radical pedagogical experiments. Indeed, during the First Intifada, when schools were closed by military order, self-organized neighborhood committees established a network of alternative education study groups within homes and car garages, where the reading list included Ghassan Kanafani, Mao, Hanna Mina, Sahar Khalifeh, Trotsky, Naji al-Ali, Karl Marx, and Emile Habibi.*[3]

While searching for the missing pieces of the puzzle, I heard from my tutor, Lara Khaldi, who was a teenager at that time, how her school in Ramallah shared a wall with a military complex. One can imagine the level of tension resulting from this unfortunate placement. Students had no choice but to be highly involved in political acts, reading condemnation and mobilising statements every morning

3 Mayssoun Sukarieh, "Decolonizing education, a view from Palestine: an interview with Munir Fasheh," *International Studies in Sociology of Education* 28, no. 2 (2019): 186–199.

on the school broadcast. Organising and innovating ways and tools of resistance, harassing their unwelcome neighbours. Her teachers were previous political prisoners, aware of the role every Palestinian should play in standing in the face of oppression and land theft, developing a pedagogy centralised around responding to urgencies of the right to self-defence and self-determination, and building personalities capable of holding on to the dream and establishing a strong foundation for armed resistance. Dabke to the melodies of traditional revolution songs was a daily activity as an attempt to preserve, celebrate, and activate the culture and identity, and to imagine a future of joy and freedom.

Uncle Mahmoud was a man of strong personality. He played the role of the principal at the boys' UN school in Dura, my hometown, although he was employed as a science teacher. His teenage sons Hasan and Ali inherited his characteristics and attributes, and never settled for his continuous reluctance against their involvement in politics and resistance. At school, he used to punish the students who gathered glass bottles to make Molotov cocktails. Little did he know that the leader of this whole movement was his son, Ali. One day, while taking his kids to school, a siren sound ascended from the car trunk. It was a megaphone that Ali had packed to lead the protest he was organising after school. Ali was busted. He was kicked out of the house to live in the room where my grandmother keeps the chickens. Years later, I sat down with my Aunt Yusra while she was rolling vine leaves and crying while singing a Tarwedeh,[4] grieving after the occupation forces broke into their house and arrested her son. Ali, the same teenager participating in

4 A sort of improvisational traditional singing.

political acts in the First Intifada. After hiding in the mountains for months and months during the Second Intifada,[5] he wanted to see his mother and family. His mother knew he loved rolled vine leaves and wanted to cook some for him. He was arrested, while she had no choice but to keep rolling.

The knowledge and practices developed during the First Intifada were born in the heat of the moment. Notions like economic autonomy practices, alternative educational endeavours, communal farms, sovereignty over food and water, and the call to self-governance were all criminalised by the occupation and so were practised in strict secrecy. As a result, it's very hard to find visual evidence or traces of such narratives. What is known today was only transferred through the stories and testimonies of people who participated in the liberation movement. When taking the legacy of the First Intifada as a reference for the deinstitutionalisation of life as a form of refusal and resistance, we look at the preserved archives and replicate whatever we find there. Again, the pictures you find when looking are the ones of physical armed resistance. The Second Intifada was a replication of those images, rather than what

5 The Second Intifada: The Second, or "Al-Aqsa", Intifada began on September 28, 2000, when Likud opposition leader Ariel Sharon made a provocative visit to the Al-Aqsa Mosque with thousands of security forces deployed in and around the Old City of Jerusalem. Clashes between Palestinian protestors and Israeli forces left five Palestinians dead and a further 200 injured during the first two days. The incident sparked a widespread armed uprising in the Occupied Palestinian Territories. During the Al-Aqsa Intifada, Israel caused unprecedented damage to the Palestinian economy and infrastructure. Israel reoccupied areas governed by the Palestinian Authority and began construction of its separation wall. By the end of 2008, the Palestinian death toll had reached almost 5,000, with over 50,000 injured. "Intifidada: Palestinian Uprising," Interactive Al Jazeera, interactive.aljazeera.com/aje/palestineremix/phone/intifada.html.

laid beneath them. The traces were also wiped from educational curricula; it's important to mention that Palestinian primary and secondary school curricula are censored by the occupying entity. Today, I wonder what happens to the opportunity to learn from such experimentation, and how it could help us imagine an alternative future while all the evidence and traces are lost?

FROM THE SUPERNOVA INTO THE BLACK HOLE

Once it became routine, not innovative, it lost its fuel. Like a star it collapsed and exploded as a 'supernova'. After all, how can one politically fragmented society maintain this autonomous lifestyle while standing alone, facing all the agendas recruiting massive resources to defeat such attempts at liberation? Once it started to be institutionalised, the Intifada lost its soul and continuation. People knew the Intifada was going to be long and that it would take time. And that the consistent efforts of swimming against the stream would be tiring. People have different opinions on when the Intifada ended. To some, it was when they lost their loved ones. To others, it was when their communal farms were invaded by the occupation forces. Then the Oslo Accords[6] came and crowned this gradual ending into a black hole. The Intifada was right, it was the right path to liberation. The fact that Palestinians were able to

6 The Oslo Accords marked the first time Israel and the Palestine Liberation Organisation (PLO) formally recognised one another. Many at that time believed this was a step in the right direction. But what followed over the next twenty years of negotiations reveals that Israel merely used the agreements to justify the further expansion of illegal settlements in the territories it occupied in 1967. Rawan Damen, "The Price of Oslo," Al Jazeera, interactive.aljazeera.com/aje/palestineremix/the-price-of-oslo.html#/14.

organise and fully govern themselves and refused the occupation was a real threat to the occupier. To prevent that threat from escalating, Oslo happened. It was the drug, the anaesthesia, and thus in turn it became the poison.

Before Oslo, the value given to a person by society was based on how much they were involved in resistance. After Oslo, the value was placed on financial and social status and class. The whole mindset of people shifted, resulting in a materialistic, pretentious, capitalist society, disconnected from the roots, living in apartments, and working for the government. The politically involved students of 'Friends School' became the elite class who live in Ramallah and work in higher positions in the Palestinian Authority, which was the main outcome of the Oslo Accords. And my cousin Ali is now working for the Palestinian Authority intelligence, and benefits from it, especially when it comes to his five million ILS business.

INTO THE BLACK HOLE

The notion of learned helplessness occupies space in my brain. I think of all the practices and strategies the occupation applies to Palestinians day after day, for decades, aiming to strip them from any means of resistance. In the context of Palestine, the word 'disarming' is very negative and frustrating; it triggers me personally. We are a disarmed nation weapon-wise (with both an old and recent shameful history)![7] The educational system in Palestine teaches helplessness, which paves the way for the occupation, by producing copies of men and

7 There have been constant attempts to disarm the Palestinian popular resistence, while arming the members of the institutionalised Palestinian Authority, which ended up protecting the security of the occupation and preventing any act of resistance against it.

women ready to melt and disappear into the mainstream.

The mainstream means to find a job in a governmental institution, find a partner, and start a family, usually with very little income and a lot of applause and cheer from society. No problem at all so far. What's problematic, in my opinion, is living in a troubled place like Palestine and having become numb enough to not try to change a thing. The number and quality[8] of individual and collective initiatives to solve problems facing society are poor and unfortunate. I wonder why? What is the problem?

In my opinion, it's education! Going to school is supposed to be an *arming* act. It should arm you with knowledge, confidence, inspiration, and hope. It should equip you to face the evolving world. With all the challenges facing the planet, Palestine has 'one more' challenge: occupation!

AN 'AHA' MOMENT

For a long time, I felt frustrated looking at the Palestinian leadership and who forms it. I thought there were no real leaders within our community, as a result of the continuous disappointment living under occupation. I lived with that belief until the morning of September 6, 2021. The morning when six Palestinian political prisoners managed to escape Gilboa, a high-security prison in the occupation entity. The leader of the group, Mahmoud Al-Ardah, has spent twenty-two years of his youth in prison and was

8 My sister works for an organisation that crowdfunds for projects with social impact. Every year she sends out an open call for people to apply with effective and innovative social enterprises in Palestine, which necessarily must have a social impact. The number and quality of applications are very poor and limited.

sentenced to life. Today he practised his right to self-determination and self-liberation under the most brutal circumstances. His body was captured between four walls, his soul and mind were free and mighty. Those who attend high-end educational institutions, such as Ivy League schools, are expected to invent radical solutions to complicated situations. However, Mahmoud Al-Ardah didn't need that fancy education to shake the grounds of a heavily militarised fascist entity. Being physically in prison could mean freedom to the brain. While being in institutional education could mean limitation and dependency. Against all expectations, Mahmoud Al-Ardah managed to replace agony and misery with hope and imagination. The resourcefulness, the responsivity, the mental strength, the refusal to be defeated; isn't this a superpower? Iron Man is fictional, Mahmoud Al-Ardah isn't.

I doubt that English words can capture the essence of the Palestinian resilience, nor that those who never experienced oppression can understand what it means, even if they spent their whole life reading about it. It's a collective agreement, a social contract. We smile when we are arrested, we innovate when we are oppressed. All the men and women who show the mindset and stamina of a leader are eventually either arrested, expelled, or killed. As the racist occupier says, "a good Arab is a dead Arab." In their understanding, there is no good Arab unless they are dead. In my understanding, the good Arab, the one who managed to escape the domestication attempts of the manipulative and blinding schooling system, gets killed or imprisoned by the fascist entity or their subcontractors, the Palestinian Authority.

STINKY DESK

Speech is the miracle of the human, however, at school, children are expected to stay silent for eight hours a day for twelve of their most formative years. Unless it's an answer to a question or a polite request, children are expected to keep their thoughts to themselves. I wonder where else they would have the chance to share their personal achievements, to question how things work or how the universe started? How many theories and explanations remain unspoken inside those little yet growing minds? And what is the fate of those ideas, those brains, and their ability to articulate? As long as these ideas are not shared or reflected upon?

In an array of three columns and seven rows of desks sit forty-two students in a UN girls' school in Palestine. Each desk is a construction of a wooden seat and a table connected together by a metal skeleton. One desk accommodates two students, sometimes three if they are younger and hence smaller students. The wooden table has a shelf where students can keep belongings – this shelf is usually used to cheat as you can easily hide an open book on it during a test. It is used also to throw away the unpalatable compulsory vitamin pills students are obligated to swallow once a week, or to hide food since it's forbidden to eat during class time. The smell of this shelf is stinky; students only clean it when there is an inspection. It's stinky because of what is kept inside, and because the desk sits in a humid and dark classroom for years and years without seeing the sun outside.

One strong memory of early life experience is the school desk. For hours students are recording their feelings and thoughts all over this dark brown canvas in multiple ways. The desk performs as a trap, like the walls of a prison cell, filled with engravings of whatever is going on within the prisoners themselves, counting down the days until they are freed.

The desk is the same for all students, no matter how different their abilities, interests, dreams, or bodies are. In the case of a school student, the singular desk design neglects the range of different needs and desires: it empowers some and paralyses others, it limits movement and therefore will. While my neighbour was thinking about her Dabke performance, which she developed and wanted to practise, she had to listen to a science class that was of no interest to her. Although I was very much enjoying the new scientific insights I was receiving from 'Miss Fatenah', I was thinking of how those rules apply in real life, and whether they come from real life at all.

School curricula are still today surreal in my memory. Sometimes I like to revisit my old textbooks, especially physics, to see how I perceive them today as an adult, to see whether I can establish this connection with a personal experience, whether I will be able to use it or be inspired by it.

A UNIQUE CLASSROOM

In a rectangular classroom, the composition of desks is oriented to face a black chalkboard stretching across the short western wall, sanctified by its position, protected and operated by an also 'sanctified' keeper, the teacher. Despite the forty-two diverse bodies and experiences seated in the room, the source of knowledge remains one. The hierarchy this setup imposes is a metaphoric representation of the whole educational system, designed to control generations after generations. It enables "illusions such as learning is the result of teaching and that a person's worth can be measured by a number on a vertical line".[9]

The door is always situated closer to the chalkboard on the right-hand side, and next to it sits the trash bin where naughty students are punished. The windows extend on the southern long side of the classroom. The sun shines its rays onto the students from the left side, so all right-handed students can write without being bothered by the shadow of their hand. On the opposite side lays a big pinboard, filled with student-made drawings of human body systems for extra credits. In the back of the class, you'll find coat hangers extending across the whole wall holding wet jackets in the winter, empty in the spring. Above will be more art projects, again made for extra credits.

Every year, the school would receive a number of new desks to replace the broken ones, and the new ones stand out because of their colour and shine. Whoever gets the new desk is crowned as the new queen, and the desk becomes a tourist attraction point to be visited in the five minutes between classes by the other students. The older desks reserve the memories, thoughts, and artworks of previous occupiers: engravings, old gum, and stickers.

In the first row sit three types of student; the short ones, those who struggle with vision, and the nerds. In the back row sit the tallest, the uninterested, and the ones who struggle with learning 'in the traditional way'. The teachers mean to seat high-achieving students next to lesser achieving students to tutor them, referring to an arabic proverb *(put the donkey and the horse in one stable, either*

9 Sukarieh, "Decolonizing education," 1.

the horse will teach the donkey to neigh, or the donkey will teach the horse to bray), hoping for the first to happen and not the latter.

The classroom itself with its array of desks ends up acting as one cell in another larger array. Identical to its neighbour, it sits back to back and shares a wall with the classroom next door, forming a row. Mirroring it is another row of the same number of classrooms, separated by a hallway, and duplicated vertically on the second floor. The rooms on the front of the school are the principal's and the teachers' rooms, overlooking the school entrance and the garden, usually the cleanest and most decorated part of the whole school. These rooms are always prepared to welcome very important guests, such as UN inspectors, people in senior positions, and parents of students.

THIRTY MINUTES A DAY

We waited for the thirty-minute break between the six forty-five-minute classes we had every day to play " حجلة" (hopscotch, hopping game). This game was the best part of the day, where my most valuable friendships were established, where I learned to strategise, where I taught my little sister to count. We organised a hopscotch league and we took it seriously. However, there were only thirty free minutes a day, which also had to be split with buying food from the canteen (it was a hassle, little girls never got the chance to buy lunch because they were not tall or strong enough to reach the canteen window, I might have to write a whole essay about this particular crazy moment), eating lunch, doing late homework, and, of course, catching up, gossiping, and speaking about personal achievements. The game territory was negotiated; the best piece of land was on soil, where you could use a stick to draw the eight rectangles.

With time the land would become hard because of the number of times girls would jump on it. There was this particular area under the pine tree which was known to be the most wanted, just because you could play in the shade, but it was always dominated by ninth-graders.[10] The second-best place to play was on the cement floor in the big schoolyard, where the floor was already hard, which was always a plus. But you needed chalk to draw the hopscotch, and you definitely needed a miracle to get some.[11] Every week the hopscotch rectangles would be cleaned away, which made it unsustainable. Most of the time it was also forbidden, and teachers made sure to punish the girl who made the drawing by forcing her to clean it publicly.

I'm writing about those thirty minutes instead of writing about the time we spent in class. The latter is still the least interesting and the least preserved in my memory. Being a student, you don't question the system, you follow it and try to master it. You are always being told to obey in order to be rewarded, or at least to avoid punishment. Rethinking my previous statement, well! We all questioned school as children, we all thought it didn't make sense and hoped it would die: "Yeah I used to wake up for Fajr prayer and pray that school dies, I know you did too."

10 UN schools have classes from first until ninth grade only, as compulsory education.

11 Every class would get a limited amount of chalks, which were kept by one student, chosen by the teacher. If you knew that student, you might be able to smuggle some chalk out of the class.

Julina Vanille Bezold

Shape-Shifters Revelation

A Mystic-Realistic Enchanted Short-Story-Thesis-Essay

PROLOGUE: BELOW THE CRUST

As the Celtic Druids' prophecy had predicted, it happened on February 22, 2022, at 22:22 at the 22nd meridian. Gaia's crust began to gently open, and snow slowly started to run down the opening just like in an hourglass. This was in Breiðafjörður, on Iceland's Westfjords peninsula. The earthlings had abandoned or forgotten the prophecy for more than 2,222 years, despite the fact that the Ogham script, engraved into prehistoric stone known as a menhir, stating the prophecy, was displayed in a small history museum in Ribe, Denmark. But the already low number of yearly visitors dismissed the small explanatory chart, if even read, as mystical gibberish.

Shortly after, sand started to run down a hole in Shabarinuru, Mongolia. It first looked like quicksand, although there was no soul in sight to witness. This phenomenon remained unnoticed in Agorgot, Mali and Abu-as-Sayyid in Syria, too. Immeasurable amounts of sand already travelled downstream in other places before it was noticed in Karlamilyi, Australia; Ancomarca, on the border of Chile and Peru; and Okomumbonde in Namibia. The same anomaly was observed in water systems such as the Arctic and Pacific Oceans; Lake Ontario, Canada; the Kitakami in Japan; and Lake Geneva, between France and Switzerland. Geologists and other scientific experts were called to make top-secret inspections assigned by the local governments, but they found no satisfactory explanation for the constant trickling down of sand, snow, and water.

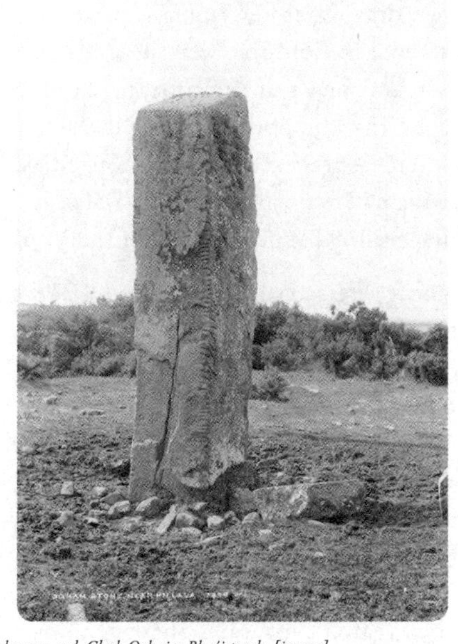

Image 1: Unknown, n.d. Cloch Oghaim Bhréisteach. [image]
Available at: www.sacredlandscapes.ie/breastagh-ogham-stone.html

A few weeks later, forests, meadows, and fields were sucked in. When the Crooked Forest in Poland, the Californian Redwood, the Bhitarkanika Mangroves in India, and the Amazon rainforest in Brazil almost completely disappeared, the authorities could no longer hide the disaster and eventually a mass panic broke out amongst most earthlings. Others, however, remained calm. An inner calling prepared them for a process of renewal. These earthlings said farewell to their loved ones, observed, or sat immersed in a state of deep meditation, awaiting.

The primary rill became a torrent, later a sprawling cascade. People and animals were dragged along. In many places, earthlings began to report that some individuals were now also disappearing in places where streams had not yet appeared at all, mainly in the cities and villages, but the police did not investigate this further as the evacuation measures exceeded their capacities. Nonetheless, those disappearing had felt reassuring, celestial peace and perceived a secure, familiar feeling in the moment of their vanishing.

What the prophecy referred to as *The Unlight*, *The Surface*, or *The Matrix* began to crumble. Enough light beings who remembered their primal root of being were able to punch holes into the scala waves and frequencies of the old matter. This process brought around forty-nine per cent of earthlings, with their related and still unharmed species and forms of life, one level closer to Gaia's core. One might imagine a rapid fall or a funnelling downwards, which was what it looked like from above. But the moment the ecological community reached a few hundred metric metres below the crust, rearrangement appeared through a phase of non-materiality. All molecules, atoms, and subatomic particles disseminated. But by no means were they invisible. One could observe with the naked eye how the matter fell down like the tiniest snowflakes in a vast snowglobe. Noiseless yet luminous. Reassembling into its habitual composition.

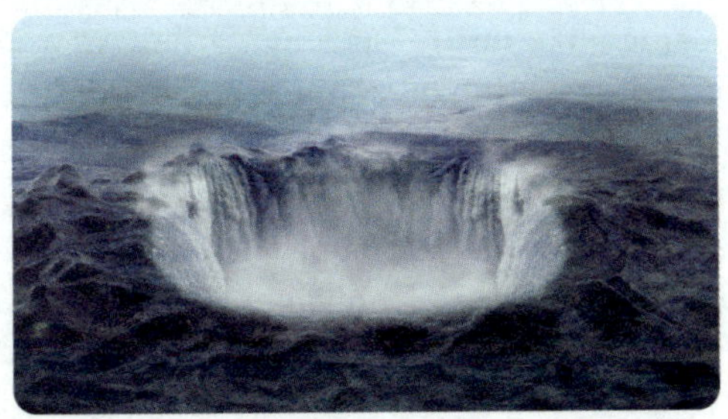

Image 2: ©Imago/Science Photo Library, 2021. Die unheimlichen Kräfte im Bermuda-Dreieck. [image] Available at: www.weltderwunder.de/artikel/die-unheimlichen-kraefte-im-bermuda-dreieck [Accessed 13 January 2022].

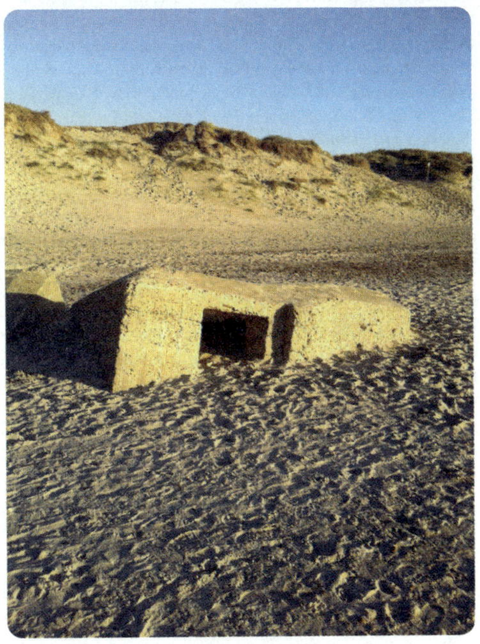

Image 3: Bezold, J., 2014. The Drowning Bunkers of Ringkøbing, Denmark.

And it remained like this for as long as the system floes, that appeared like large, chunky, concrete-grey clouds in the sky, remained. The ecological community of Deep Gaia wasn't asleep in the meantime; it was in a state of *super consciousness*.[1] One day these chunks finally dissolved completely, and Deep Gaia was for the first time fully covered in sunlight. Climatic conditions were restored, depending on the new grounds, forests, fields, lakes, and

1 Michael Newton, *Journeys of the Souls: Case Studies of Lives Between Lives* (St Paul, Minn: Llewellyn Publications, 1994). Michael Newton, Ph.D., directly talked to souls through his own hypnosis technique that he developed over forty years. Thus, he is able to place people in a superconscious state of awareness to reach his subjects' hidden memories of life in the spirit world after physical death. If the mind had three concentric circles, each smaller than the last and within the other, the first outer layer is represented by the conscious mind, which is our critical, analytic reasoning source. The second layer is the subconscious, where we initially go in hypnosis to tap into the storage area for all the memories of everything that ever happened to us in this life and former lives. The third, the innermost core, is what we are now calling the superconscious mind. This level exposes the highest centre of Self where we are an expression of a higher power. The superconscious houses our real identity, augmented by the subconscious, which contains the memories of the many alter-egos assumed by us in our former human bodies. The superconscious may not be a level at all, but the soul itself. It represents our highest centre of wisdom and perspective, and all information about life after death comes from this source of intelligent energy.

When subjects are placed in trance, their brain waves slow from the Beta wake state and continue to change vibration down past the meditative Alpha stage into various levels within the Theta range. Theta is hypnosis, not sleep. When we sleep we go to the final Delta state, where messages from the brain are dropped into the subconscious and vented through our dreams. In Theta, however, the conscious mind is not unconscious, so we are able to receive as well as send messages with all memory channels open.

I would hereby like to thank Naomi Pire for really spelling this book out for me. It has been one of the most transforming and ethereal reads ever. [And damn, girl, if stuff in the heavens is really like that, I guess we (souls) are fine; and no one is ever truly gone *alien emoji*.]

oceans that were distributed and reshaped while they still carried their ancient wisdom from previous constellations.

When life started waking up in Deep Gaia, no living being felt estranged from itself or its environment. Immediate recognition of old, new grounds arose. Deep Gaia inhabitants came from all places of the crust. There was a redistributed balance in the diversity of what was previously called [ethnicity], *nationality, sexuality, gender, physicality, age, or place.*[2] The occurrence of the prophecy was the first time in all of human history where their consciousness had reached a level of evolution where they could actually see from each other's eyes. The eyes of the serpent could see through the eyes of the eagle. The eyes of the earlier North and South of Gaia could now see through one another's eyes and begin to work together, understanding each other's entities. Senses in the light

2 Rebecca Tamás, "On Watermelon" in *Strangers: Essays on the Human and Nonhuman,* 2nd ed. (London: Makina Books, 2020), p.13, 21.
I took over this list from Rebecca Tamás to describe the clusters of political identity. They belong to the concepts of the old world. To elaborate further using her own words:
"We are in a state of emergency, environmental emergency, extinction emergency. Yet this 'state of emergency' did not arrive unbidden or suddenly. This state of emergency has been existent throughout history – in the land enclosures that impoverished peasants, in the growth of Western economic power through the exploitation of the Atlantic slave trade, in the violence of colonial oppression, in the viciousness of global patriarchy and female silencing, in the abuse of natural resources by industrialist and post-industrialist land oweners and businesses, in the cruelty meted out to the animals we eat – the crisis was always already occuring. The rising temperatures, natural disasters and bleached corals we see now, are only a new manifestation of the crisis of equality that is, as Benjamin says, 'the rule'. That does not mean that all of history has been the same, or that it can never change. Merely that our current crisis is not new, never could be new. The Anthropocene is a useful way to understand the start of the material change of the environment due to human action; but it only marks the visible appearance of systems of inequality that are much, much older." 21.

beings had heightened to such a degree that the subtle aura of other species had become palpable. The secondary part of the prophecy entailed that each and every being who arrived in Deep Gaia came for a specific reason, with gifts that were needed to engage in the duties they had laid out in front of them ...

I. UNTIL THE LIGHT TAKES US [AXIS MUNDI][3]

October 15, 2038

He who, dwelling in all things,
Yet is other than all things,
Whom all things do not know,
Whose body all things are,
Who controls all things from within
– [Them] is your Soul, the Inner Controller, The Immortal.
– Thus far with reference to material existence.
Now with reference to the Self.[4]

– Upanishad, 3.7.15.

"Catch!" With great stamina, after thoroughly examining its ripeness, she snapped another one off the limb and smoothly pitched it from the tree. The fuzzy abundance landed in my palms. I carefully put it in the basket, soaking up the odour of generosity. "I think we've had enough for now," Lelibela said. "The other ones are still too yellow." She climbed down the tree as skillfully as a little monkey.

3 Its roots reach down to the underworld, its trunk sits on the Earth, and its branches extend up to the heavens. Many cultures share a belief that this tree is the *Axis Mundi* or *World Axis*, which supports or holds up the cosmos.

4 Brihad-aranyaka, *Upanishad*, 3.7.15.

"Wow,[5] that's a lot of them," she said, and we hoisted the numerous baskets full of juicy, plump peaches[6] onto our wooden cart and made our way home.

A single focused beam of light fell on a moss clearing as we walked along the path. Numerous insects and plant dust danced in it in microgravity, and the steam rising from the moss carpet palpitated, opening and clearing our lungs. We both began to breathe more deeply and evenly, in synergy. The end of the light beam fell on a thick oak tree whose colossal surface roots were equally overgrown with moss. I couldn't identify where the ground ended and the tree began, just like I used to be unable to distinguish where opinions ended and judgements began. We paused, both watching the sensation inquisitively. A carousel of great vitality and regeneration played out before our eyes. Almost no breeze was blowing, and yet the space was filled with vastness. Molecules and atoms, the sun's spotlight, the stream vibrating in the background; we felt on our

5 My dear Marouf Alhassan, thank you for the conversation we had on December 28, 2021, in which you noticed that the word 'wow', when turned upside down, spells 'mom', and consequently that this expression of cheering abundance could have its source in the divine mother or feminine.

6 "In China and Japan the symbolism of the peach is extensive, uniting the sensual with the esoteric, the human with the divine. In appearance and taste, the peach suggests a juicy abundance that is both natural and sacred. Blossoming in the early spring, the peach tree is a sure sign of nature's regeneration. The peach, with its cleft, rounded forms has long been associated, in east and west, with the female genitalia, and with the feminine principle of fecundity and renewal (Stevens 388). Even feminine complexions resembling the coloring and texture of the peach are described as 'peaches and cream', and girls blossoming into womanhood are sometimes referred to as 'peaches'."

Ami Ronnberg and Kathleen Martin, *The Book of Symbols: Reflections on Archetypal Images*, The Archive for Research in Archetypal Symbolism (Köln: Taschen, 2010), 172.

skin and in our electromagnetic fields how the particles interacted with one another. These particles were constantly destroying and recreating themselves, and we had come at just the right time.

"What is that tree doing?", I asked my daughter.
"Why is it so bright?"
"It's in photosynthesis, Ma."
And she caught hold of my hand.
"I mean ... I know what it is, but I think it's tickling me."

With a chuckle Lelibela replied: "The light you're sensing is our Creator, *Oryan*. The tree absorbs the energy in the sunlight and converts it into glucose, so it can store it for later use or sweeten the flesh of juicy fruits." She shrugged her shoulders, knowing I knew. "Trees and plants are doing this so exuberantly, almost altruistically. It's interesting how you start perceiving these sensations more, Ma. Last year when we came to pick peaches you were still overlooking them. Remember?"

I averted my gaze from the tree and looked down for her but she was suddenly at my eye-level. Her eyes were wide, reminding me of those of her deceased father. Her right eye blue, the left one green, as always,[7] yet in the setting of the trees they both looked like the forest itself. She was radiant. Copiously overflowing with glow. Her fingers were almost the size of mine by now. From her fingertips, microscopic golden sparks were released, slowly floating towards the luminous clearing, mingling there. A heartbeat later, ultraviolet flares streamed back at her, funnelling into where Lelibela

7 As a kid, I thought you were either an angel or an alien. This is an ode to you, David Bowie; the inspiring, encouraging shape-shifter of my time. Reincarnate back soon!

had told me earlier her thymus gland[8] sat. She remained like this for a moment, her eyes closed. Then she opened them and asked: "Would you like to go in there for a moment and ask if you can meet the tree?" I nodded silently, slightly awe-inspired. "Don't be timid, I'll show you. Come, sit on the moss." We left the cart with the peaches by the path as Lelibela beckoned me towards the moss carpet, right at the foot of the woodlands' heroic senior.

"Human people are the younger siblings of Creation, you know. We have the least experience of how to live and thus the most to learn – *sometimes we must look to our teachers among the other species*

8 "Originally, the thymus gland was the source of sensory perception. It is part of the human immune system until puberty. Then it shuts down. It is a vestigium. After puberty, the third eye is used as the center for receiving visions and consciousness. The thymus gland becomes dusty. However, you can reactivate it through special body processes and thus receive energy and awareness from this place."

Gary Douglas and Dr. Dain Heer, n.d. Access Consciousness® Workbook for Access Bars®.

I would like to add that I am aware that in modern medicine, during thoracic or cardiac surgery, the thymus gland, which is rudimentary and supposedly non-functional, is often unnecessarily removed. However, removal due to necessity, such as disease, may also occur. I would find it interesting, when considering the thymus gland as an organ of intuition and consciousness, to hear the experiences of those affected.

Thanks to my mother, Claudia Bruppacher, and Amineh Tekiyeh for introducing me to this incredible toolbox and method, and for everything I was allowed to learn, know, and experience from and through you so far.

for guidance.[9] *Your intent produces an energy field.*[10] *Gentleness is the key to understanding.*[11] Make yourself comfortable and close your eyes," she said, while she too sat down cross-legged on the moss, so that my daughter, the oak, and I formed a triangle.

The moment I saw the void on the inside of my eyelids I remembered how my former folks were denying their dependency. I remembered when other life forms were under ownership, under force. I remembered how we were in the position as humans to theoretically grant rights to other entities. But you can't grant emancipation to them, we were depending on them already. So they fought back,

9 [Quote] Robin Wall Kimmerer, *Braiding Sweetgrass: Indigenous Wisdom, Scientific Knowledge and the Teachings of Plant*s (London: Penguin Books, 2013), 9.

In Kimmerer's work I find it compelling that her ecological knowledge is inherent. It appears through intuition and tradition in a style of enchanted writing and braided storytelling. Her point of departure – and the one of the Potawatomi Nation she is a member of – never separated the concepts of 'society' and 'nature' in the first place and, consequently, when she studied Botany she realised that looking at a plant through the lenses of science can be a limitation as a way to understand life itself. Her engagement in the way she is writing comes from a source of intra-acting in the world, where botanical names, for example, are not given to plants in order to master them or to foster a behaviour governed by efficiency or effectiveness, but rather to re-enact creativity and accountability towards Mother Nature and to learn from our intra-actions with her, in order to consequently generate possibilities for new futures. In addition, I am mesmerised by how she narrates the world as an entity of entangled occurrences and not necessarily of cause and effect in a separated, linear structure.

10 [Quote] Peter Tompkins and Christopher Bird, *The Secret Life of Plants* (New York: Harper Collins, 1989), pp.17–33; 163–178.

Thanks to my dear Darcy Neven for lending me this book while hosting me in your garden-home and inspiring my writing through the input from, and invitation to, the exhibition *A Letter to Elizabeth Tibbots*, at The School in Hasselt, Belgium, in collaboration with Pablo Hannon, in November 2021.

11 [Quote] *My Octopus Teacher*, directed by Pippa Ehrlich and James Reed (Netflix, 2020), 1:25:00, www.netflix.com/title/81045007.

requesting their standing.[12] It was on humans asking permission and rights from our owners. It was on us including and welcoming them into conversations and extending democracy.[13] And now, just one generation further, this ontology has become a reality. When a physical body is filled with as much light as that of my daughter's, the gift of discerning the light in other things and beings is immeasurably expanded, as the inner state determines what one can recognise in the other.

My daughter snapped me out of my thoughts with her words: "I am going to introduce you to an exercise now. It can demonstrate the sensitivity of trees, transfer you to understanding how to move in and out of their living space, and allow you to introduce yourself to them. Don't stay longer than a few moments. This way, the plant has a full signature of your thought-forms and you have the one of the oak. This is the beginning of your communication. Again, be gentle, Ma, if you push your thoughts too forcefully, it can get sick.

So, now, take a few deep breaths.
Ground, centre yourself.
Allow your points of views to leave you now.
Let your barriers down. Also the ones in your back
and the ones you're not aware of.
Then, begin by sending your focus down into the
centre of Mother Gaia, part of All That Is.
Say "Hi Gaia, hi molecules, thanks for having me.
How can I contribute to you today?"

12 Christopher Stone, *Should Trees Have Standing?: Law, Morality, and the Environment* (Oxford: Oxford University Press, 2010).

13 Radboud Reflects, "The Parliament of Things | Philosopher Bruno Latour, lecture," November 25, 2020, video, 1:28:50, youtu.be/zZF9gbQ7iCs.

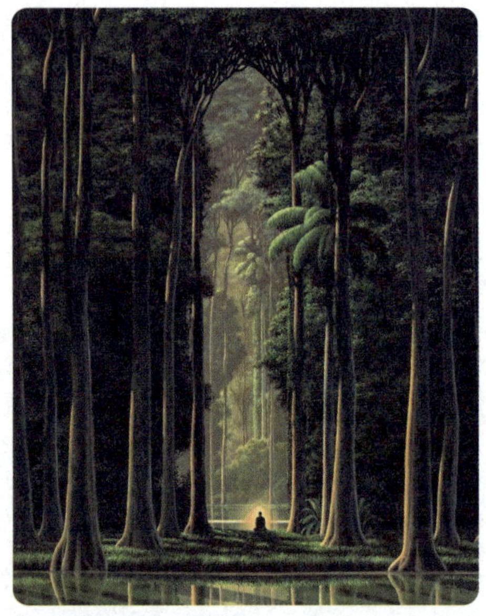

Image 4: Tomás Sánchez, 1995. Meditador. [image]
Available at: www.artnet.de/künstler/tomás- sánchez/2 [Accessed 11 December 2021].

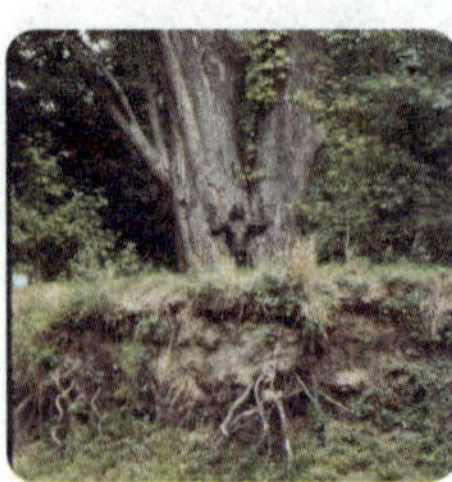

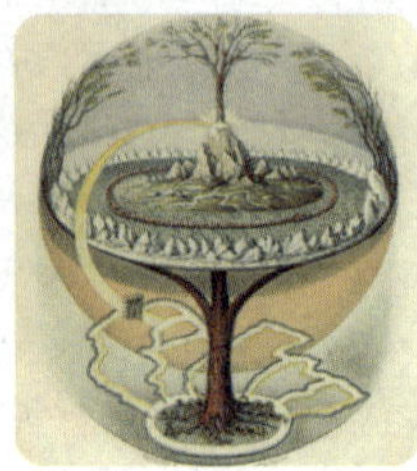

Image 5: Ana Mendieta, Richard Saltoun Gallery, 1976. Arbol de la Vida (Tree of Life), "Silueta" Series in Iowa. [video] Available at: www.artnet.de/künstler/ana-mendieta [Accessed 24 January 2022].

Image 6: Oluf Olufsen Bagge, 1847. Yggdrasil, Prose Edda, 1847, print graphic. [image] Available at: int. artloft.co/de/was-ist-der-ursprung-vom-mai-tag-und-seine-bedeutung [Accessed 24 January 2022].

Bring the energy you receive here up through the
points where your body touches the ground;
bring it up through your entire body, fill it,
bring it up through all your chakras, slowly.
Ultimately, go up through your crown chakra
in an alluring ball of light.
Now imagine that ball of light going
out past the stars
and through the universe.
Go beyond the universe, past the layers of light,
through a golden light,
past the sticky substance that is the Laws,
past a deep blue light, past a pink mist
and into a pearlescent white light,
the pure energy of Creation.
This is the energy that creates the particles
that create the atoms.
Take another deep breath in.
Imagine that you and the moss below you have
become one on a molecular level.
Your molecules and those of the moss are
transferring back and forth between one another.
You are connecting to them, becoming one with
them. Now imagine that on the molecular
level you are part of everything in this forest.
Expand your being and become one with the
outside world. Imagine that you
are part of our area here,
our home village Almanac,

then Øm, the land, and then you are part of
whole Gaia, connecting to her, the land and sea,
every creature, every people on and in it,
until you and Gaia are one.
Imagine that you and the universe are one.
Imagine that you are part of all layers.
Fully become one with it.
Think to yourself,
Creator of All That Is, Oryan,
thank you for my life.
Take another deep breath.
Welcome to Oryan's Plane of Existence.
Behold, you are not separate,
you are part of All That Is.
With this being done, you may now ask the oak:
I seek to scan you;
Please, show me what I need to see.
Go to the oak as gently as a feather on a summer
breeze. Remember, if you go in with too much force,
you can harm it. Now imagine going in, entering
through the bark, its skin, take a quick look,
go into its veins where Mami Wata[14] is endemic,

14 Henning Christoph and Hans Oberländer, *Voodoo* (Köln: Taschen, 1995). See also www.soul-of-africa.com/en/exhibitions/mami-wata.html.

From a young age I was fascinated by the practice of voodoo. I soon found out that voodoo with dark magic is really only a very small percentage and also in most cases only meant to provide justice.

The only voodoo museum in Europe is located in my hometown of Essen, Germany, and is called The Soul of Africa Museum. It sees itself as a cultural organisation and does not pursue any commercial interests. Henning Christoph, ethnologist, anthropologist, photographer, and filmmaker, runs and maintains the museum, and here I was able to learn about the voduns'

she rushes through,
go into its massive trunk characteristics,
its commanding presence,
up into its twisted branches and limbs that get
finer and finer, just like our veins do.
Go up all the way until you reach the oak's broad
leaves and stippled fruits, the tiny acorns.
Now quickly fly down its trunk again, into its
roots, standing firm and entrenched in the soil,
getting more delicate with every interval, just like
its top, but below, into the underworld.
Arrive at the point where roots touch earth and
eventually soak up nutrients and minerals,
stay here for one breath longer,
and then take yourself out of its space again.
Rinse yourself off with Oryan and oak energy,
yet stay connected to it.
In your pace come back and gently open your eyes."[15]

healing, protection, and worship rituals a little bit more. The exhibits were given or sold to him by voodoo followers or priests, mostly from West and Central Africa. He also maintains a Mami Wata altar, which, for unknowing visitors, seems like an exhibit, but for members of the African diaspora, it is an altar for tributes. People often bring their offerings and sacrifices here after hours.

Mami Wata is the goddess of the seas and water and is often uncharacteristically depicted as a mermaid who loves beauty, wealth, and cleanliness. Water spirit cults were practised in many places in Africa and Latin America and later continued worldwide, mostly as a result of slavery. She is depicted as a feminine and beautiful nature deity, and since I believe her to be one of the primordial mothers of the element water, I wanted to give her a place in my narrative as a power source, nourishing the tree.

15 The meditation is partially inspired by the processes in: *Vianna Stibal, Seven Planes of Existence: The Philosophy of the ThetaHealing® Technique*

My consciousness returned to me with a rapid *choonk*. Suddenly I was in myself again, looking out of the windows I was given. The weightless levitation and my former thriving greenery were replaced with tingling sensations in my limbs, almost crackling. A crispy realisation that the gauzy exaltation of this voyage was quickly taken over by thoughts on words I once read, ages ago:

> *Like the oak whose roots extend into the mineral realm, the self is rooted in the chemical elements of the body and extends [...] into infinite heights and depths. As a mature oak unfolds from an acorn, so does psychic individuality unfold from some small intimation of self that, brought into consciousness, grows and gives leaf over time to a multiplicity of images. Mirroring the oak's solidity, the self is the perduring centre that can withstand fiery outbursts of affect and psychic flooding. 'Oak' transports, and humbles – so perfectly is [sovereign] nature embodied in its form.*[16]

I sat on the moss until my daughter stood up and softly lifted my body, while the oak's dignity was still imprinted in my neocortex.

(London: Hay House, 2016), pp.13–14; 186–187.

Again, thanks to my mother and Naomi Pire for their books and bottomless input.

16 [Quote] These aren't my words, they're C.G. Jungs', from "The Oak and Human Consciousness", found through: John Williamson, *The Oak King, The Holly King and The Unicorn* (New York: Harper & Row, 1986).

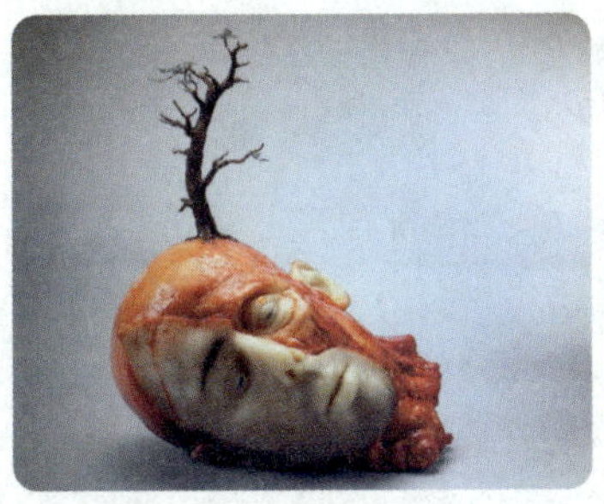

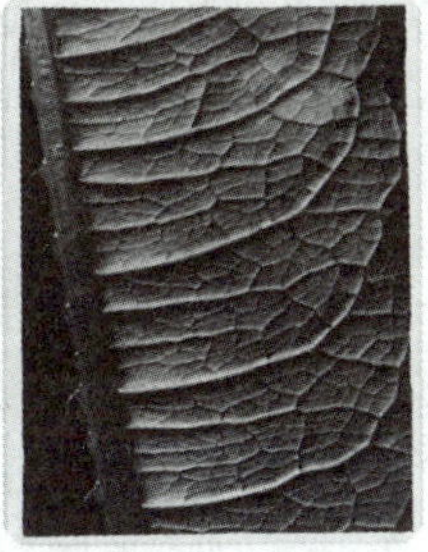

Image 7: John Isaacs, Thinking about it, 2002; as found in Fischer, H., Olbricht, T. and Eskildsen, U., 2007. Rockers Island. Göttingen: Steidl.

Image 8: Lotte Jacobi, Folkwang Auriga Publishing House, 1930. Untitled (Dipsacus, leaf), Silver Gelatin Print on baryta paper, 23.8 x 17.8 cm. [image] Available at: sammlung.staedelmuseum.de/en/work/untitled- dipsacus-leaf [Accessed 19 January 2022].

II. [AMONGST] THE FATHERS OF DESTRUCTION,[17] OR: THE ART OF CHANNELLING THE PEACH OF PATRIARCHY

October 15, 2038

But the new barbarian is no uncouth Desert dweller;
he does not emerge From fir forests; factories bred him;
Corporate companies, college towns [Fathered] his mind,
and many journals Backed his beliefs.
Lies and lethargies police the world In its periods of peace.
... life after life lapses out of
Its essential self and sinks into
One press applauded public untruth

17 I borrowed this term "Fathers of Destruction" from Farida Akhter, *Seeds of Movements: On Women's Issues in Banglades*h (Dhaka: Narigrantha Prabartana, 2007), found through: Vandana Shiva, and Maria Mies with Ariel Salleh, *Ecofeminism* (London and New York: Zed Books, 2014).

And, massed to its music, all march in step
Led by that liar, the lukewarm Spirit
Of the Escalator[18]

– Wystan H. Auden from *The Age of Anxiety: A Baroque Eclogue*

We returned to Almanac. Someone had already prepared a fire in the atrium where the tent stood. It was getting to be autumn, a chilly breeze was in the air, slightly freezing the tiny hairs in my nostrils, giving steam to my breath. The sky looked like the peaches we picked and took down to the pantry, putting some aside for dessert before joining the others to prepare dinner.

After supper, we gathered in the assembly yurt. A new woman in Almanac, Afagh, who had joined us only a few weeks ago with her sons, had named it recently.

It was now called *Mantiq al-Tayr.*[19] For me it was still hard to pronounce but it meant 'the conference of birds', and she told us she had found it in a book of poems from her childhood about the pilgrimage of birds in search of enlightenment. Sometimes, in the evenings, she would read to us from the book in her mother tongue, Farsi. The more I understood the mystic allegory, the more appropriate the name revealed itself to be.

We sat down in a circle in *Mantiq-al Tayr*. Some children, weary from day and digestion, rested down their heads into the laps of their parents. They stroked the heads of those at their mercy, slowly

18 W. H. Auden, *Age of Anxiety: A Baroque Eclogue*, edited by Alan Jacobs (Princeton, NJ: Princeton University Press, 2011).

19 Farid-ud-Din Attār, *Conference of the Birds: A Seeker's Journey to God*, translated by Rustom Pestonji Masani with an introduction by Andrew Harvey (York Beach, ME: Weiser Books, 2001).

running their fingers through hair of all sorts of colours, lengths, and textures, gazing into the fire with distraction. Alma placed a tray on the carpet and slowly started pouring tea into tiny ceramic cups. She distributed them amongst everyone, asking: "What would we like to channel[20] tonight?" Lelibela twitched, then slowly raised her head from my lap and gestured toward the wicker basket full of peaches. "Now, we've been picking peaches for years but never consulted one." Alma's face was suddenly drenched in a toothy grin. "Would you like to channel one for us tonight, Leli?"

I could feel my daughter's nervous sweat on my own back as she walked towards the fire. As unbothered as she was about sharing understandings in the forest with only me, she was reluctant to reveal her gift to the community. Alma reached out her arm and welcomed her into the midst.

20 Pamela Kribbe, *Earth Speaks* (St. Petersburg, Florida: BookLocker.com Inc., 2021), 6–7, retrieved from: booklocker.com/books/11562.html.

"When you channel, you find yourself in a state of spiritual relaxation, which is comparable to the sense of flow that you can have when you are inspired by something; for example creating music, doing a sport or painting. You are outside of your mind and deep in your bodily feeling. As a channeler, you are also actively present in this open and receiving state because you form the bridge between the intuitively felt insights and their representation in human language. The channeler is the interpreter who translates the intuitively received and felt insights into words and concepts. [...] The best thing you have to give is your trust, openness, and courage. These qualities make you surrender, as unbiased as possible, to the flow of spiritual energy that seeks to manifest itself through you. In receiving that flow, you will work with your mind and intellect to best share the energy and insights that you feel in human language. Words, concepts, and language belong to earthly reality. The contact with the spiritual world is often very direct and emotional. We need a human translator who gives this energy an earthly form. In this translation some distortions can and will occur. Purity does not stand or fall with perfection, but with sincerity and a sense of one's own limitations."

"I mean ... I might as well try an acorn first." And she looked down at her hand, opening the fist in which a small fruit from today's visit was disclosed. "You know, something from the past tells me this fruit is more related to me than the peach. I don't want it to be inaccurate."

"Mhm ...", hummed Alma with a frown, looking directly into my daughter's eyes: "Is your uncertainty of not having much shared history with that peach greater than your desire for belonging?"

Immediately she shook her head vehemently, so that her curls swung back and forth. "Well, then ask if it grants you permission to dive into its being." Leli carefully and with consideration reached for a peach from the basket, placed it on a low, wood-carved stool, sat cross-legged in front of it, the fire at her back, rubbed her hands together, exhaled heavily, and held her hands a few inches above the soft-shimmering fruit. Her breath heaved and lowered her chest as all of Almanac was watching her. She squinted her eyes, whereupon her features softened. Then she opened them, looked around, almost looked at each of us silently, before she said, "I have permission."

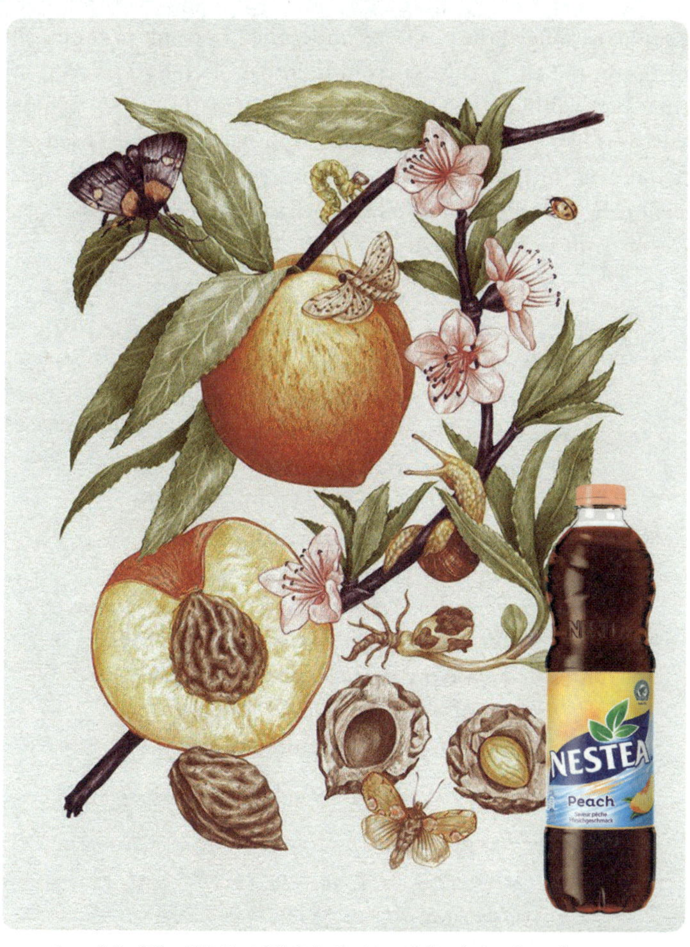

Image 9: Zoe Keller, 2014. Peach Life Cycle, Graphite with digital colour. [image] Available at: www.behance.net/gallery/22309365/Peach-Life-Cycle [Accessed 14 August 2019].

Image 10: Nestlé, 2022. Nestea Peach 500ml EW PET Bottle. [image] Available at: www.worldofsweets.de/Nestea-Pfirsich-500ml.321692.html [Accessed 23 January 2022].

People rearranged the cushions under their bottoms or took a sip of tea. Some children rose from their pre-sleep and pricked up their ears, rubbing their eyes into wakefulness. The tension in the yurt was like a taut balloon. Once again my daughter raised her hands over the plump beauty and lingered for minutes, breathing shallowly in absolute immobility, until she opened her lips to speak for the fruit in front of her:

My plant is self-pollinating,
containing both reproductive parts.
It only takes a modest breath of air
for the pollen to blow sideways.
In spring I carry stunning pink flowers,
but when there is a late spring frost I won't
carry fruit in the late summer at all.
If conditions are right, the fertilised
ovary develops into a fruit.
Sometimes our flowers have to be picked or eaten,
as all of them turn into fruits and might make
our tree too heavy and the harvest disquieting.
We need a warm, temperate climate
and abundant sunshine.

[mumbling, the tone of voice becoming sinister]

Some predecessors of mine shared graves with men
and women over a time span of 10,000 years just
outside of the city of Shenzhen, China.[21]
They were resembling funerary goods.

21 "Geschlechterkonflikt – Frauenbilder der Geschichte," August 24, 2020, video, 1:01:24, available at: youtu.be/hlEMHRsB7Ss.

The genesis of disparity can be traced back here. 4,000 years ago, while decaying in the underground, our pits witnessed gender-based nutrition for the first time.[22]
It was dark. This was news to us. Female bones were no longer of equal quality to those of Men.

Original video was in the mediathek of arte: "Frauen, Frauen, Frauen! Im März schaut ARTE mit einem weiblichen Blick auf die Welt," ARTE Presse, March 4, 2020, available at: www.arte.tv/sites/presse/meldungen-dossiers/frauen-frauen-frauen-im-maerz-schaut-arte-mit-einem-weiblichen-blick-auf-die-welt/.

22 Yu Dong, et al., "Shifting diets and the rise of male-biased inequality on the Central Plains of China during Eastern Zhou," *Proceedings of the National Academy of Sciences of the United States of America*, 114.5 (2017): 932–937.

Kate Pechenkina [Professor, Ph.D. University of Missouri, Columbia, 2002] is an anthropologist and archeologist who traced back the date in history where an egalitarian society became a hierarchical one. She worked on human ecology in continental and insular East Asia.

It is no news that women were worshipped in Ancient cultures. For thousands of years gender roles were not prevalent, and there was no significance or judgement about being male or female in most cultures. Everyone in a community had to contribute in order to maintain its existence. In the Neolithic period, hunting and gathering were not as separate as once thought, nor was gender so divided. It seems that about 4,000 years ago a shift took place. During the start of the Bronze Age, it could be seen from bone findings just outside of the province of Zhejiang, China (and similarly in findings on Malta, for example) that for the first time there was inequality in nutrition that caused sexual dimorphism. Carbon in bones indicates the consumption of plants, and nitrogen shows the consumption of animal products and fish. The procedure used to uncover this information is called isotope analysis. So while women, men, and children ate the same diets in the Neolithic Era, around the Bronze Age women's bones were significantly deficient in various nutrients, while men maintained a balanced diet at all times. This theory is further proven by the ways burials were arranged differently. In the Neolithic Era, graves were similarly richly stocked with all kinds of different grave goods. Yet from the Bronze Age onwards, graves of females contained very little or no grave goods, while those of men remained equally opulent.

Man was entitled to my ancestor's juicy
flesh as well as animal flesh.
Slowly creeping poison, causing
an unstoppable downward spiral.
It is this domination that gave birth to
all forms of slavery that came after.

[sighing, then continuing in a lighter tone of voice]

I have many names,
One of them is Prunus Persica, the Persian plum,
Which is odd 'cause I grew originally in China,
where I was first looking like what
you would call a cherry today.
It took 3,000 years of human selection
to turn me into the abundant fruit you see now.
I had many faces.
In China, my coveted tenderness was long enjoyed
solely by royalty, not by the farmers picking us.
Celebrated by privilege, until taken for granted.

From China our delectableness spread
to India and Western Asia.
I remember the day Alexander the Great fell in
love with us, so he moved countless of my siblings to
Europe after he conquered Persia.[23]
And later, in the 1500s, European colonisers
brought us to America, where we turned into the

23 Marion Eugene Ensminger and Audrey H. Ensminger et al., *Foods & Nutrition Encyclopedia*, 2nd Edition (Boca Raton, Florida: CRC Press, 1993), 1040.

Nation's first commercial fruit crops.
Our delicate fleecy fuzz is essential for our health.
Its protective coating safeguards us through times
of insect invasions, rot, wind, fungus, and it locks
in our succulent moisture.
The human eye didn't like it, so in
the 1950s we were shaved after harvest.
Half of us were marketed as fresh, naked, yet
aesthetically pleasing fruit.
The other half were processed into
cocktail fruits in metal cans or plastic bottled
iced tea, among other forms.
We had no chance but to surrender
for the time being.
One day, our skin was intoxicated with poison
under the assumption that these pesticides would
protect the food plant from undesirable organisms.[24]
As if we couldn't have taken care of that ourselves.
The toxins contaminated the ecosystems we were
part of, hindered biodiversity from emerging,
wiped out over sixty per cent of the animal
kingdom and the majority of water species,[25]
it contaminated the soil our
roots were connected to,
and slowly it contaminated people's

24 San Telmo Museoa, "Vandana Shiva | Ecofeminism and the decolonization of women, nature and the future," March 25, 2020, video, 53:24, available at: www.youtube.com/watch?v=hVbbov9Rfjg.

25 "Living Planet Report 2020," World Wide Fund For Nature, Living Planet Report, accessed December 7, 2021, available at: livingplanet.panda.org.

guts, and then finally their psyches.
When we were eaten, before the era
of toxication, we met over 100 trillion
microbes in human stomachs.
Those were very diverse and complex intelligent
systems; we learned a lot from them.
But after contamination our toxins
started destroying them.[26]
Nature is the – female – enemy, which
must be forced into Man's service.[27]

Lelibela's hands, still generously spread over the peach, shivered. Her closed eyes were moving rapidly as though she were having a bad dream. Small beads of perspiration on her frowning forehead shimmered in the light of the fire. There was a jittering in the sound of her breath now. It took a few moments until she recovered. Some people in the circle, first and foremost myself, were clearly tempted to wake her up to release her from the burden she was experiencing. When I could hardly bear my daughter's agony any longer and rose up to stand by her, her body calmed down and spoke words in an old, forgotten language that no one had ever taught her:

26 "UN human rights experts call for global treaty to regulate dangerous pesticides," UN News, March 7, 2017, available at: news.un.org/en/story/2017/03/552872-un-human-rights-experts-call-global-treaty-regulate-dangerous-pesticides.

200,000 people per year are dying from the consequences of pesticide poisoning and the numbers of people suffering with chronic diseases such as cancer and diabetes are exploding. Many children are being born with neurodegenerative diseases as a result of this.

27 Carolyn Merchant, *The Death of Nature: Women, Ecology and the Scientific Revolution* (San Francisco: Harper & Row, 1983).

Ipsa suos onerat meliori germine ramos persicus et pruno scit sociare genus imponitque leues in stipite phyllidis umbras et tali discit fortior esse gradu.[28]

EPILOGUE: NOT THE END, OR: BEYOND THE ANTHROPOCENE

July 2, 2055

We are all Godseed, but no more or
less so than any other aspect of the universe,
Godseed is all there is – all that Changes.
Earthseed is all that spreads Earthlife to new earths.
The universe is Godseed. Only we are Earthseed. And
the Destiny of Earthseed is to take root among the stars.[29]

– Octavia E. Butler, from "The Books of the Living", in *Parable of the Sower*

It was Lelibela's thirty-first birthday. She had decided to take a walk in solitude, roaming beyond the fields of Øm towards the desert. Her ever-growing belly did not prevent her from travelling long distances every day. She was determined to retreat before motherhood.

28 [Quote] Palladius Rutilius Taurus Aemilianus, *Opus agriculturae*, Book 14, ll, edited by J. C. Schmitt (Leipzig: Teubner, 1898), 94–98.
"Of the peach:
Better shoots load the branches of the peach,
Which with the plum to unite its kind doth teach:
On Phyllis's stem light shades it kindly throws,
Which, by this step, to be much stronger grows."

29 Octavia E. Butler, *Parable of the Sower* (London: Headline, 2019), 73.

Fewer and fewer plants were visible; the vegetation reduced until she couldn't see a single hint of greenery anymore. The climate became drier and warmer. The wind was still, while the sand burnt in crimson during the last moments before the sun departed. Lelibela set up her night shelter, so she barely saw the hot planet disappearing behind a massive sand mountain. She built a fire as the nights became bitterly cold here. She settled next to it, wrapped in a blanket, and soon drifted away in her evening meditation. It was dark and utterly peaceful. She had by now gotten used to the energy living under her ribcage, but it was something different. Pulling. Downwards yet upwards. She could sense tranquil frequencies from her home village Almanac, and while muffled into this hunch of reassurance she fell asleep under the grand lunar halo.

Her dreams were serene but wild. She met people she knew she had known for a long time. But there was no particular face yet. Someone called her home. To a home very different from Almanac. A vastness opened up that she had never experienced before. And then her father appeared in front of her, reaching out his hand, saying: "Lelibela, people may vary in their ability to handle revelations. But you know."

Blinded by the sun she woke up the next morning. She slowly rose, gratefully emptying her water flask. She took off her shoes to feel the sand between her toes, stood up, stretched, and yawned. Her eyes lingered on the massive sand mountain that had shrunk considerably overnight. She ran up the hill. On the crest she paused to observe. She saw sand trickling down, as if in a funnel. From all sides it poured downward. A hard kick hit her belly from the inside. Vary. In. Ability. To. Handle. Revelations. She looked at the tiny opening through which the sand ran. A tiny hole, barely larger than a peach. She inhaled, exhaled. Arms open, she threw herself backward and rolled down the hill toward her sleeping place. Her belly laughed. She left everything but provisions, even her shoes. She had five days to reach the others, but she knew it was enough.

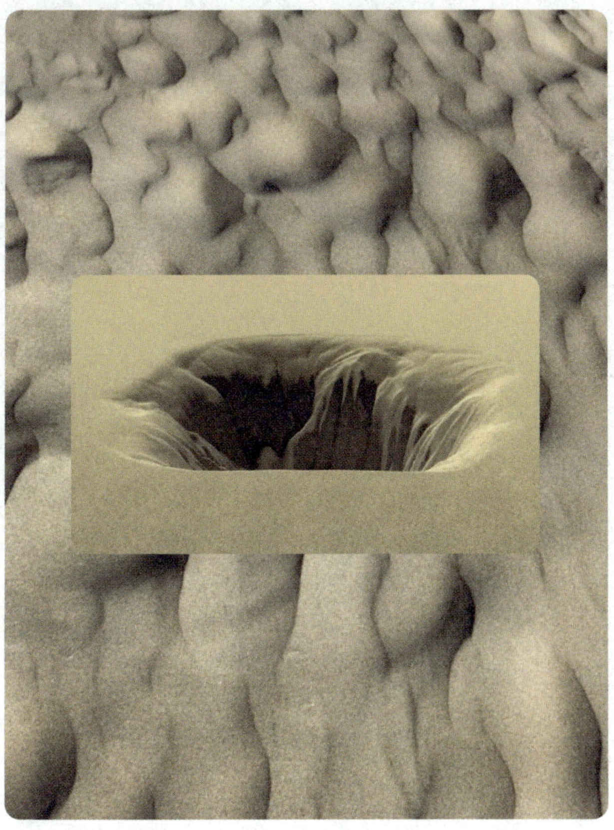

Image 11: Unknown, free license.

Image 12: Unknown, free license, n.d. Pit in the Desert, 3D rendering.

Lama Aloul

Running in a Marathon

The witnessing body, the narrator, the second body, builds its knowledge through the senses in seeing, feeling, tasting, and hearing. Its voice stretches from the past.

The science body, the third body, relies on rational and logical thinking. In direct conversation with the witnessing body, its voice stretches from the past to the present reciprocally, though it is influenced by the past and by societal norms and biases.

The critical body, the fourth body, uses logical thinking to influence other fixed logical thinking. Its voice stretches from the past to the present and to the future.

The spiritual body, the fifth body, the all-knowing body, learns from everything and its knowledge is embedded in everything. Its voice stretches from all dimensions and is not confined within time.

The alternative body, the sixth body, uses both logical and intuitive thinking, and is open to non-conventional ways of thinking. Its voice stretches from the present to the future.

You are running in a marathon.
A marathon,
you lost track of how or when it started.
A marathon, you could only see its runners;
symptoms running one after the other, and together
they are not easy to chase or identify,
running together
in a group of marathons,
in a syndrome.
syn is to-run,
and to *drome* is together.

"a syndrome; is a group of symptoms that consistently occur together,
or a condition characterised by a set of associated symptoms."
said the science body

You are not sure why and for how
long you have been running like that.

You had to stop running, and went off track,
why are these runners still running like that?

But this marathon didn't start here and now, it started before and then.

Let us embark on a journey, where we explore
these runners, understand them better,
and dig a little deeper.

Shall we begin? Said the witnessing body.

INTRODUCING OUR FIRST RUNNER

"This runner is the oldest one, it is fast and vigorous. As soon as you stop it, it multiplies into another," said the witnessing body.

Acne was a big struggle for you, it affected your self-esteem and overall mental health. You once had a trip with your family to Tiberias, you had been planning this trip for some time; the israeli occupation approved your permit and papers to visit. But as usual, a vigorous pimple popped out at the right time. So you opened your laptop on top of your lap and searched home remedies to clear out pimples fast, you saw one remedy that you thought would be most effective, the remedy says, mix garlic with lemon and dip a cotton pad, place it for a few minutes on the pimple, and it will diminish in size. That's what you did. Except you might have left it for too long, it started burning, so you removed it immediately but it was too late, now the pimple was not only swollen but doubled in size. Oh what a disguise. At least your sister thought it was funny.

Your dermatologist thought it was funny too. That's when your mom booked you an appointment to finally see one. You were excited because you heard of amazing results of women who cleared up their acne after being treated by that doctor. Some women even got marriage proposals after, because their skin was perfect, according to some gossip.

You have tried different treatments for your acne, some worked but only for a short time, you started feeling really frustrated and you were ready to do what it takes to have clear skin.

"Let's get you on accutane," said the science body. Accutane/Isotretinoin capsules are usually the last treatment we use in treating acne, we usually prescribe it when all the other treatments fail. It is a very effective treatment for severe acne. However, this medicine can have serious side effects, so it must be prescribed and supervised by a specialist doctor, tell your doctor straight away if you become depressed or think about ending your life while taking this drug," said the science body.

You knew about the serious risks that can accompany this drug, but you still wanted to take the medication, and take the risk. It was not until the accutane failed to treat your acne that your dermatologist predicted it could be a hormonal problem, and for treatment you needed to see a gynaecologist.

But you have been seeing gynaecologists during the same time for another symptom. You thought your acne could be treated separately without associating it with the other symptom.

It became clear to you that acne is never a problem on its own, but it is almost always a signal of something deeper.

"It only took you a few years, several failed experiments, and a few salaries, to finally see that it isn't a problem of the skin alone, but it is much deeper than that. Our skin is only part of a multi-organ system. It is only one leaf on the tree. An imbalance of your skin is also an imbalance of another tissue, another system, another body.

Can't you see?" said the spiritual body.

INTRODUCING OUR SECOND RUNNER

Another runner, this one is unpredictable and is not punctual, it sometimes runs off track. You have been dealing with this runner in parallel with another, but never together.

You just graduated from high school and moved to a new city. It was a big change for you. After a few months, you noticed your menstrual cycle had stopped. This was confusing, as you've always seen yourself as healthy. You ate well and had a good lifestyle, or so you thought. What could have gone wrong? You wondered.

You started seeing some gynaecologists, looking for some answers. The doctors didn't seem to agree on a single diagnosis. Some were stating you were completely healthy despite the symptoms that were showing, some were requesting more tests, and others were keen on a specific diagnosis. Why was there such a contradiction in the diagnosis? You wondered.

It took you not less than a year, several visits to different gynaecologists in Palestine, Jordan, and Egypt, to reach a final diagnosis that seemed most coherent; Polycystic Ovarian Syndrome, PCOS.

So you took your laptop on top of your lap and searched;

What is PCOS?

"Polycystic Ovarian Syndrome, PCOS, is a syndrome affecting the reproductive system of a woman's body, embodying several symptoms such as excess androgens, insulin resistance, acne, excess hair growth, and can cause anxiety and depression," said the science body.

What causes PCOS?

"PCOS is still not completely understood by medicine. It is a heterogeneous disorder, the symptoms PCOS is associated with are various and can have various potential causes. They can also be similar to symptoms of other health conditions. This makes it hard to diagnose. Doctors use a diagnosis of exclusion by leaving out all other possible conditions or diseases that could be associated with the symptoms of PCOS," said science body.

How does modern medicine understand PCOS?

There are several approaches to define or understand syndromes as suggested by Ricardo Aziz. The first is through expert knowledge and consensus (Aziz, 2006). The Rotterdam Criteria, which has been used to define, diagnose, and further treat PCOS was based on expert meetings and consensus.

In 2003 a panel of experts from the American Society for Reproductive Medicine (ASRM) and the European Society for Human Reproduction and Embryology (ESHRE) met in Rotterdam in a consensus workshop to provide a more unified diagnostic criteria for PCOS; called the Rotterdam Criteria. The Rotterdam Criteria expanded on the guidelines criteria of the National institute of Health, NIH, that were created in the 1990s, which was used before the Rotterdam Criteria and added two new types of this syndrome.

How is PCOS diagnosed in modern medicine?

There isn't a test to definitively diagnose PCOS. It usually starts by the doctor asking questions that look for symptoms, such as abnormalities in the menstrual cycle or weight changes. The doctor will also look at physical signs, such as acne, signs of excess hair growth, or insulin resistance. Additional exams are usually conducted such as blood tests and ultrasound to confirm specific symptoms. If two of the three main symptoms were found; excess hair growth, Polycystic ovaries visible on ultrasound, and irregular-absent periods, then the patient is diagnosed with PCOS.

This diagnosis criteria is clearly not solid, and that is clear through your own experience, which made you reach out to the critical body, and you asked;

Are we in need of new criteria for diagnosing and treating PCOS?

"A lot of women only learn they have PCOS when they are trying to get pregnant but are having difficulties, so they learn they have PCOS upon their visit to the gynaecologist. This comes after years of living with a wide range of symptoms and health concerns before getting diagnosed or before their symptoms are treated, which can really affect their quality of life and wellbeing. A lot of these symptoms are even normalised for women to experience," said the critical body.

How efficient is this criteria for diagnosing PCOS?

As more patients are left misdiagnosed and sometimes mistreated, many doctors are arguing against the usage of the Rotterdam Criteria to define, diagnose, and treat PCOS. Some argue that it should be revisited, since the development of these criteria was based on expert meetings and on consensus, and not on evidence-based treatment. (Mol & Wang, 2017).

As Michael Crichton argues, "The work of science has nothing to do with consensus. Consensus is the business of politics. Science, on the contrary, requires only one investigator who happens to be right, which means that he/she/they have results that are verifiable by reference to the real world. In science, consensus is irrelevant. What is relevant is reproducible results."

Some also added that the criteria is premature as it does not adequately define or characterise this syndrome. These two new additions in the criteria indicate that science understands these new phenotypes, which is not true, this could affect any future research and investigation on these types; consequently decreasing the potentiality of further studies to understand these two new types. Moreover, as stated by Aziz, "The data we have on the health implication associated with the new added phenotypes are unclear and relatively poorly characterised." (Aziz, 2006)

How did we name this Syndrome?

The name PCOS was first named 'Stein-Leventhal syndrome' referring to Stein and Leventhal, and then changed to PCOD (Polycystic Ovary Disorder), and then to Polycystic Ovarian Syndrome (PCOS). Historically, medical disorders are given the name of the individual that was able to describe the features of a disorder. These names are peripheral and many times not intuitive nor are they instinctual in nature.

There have been several calls to change its name, and these proposals are on the rise as the need for medical efficiency is growing with the increasing number of health problems. The proposals are suggesting a name that is more informative, and doesn't confuse or divide.

Why should we change the name of PCOS?

As noted and recommended by the National Institute of Health consensus meeting in 2012, "We believe the name PCOS is a distraction and an impediment to progress. It causes confusion and is a barrier to effective education of clinicians and communication with the public and research funders. It is time to expeditiously assign a name that reflects its complexity." The name PCOS centres the condition around symptoms in the reproductive system of women despite its heavy relations to its metabolic dysfunction. This affects how this syndrome is viewed especially by women, and therefore they often worry too much about the cysts or even relate them to tumours, which causes more stress and anxiety. (Aziz)

Another negative influence of the name is that it affects the amount of funding and research support from corporate or governmental agencies.

You were happy you found strong voices in the medical field who are trying to have a positive influence from within the medical and scientific system.

Later, you reached out to the alternative body, looking for some solutions and alternatives, and you asked,

What are the potential names of this syndrome?

"Several investigators and individuals are suggesting to rename it. Since the etiology of this syndrome is still not even completely understood, it makes it even more complex to choose a name that informs patients, the public, and health care providers about what it really is. Since this syndrome primarily affects the reproductive system and/or the metabolic system, some suggested giving the name a two-state solution.

One name reflects the reproductive consequences that are cared for by gynaecologists, and the other name reflects the metabolic symptoms that are cared for by internists, physicians, and sub-specialists who deal with the metabolic consequences of the syndrome. However, as stated by Aziz, this naming suggestion does not work, as the symptoms of both the metabolic and the reproductive are linked and can not be viewed separately," said the alternative body.

"When there seems to be some mystery and rising conflict in a situation, perhaps it is wise to look at the ways and tools we are using to deal with it. Perhaps the conflict isn't in the situation itself but it is in the tools and systems we created to deal with it," said the spiritual body.

Instead, Aziz is suggesting to give three name differentiations based on the characteristics or the main symptoms of the syndrome. This way, instead of giving the individual physician's the agency to diagnose, the diagnosis is based on clinical characterisation.

Another alternative for naming PCOS was suggested by Aziz, since science still can't fully understand the syndrome's causes; so instead of defining PCOS by its associated symptoms, alternatively, it should be defined by its long-term implications and the health consequences, which are clearer to scientists; for example, a metabolic syndrome that puts the patients at risk of heart disease. (Aziz 2006)

"Changing the name has a huge political influence; if done right, it will enhance the awareness of this public health condition, and encourage more fundings for research," said the alternative body.

"Syndromes are only a label you created to comprehend what you still can't comprehend. The closer you look, the farther you get. You can't treat what you don't understand," said the spiritual body.

After identifying some of the symptoms and revealing some of the runners, it was time to start the treatment process.

You were given contraceptive pills to help regulate your period. Your father, expressed his concern with these hormonal pills, and their long-term side effects, but at that time you didn't care, because you started menstruating again and your acne, to your surprise, was clearing up for the first time!

"Patients with PCOS are usually given oral contraceptive pills like Diane-35 ED. It's used for the treatment of signs of physical male characteristics caused by the male sex hormone, androgen, such as, severe acne, facial hair, and irregular periods," said the science body.

After stopping the pill, some of the symptoms returned, and you later realised that this wasn't a long-term treatment, and in fact, there aren't any. All the treatments are like bandages to these symptoms and none confront the root cause. You took your laptop on top of your lap and searched, and as usual the science body replied.

How does modern medicine approach and treat illnesses?

Modern medicine is really efficient at handling infectious diseases and emergencies. It also proves successful in increasing longevity, decreasing infant mortality, and lessening the stresses of life by medical interventions.

How does modern medicine treat PCOS?

There is no cure for PCOS. However, a variety of medications can provide relief. Lifestyle and diet change is advised by doctors, especially for patients who are considered overweight or are trying to get pregnant in order to achieve hormonal balance, improve metabolism, and combat insulin resistance. Medications are also used to provide relief or prevent development of serious health risks, including birth control pills, progesterone pills, spironolactone (a blood pressure medication), clomid (an ovulation-stimulating medication), and metformin (a medication used to treat Type 2 diabetes).

Its focus is on preserving and restoring fertility, reducing symptoms, and preventing complications that can develop in women with PCOS from adolescence to the post-menopausal period. Historically, science was developed as disease-based. In this approach, the diagnosis and treatment is straightforward as it is focused on disease-causing agents.

"Don't get too distracted by the leaves of a tree, if you want to understand better, maybe you should try to look deeper, can't you see?"

You felt disappointed and deceived with how modern medicine approached the treatment. So you took your laptop on top of your lap and reached out to the critical body:

What is wrong with the current approach of modern medicine?

Cure in modern medicine, in most cases, is not the priority, and prevention as a methodology is not embedded in the consciousness of biomedical researchers. According to MD, Ajai, "It's probably because it would ultimately make them redundant." And so the approach of modern medicine is mostly palliative; meaning it aims to reduce pain and distress without targeting the cause of the condition. It's disease-based approach works to control, and not prevent or cure, except curing infectious diseases (MD, Ajai). This approach views individuals as cases and undervalues the sociocultural and humanistic aspects of patient care." (West J Med, 2002)

"Medicine means nothing if not this: to cure sometimes, to comfort always, to hurt little, to harm never." (Kaplan, 2009)

"All knowledge is one, the division in knowledge is only an illusion. Knowledge manifests itself in separation to make the process of understanding it a little easier. Knowledge is interconnected and so are the bodies and everything in this world," said the spiritual body.

EXPERIENCE OF MODERN MEDICINE IN THE NETHERLANDS

You were excited upon your first visit to the general practitioner in the Netherlands. You had good expectations of the healthcare system as the Netherlands is considered a first world country. When you told him about your already worsening symptoms, he immediately started comforting you and said,

"You do not need to see a gynaecologist, this is very common, and seeing a gynaecologist is too expensive in attempts to convince you that you don't need to see one," said the science body.

This was very disappointing to you. So you asked for a female practitioner, hoping she might be able to understand, but this time you were ready, you brought some documents with all the tests you need to take for a PCOS check-up with a note from a PCOS nutritionist that you found on the internet; in hopes that she might be able to understand.

After talking to her about all your symptoms and experiences along with the tests you need to take, she tried to comfort you by saying,

"You do not need to worry, a lot of women have it too, I also have it but I'm married now and was able to get pregnant."

She only agreed to do some of the tests in their lab, the rest of the tests were not available in their lab.

You asked her about the reason she can't give you a referral to the gynaecologist, she apologised and said,

"I once had a patient like you, and I sent them to a gynaecologist, but that got me in trouble as the gynaecologist was very upset with me for giving that patient a referral, but if you know any gynaecologist who can help you, then I can give you a referral," said the science body.

This is when you learnt that cases like yourself are not taken seriously by doctors, at least in the Netherlands; only women who are pregnant, or are trying to conceive, or women who are overweight, since they seem to have a higher risk of diabetes than women who are lean, are taken seriously.

"It seems that the health of a woman is only taken seriously when it involves the health of a fetus; the health of a potential human being. Or when her health condition involves another human being like her husband, in this case when it involves the quality of life of a man. And so it seems that the value of the health of women increases when there is another human involved, and so her wellness and well-being alone is not prioritised or valued by the health care system in the Netherlands at least," said the critical body.

But that didn't stop you, so you went to see another general practitioner in another medical centre, hoping it would be different. You brought with you once again the list of tests to do, along with backing evidence and statistics as advised by a PCOS nutritionist. The general practitioner finally agreed to do some of the tests that you requested in their lab. He said that if they found some marks on hormonal imbalances then they can continue with the list and the other tests. You agreed. When the tests were out, they were all normal to your surprise, so you couldn't continue with the rest of the tests and they definitely were not going to send you to a gynaecologist.

"Lab tests are important to determine the health state of the patient. The results are shown in a set of numbers called the reference range or the normal values. These values are determined by testing a large group of healthy people whose results are considered typical and normal," said the science body.

"It is indeed possible for healthy people to test outside the normal range, while people with problems to have results inside the normal values. In this case, you will likely need more testing. Lab tests alone are not enough to provide information about the health of the person. Additional

physical exams, or looking at the person's health history and other tests, should be done for complete diagnosis and treatment," *said the critical body.*

"The perception that there is one medical system that is right and other systems are wrong is diminishing, instead of dismissing or completely cancelling, perhaps it is wise to re-shift the focus, re-evaluate the results, and look at what is working."
The spiritual body.

"More people are turning towards alternative medicine as their faith in the modern medical system is diminishing. The need for a medical system that allows physicians to put the patient's unique experience of illness as the focus is becoming more urgent than ever."

Does funding in modern medicine affect the way we approach the patients?

"Funding and research mostly goes to treatment for those who are already sick, and little is invested in prevention or understanding the causes. Doctors would benefit from tests and research to understand a certain disease rather than having the right medications to treat the symptoms. There is also some resistance from insurers around paying for screens and tests to diagnose earlier," said the critical body.

Researchers and investigators should turn their focus on researching alternative and non-conventional medicine, which promotes lifestyle change such as yoga, meditation, and spirituality in preventing disease. (MD, Ajai) alternative body.

What can change in the approach of modern medicine?

MD, Ajai imposes that the approach of medicine should be one that is based on prevention. "The first goal of medicine is that no one has to reach a clinic or a hospital except of course for secondary and tertiary prevention. This should be the very first goal and not the last."

He also adds that for true prevention of disease and pursuit of longevity and wellness, there are values that we should prioritise; "Clean water, nutritious food, clean and disaster-free habitation, proper sanitation, control of pollution, poverty alleviation, empowerment of the deprived and disadvantaged, life-style modifications." This definitely makes it a complex process of prevention as it requires the efforts of agencies that are not in control of medicine.

"Pharmacology can be a very potent tool for prevention, cure and well-being, but most of it is directed towards palliation and control at present. It must be marshalled towards cure, and prevention. This is its big challenge, if it can transcend economic compulsions and awaken to its true role in medicine," said Aziz.

What's next for PCOS?

"Let's embrace the call to action and identify leadership, stakeholders, and sponsors to drive the process, develop clear global engagement and education plans, and identify the resources necessary to effect these," said Aziz.

Your journey didn't come to an end, and probably will never do. You decided to take a new path in the treatment process through alternative medicine and ancient wisdom. You have already been seeing positive changes.

You started reaching out to other fellow women who are also experiencing the same syndrome, in hopes to learn and exchange knowledge together to increase awareness of our bodies, the surrounding ecologies, and the reciprocal connections between the two.

WRITER'S NOTE

This essay might never have an ending, it will keep on growing as more experiences and learnings are undertaken by the writer and the witnessing body, as more research and development in modern medicine proceeds, and as our consciousness towards our health, body, and ecology grows.

I would also like to invite you to build on this essay with me, collectively sharing our experiences, reflections, and learnings together.

To have access on the development of the essay, along with the references, please write to me lamaloul97@gmail.com

Naira Nigrelli

how to common the art academy

a case study on gerrit rietveld academie and sandberg instituut

SUMMARY

a student that seeks to undertake their education abroad, most often, would not in the slightest invest time into investigating and contributing to the decisional infrastructures the hosting system provides: almost parasitically, most (student) members feeds off of it, graduate, and leave. while the opposite is less frequently true, students almost reflexively adopt the idea of a drive-through academy, and in decision-making are increasingly dependent on the representative bodies. an institution is worthy of being commoned, collectively governed, because getting acquainted with the functioning powers of an educational art institution could educate a critical view on the institutions that lie before our eyes, in the *life after sandberg*. but what would it take to common our cultural institutions? who is the academy *really*? within the parameters of my experience as a student representative, in this essay i will attempt to describe what tools of relation i see possible to facilitate together and how each moment is worthy of being harvested or mobilised. ultimately, forms of self-empowerment are in the bridging of these tools. this essay is a field-research that takes the sandberg instituut and the gerrit rietveld academie as a point of departure. in the first section, i explain how my collaborator, lila bullen-smith, and i see the practice of commoning. specifically what is the urgency in our cultural institutions. subsequently, i describe what work is already being done as a primordial form of informal, parallel governance: a conglomerate of unions and initiatives that intertwine with formal decision-making, reinforcing the formal representation bodies (which i will list and contextualise). finally, in the last sections, i propose an informal institutional glossary that could support this informal, parallel work, and how it could improve institutional relationships beyond contracted mandates. harvesting a new glossary is a speculation on new forms of institutional cooperatising and positioning: a better grasp of institutionalisation. to bring forward an example of interdepartmental efforts is to identify and untangle the knots we encounter throughout our time at school, as an essential component of our educational journey, after education. without a lineage, how are we represented in the organisational infrastructure and in the curricula? and further, how, in these circumstances, can we raise our bar of ownership with a greater sense of civic responsibility, ultimately leading to forms of co-governance? it is exactly in this independent, small-scale institution that one can start to address enquiries on *cooperatising* and collectively governing, actions that immediately self-empower and take care of our global culture.

WHAT DOES IT MEAN TO COMMON?

acts of *commoning* at the gerrit rietveld academie takes place both formally (in the boards and the participation council) and informally (student-led initiatives such as the unions, the student council, and other interdepartmental activities, some of which are facilitated by institutional funds). formally, they happen at an administrative or representative level (via democratic election). informally, there are no elections, at least not across all student and teacher members (for example, anyone can join the existing, or spontaneously initiate, a union). the student council, however has a self-standing and self-governed decision structure. it was born as a union but does not act as others in terms of membership: new members are elected by current members and once part of this council, the student acquires a contract, issued by the institution. in this way, despite being "institutionalised", it differs greatly from the formal participation council (mr), which operates within the legal framework of the school. here instead, members are democratically elected by the members of the institution who, upon membership, do not receive a contract (but a "donation" known as IB-47). hence members inherits a different legal status than a student in the student council. this non-linear approach and legal mandates and recognition across representative bodies can be confusing for new members. in terms of mandates and responsibilities, the challenges of being politically engaged in these cultural institutions is increasingly demanding. on the long run, however, not only could this consolidate the decision-making infrastructures of the organisation but elaborate the morphology of a more incluse institution.

but in the western world, political engagement rests as a privilege on many layers within society. even though there are numerous informal ways of getting involved in the politics of sandberg and rietveld, i find that such a meagre selection of candidates is problematic because, in a way, it means presented with the choice, most art and design students would deny access to information on the functioning of the institution in a individualistic and not commoning approach. it is particularly here, at our cultural, educational institutions, that this positionality begins. art and design can support the integrity of society as a whole, provided they offer space for cultural discourse. subjects relevant to society, hence, start with critique at the institutional level. not as a war of fronts but in using art to build bridges from within. art in conflict situations are a perfect example of positionality. so where do we find the incentive to participate in the decision-making structures, ultimately as an act of care towards our future generations? and what is meant by *commoning*, exactly?

the problem is not in the possibility to represent and hence influence the decision structures, but the way this workload is distributed. informally, too much is expected from the representatives, resulting in an unequal distribution of tasks and unbalanced social-institutional engagement. for this reason it is important to create *tools of relation* that derive from a traceable past and harvested present: the important missing link with the generations of the future is exactly the cause of an alienating present.

the jaarverslag 2020 (2021 is still in the process of being published), very well describes the current contractual relationships with the people working and studying at school. when looking at their lifespan, on average, students remain enrolled at the academy mostly for under five years in the case of the bachelor's and above two years in the case of the masters. particularly, one to ten years for the members involved with the more administrative work, very similar to the timespan of heads of departments and distant to that of freelancers (better known as "professional advisors"[1]). within the legal framework of action, instead, the supervisory board (rvt), the board of governors (cvb), and the participation council (mr) do not differ much. in fact, the chair of the rvt can be in office for a length of four years, up to a total of eight years. the same rule applies to the members of the cvb and the chair of the mr. currently, all members in the formal roles of sandberg and rietveld are in their last years of maximum office. when these numbers are compared

1 freelance contracts.

with the average institutional life-span of students, one can quickly realise how little influence each student can make when there is no traceable past of forms of agency. for this reason, particularly in these times of transition to a new governance model, it is imperative to invest time now in methods of passing on the relay.

ways to deal with the harshness of reality is a real attempt at commoning relayed activities. particularly at the academy, tradeable generations can equip us into asking better questions to understand our collective culture.[2] particularly, how they manifest within institutions and how in turn they affect education. what is needed are supplements to the work that is already being done. lila and i have already started mapping the institutional network of sandberg and rieveld and are working towards increasing accessibility and contributions, from the formal platforms (such as the intranet) to the informal.

A FIRST ATTEMPT AT COMMONING

what is the current organisational status of the art academy and how does this conflict with the desires and work of its students?

while the intranet is busy explaining the formal doings of the school, the navigational map is its informal and independent counterpart. efforts in this category are also the roles of unions, student circles, "*unsettling*", as well as the lineage of the chair of a board or of a department. they provide small-scale, internal mutual-aid projects that turn into a source of great support to the bodies that operate

2 david bollier and silke helfrich, *free, fair, and alive: the insurgent power of the commons* (gabriola island, bc: new society publishers, 2019).

within the legal frameworks. these, all together, ultimately build our institutional genealogy.

you might be wondering about privacy, but the collection of data is not necessarily a *bad thing*. it is the privatisation of it that could threaten our cultural work and the people it supports. for this reason it is important that this archive be open source and internal. lila and i envision a longterm harvesting[3] process that can give depth to our institutional lineage. agency is about exercising our culture-specific free will. *take the diploma and run* isn't what we have in mind because, while we are running, we could maybe slow down and realise that the time is right to start now.

Organogram Gerrit Rietveld Academie

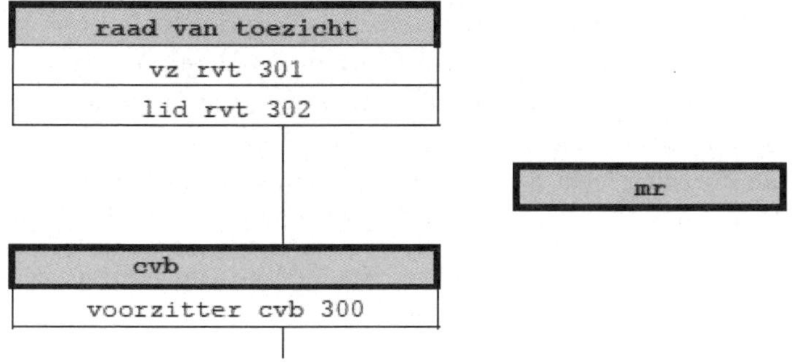

3 "glossary," documenta15, accessed december 7, 2021, documenta-fifteen.de/en/glossary/.

via democratic election, the mr welcomes all members of the academy to review, approve, or advise both executive and supervisory governing boards. in turn, these strive to provide a clear outline of all decisions that ultimately affect the socio-political life of the institution and its members. being part of the participation council is essential to the empowering of coordinators, educators, and learners across all the institution. furthermore, commissions are in place and within the mr focus groups take a closer look into the 'student charter', the priorities, and the regulations. the importance of the mr meetings are accessible by all members. attending them can provide training on political science. as a member of the mr you will receive trainings that focus on financial readings or legal advice as well as take part in regular meetings with the boards, as a representative. actively working in these positions has informed myself to be able to ask better questions; questions that are more informed and that navigate a web of institutional interdependencies. i am very far from having mastered these skills, but the knowledge one can acquire here can make education all the more approachable. but does that make it a more inclusive environment? or more of a "safe space"?

contrarily to most institutions in the netherlands, the gerrit rietveld academies are a joint, independent academy of arts. it does not share a supervisory board (*rvt*) with other institutions. in other words, its approachability and scalability embodies the essential leverage that representative bodies can have on final decisions. this labour is highly specific to the institution itself. as opposed to the university of applied arts of the hague (the *kabk* and the *kc*), the rietveld and sandberg is still formally and informally more approachable, even to those who are less politically involved. for example, this year, this rvt has supported the appointment advisory committee (bac). in this committee, chairs the chair of the supervisory board, another member of the supervisory board, the head of operation, head of workshops, head of human resources (secretary), an mr representative, one head of one masters programme, one head of one bachelor's programme, one student from rietveld and one from sandberg, myself. the *bac* has been installed to write and appoint (the profile of and) the new chair of the executive board. in addressing the points to put forward, as the student representative of sandberg, i became aware of the lineage of the past, present, and its importance in the future. the representative work expected of me had me reflect on and suggest how this lineage looked, in representing those whom i can speak for, looking forward. in theory, participation in the political dynamics of the school, in practice, how to secure these dynamics as we move towards the future.

in addition to representation, the independent academy is known for self-managing its funds. since the start of the loan system in holland, the academy receives money from the *quality agreements*; the agreement by which the government financially but indirectly supports the art students. these are important interdepartmental programs, one of which is the *extra-intra fund*. what is great is that short-term projects have immediate effect on the small-scale institution. the scalability is also very important for cultural institutions. particularly in education, the decision-making process of democratically elected bodies provide faster communication pathways not only in the spontaneous *corridor talks* but also in the number of people involved. but we cannot expect that our "participation" will make substantial changes and immediately. it is certainly not a reason to turn one's back to "yet another bureaucratic system" because commoning an art academy doesn't happen overnight.

so far i have described what are a few points in favour of an independent cultural institution. and while until now i have attempted to outline the internal politics, the institution does not function in a vacuum. in fact, the demographic of this academy describes that seventy per cent of its students are non-dutch.[4] this already is important to harvest and dissect as we go. it informs us about the global tendency of this cultural institution. questions of ownership and (self-)governance may have already been asked. these are also informed by our classes or exhibitions on decoloniality of power. they all take part in the critical art practices that when replicated can encourage unionising.[5]

the digital archive lila and i have been developing can provide material to the interdepartmental resources that helps us to respond to the question: "who is the academy, *really*?" a changing relationship, surely, is about our positionality. so while you might have the feeling the proposal recalls existing activities, the good news is that the work is already being done. forms of self-governance are particularly concerned with building upon this, and the fact that the gerrit rietveld and sandberg instituut, jointly, is an independent art academy makes the building of an archive all the more exciting.

4 jaarverslaag, gerrit rietveld academie, 2021.

5 see appendix: extra-intra application document (national art student union) – in appendix.

WHAT IS THE URGENCY OF (PARALLEL) MAPPING OUR INSTITUTIONAL WORK?

is it true that the institution as a system is learning and evolving in the same way as the people it hosts? could a student provide an educational exchange from which the institution can "graduate"? the institutional plan clearly identifies education as intrinsically hierarchical,[6] and whilst it is true if we continue to use terminology such as "bottom-up" or "(de)centralised approach" (which still implies centralisation), what would change in the narratives of the institution, beyond its formalities? the creation of a social contract[7] similarly to that described by rousseau, in a small-scale academy, can constitute the first step of counter- (or parallel) mapping. our institutional social contract reveals the annexes between written and oral history, within and across administrative and educational departments. the corridor talks that have been taken away from us in these times of pandemic uncertainties have turned out to be important resources of spontaneity or gossip as the utmost informal institutional work. gossip not in the narrow sense, but in a sense that smooths formal edges. one that gives depth to our sense of belonging. so how can we, in such a prolific cultural environment, start positioning ourselves within the academy, ultimately to find ownership? which visual lineage or forms of unionising could nurture institutional, emancipatory practices? we can find strength in imagining inter-disciplines not as negative spaces but provocative ones; language and the politics of translation can identify fundamental descriptions of our institutional reality.

6 see appendix: institutional plan, gerrit rietveld academie 2020-2025, p. 58.

7 jean-jacques rousseau, *the social contract* (indianapolis: hackett publishing company, inc., 2019).

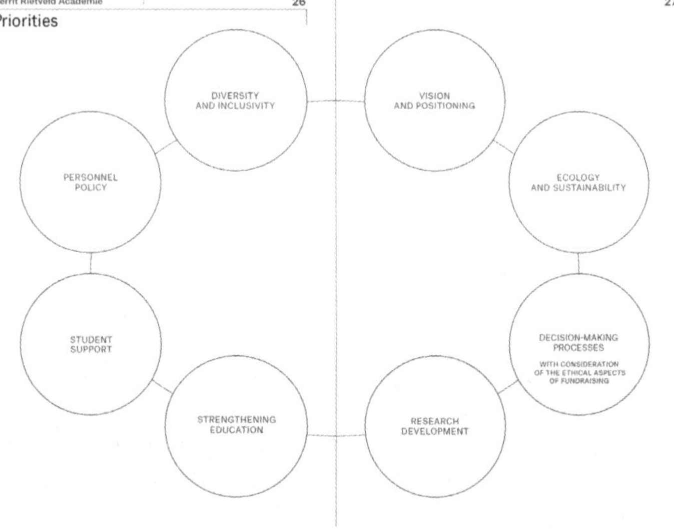

as seen above, parallel, institutional mapping is a way to carry out the eight priorities in the institutional plan for which the mr divides into complementary working groups (the commissions). in general, the institutional plan gives insight in to the prospects, educational targets, and curriculum of the rietveld and sandberg instituut. from 2020–2025, it aims to describe the vision of this art academy, after a long-term, joint effort of many pillars and representatives of the school, it gave life to an enormous effort of (formal) commoning. even though it is partly outdated due to the research done before the pandemic, it is also lila and i's idea of safe space. in fact, the ultimate participatory, emancipatory practice of curatorial practices is not about being right, but one that teaches us how to allow dissensus and failure of the real in taking decisions and performing our freedom of speech. and not, instead, by pondering on the fine lines that divide trust from transparency, concepts often swapped in daily exchanges but critical in formal discussions.[8] free speech as another form of political correctness undermines spaces for criticism as cultural growth. and especially within these walls, it is our defence from reflexive adopting of the culture of integration. in short, not guaranteeing the space for the parallel work, may threaten: "*a well-functioning democracy (...) organising contradiction is a very important social function of an art academy.*"[9]

a maxim of mutual-aid can be dated back to may 2020. the "harshness of reality"[10] confronted the institution's idea of "safe space" as its political position remained unclear. the class of disarming design issued a public statement addressing the public silence of the institution, opposite to other art institutions in holland. and while initially it might have seemed like a demand for a public, political positioning, this letter was instead an invitation to understand the institutional "silence".

should our cultural institutions be explicitly political, or should they be striving, together, to align theory and practice, formal and the informal, in an endless process of becoming? what does it mean to be a "political" cultural, educational institution? the statement went as follows:

8 sandberg instituut internal archive (intranet): medezeggeschapsraad / minutes 25 november 2021.

9 institutional plan gerrit rietveld and sandberg instituut 2020-2025, p 15.

10 open letter to director of sandberg instituut: request tuition fee reduction, spring 2020.

>> dear executive board of the gerrit rietveld academie,

in light of the current international liberation movement for palestine, and the historical and monumental reclamation of established discourses and narratives, we, the students of the disarming design department at the sandberg instituut, find it immoral that sandberg and rietveld have remained publicly silent so far. you claim to teach decolonial theory and yet have failed to take even the smallest of action in solidarity with palestine. (...) there can be no neutral position today. it is very simple. silence aligns you with the oppressor.

we demand your immediate action through a public statement (...)

decolonial theory is nothing without decolonial practice.

sincerely,
the students of disarming design

the efforts to produce this statement identified an important aspect of commoning a cultural institution. the statement was published as a class and publicly addressed to the executive board. it marked an important moment of self-legitimisation; a great act of responsibility, positioning, and openness to incongruences and misunderstandings. this work is informal, interdepartmental, and must be recorded for the future lineage of sandberg. because there are no fronts, the publishing of a statement must not be seen as a "won battle", but as an example of publicly relevant work that happened behind doors and that should have been dealt with openly, practising space for mutual-aid. a space between the "bottom and the top", to thrive together. but in the nature of institutional collectivising, top and bottom are a matter of perspective in this cultural melting pot. and expectations must to be managed as that act of care. "*it is not my responsibility to teach the europeans about oppression (...)*", if not our cultural institutions, whose duty is it then to listen to and support forms of emancipation, especially in times of uncertainty? or in this governance-transition? it is in the micro-politics of the interregnum where resistance as emancipatory practice can better operate.[11] the possibility of a paradigm shift proposes, therefore, that the interregnum be a place where principles of hegemonic coordinates are temporarily suspended, and where activism can take its space within these liminalities. the monsters that appear here, as gramsci would describe them, are moments before the future can identify its new lineaments.[12] moments when we can act, in the infinite spaces of the interregnum. a chance we must not lose.

THE MUSEUM OF COMMON WORK

on self-governing and ~~bottom-up centralised~~ distributed decision-making processes

since human nature is the true community of men, those who produce thereby affirm their nature, human-community, and social being which, rather than an abstract, general power in opposition to the isolated individual, is the being of each individual, his own activity, his own life, his own joy, his own richness. to say

11 antonio gramsci, *lettere dal carcere* (palermo: sellerio, 1996).

12 steven henry madoff, ed., *what about activism?* (berlin: sternberg press, 2019).

that a man is alienated from himself is to say that the society of this alienated man is the caricature of his real community.

– karl marx

whereby my representative roles were democratically elected, and public consultation could have taken place in the organising of assemblies, i was often told that my consultation with those i represent is formally just a *courtesy*. and while time restrictions often give no option, it is often the case within vertical hierarchies and centralised governance. this *modus-operandi* seems to leave little room to reflect profoundly together, upon politically and socially relevant decisions at school. in fact, similarly to a governmental *referendum*, the act of assembling rarely happen because of these temporal asymmetries. so much, that we increasingly start to rely on representative bodies, that paradoxically distance ourselves from developing our sense of ownership. for these reasons, a continuation of the "tools of relation" database and data visualisation networking aims to lay the foundations of distributed decision-making processes. taking advantage of the modern blockchain technology, its distributed system becomes clear as it serves the purpose of building technological trust. similarly, a distributed decision-making process allows them all to be centres of culture-production (in the case of "tools of relation", spoken of as "activations"), to close what i would call a "decision-making loop", and not a decision in itself, after all centres have confirmed its sequence of approvals. the european union is already thinking about a blockchain voting system, something that might be happening in the near future.[13]

13 european parliamentary research service, "blockchain voting," september 19, 2018, video, 3:12, www.youtube.com/watch?v=2rgbOv_ab4c.

particularly in cryptocurrencies, blockchain technology works in a more complex distributed system. the beauty of this is that the traceable lineage becomes visible and therefore observed.[14] this logic can be applied in many branches of cultural practices, not as monetisation (as they are already busy with), but for example in the creation of an informal glossary. when passed through (not legitimised) to each member, it can be written and finalised.

a similar example i succeeded to pass through was the following standpoint in the bac profiles:

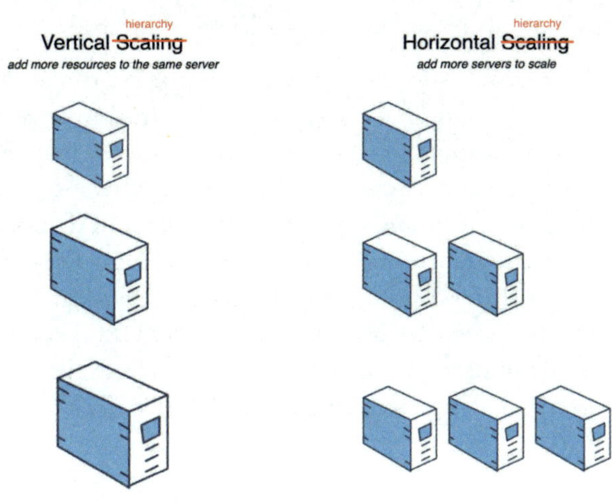

14 nitish srivastava, "what is blockchain technology, and how does it work?" blockchain council, accessed october 23, 2020, www.blockchain-council.org/blockchain/what-is-blockchain-technology-and-how-does-it-work.

the interspaces of the "tools of relation", are the spaces that make the academy stronger under a culturally aware perspective, for example archiving the palestinian statement, or the process of its becoming (meetings with the board and flag-banning, etc.). so what is proudly called a "decentralised" system, the rietveld and the sandberg, leads us back to work that is lost in the informal centres of culture, where information, lineage, is not yet archived. the urgency of an interspace of this kind manifests proactivity and collective intervention, as well as ownership and sensitivity. so how can we easily provide trainings in a distributed manner? for example, in forms of mutual-aid programs, described by dean spade.[15]

"tools of relation"[16] was born from the input of groups and/or people. the archival backbone is a database in its visual representation of institutional mapping. as described earlier, all active members of the academy can identify their practice, or better activation, within the walls of the institution. we were not short of ethical questions, in naming these affiliations. they instigated an immense sense of responsibility that, while working, our agency or personal thoughts had to be developed with other forms of collectivity. that explains the external input. the database also includes an informal glossary, part of which will be presented at the end of this essay.

15 dean spade: *mutual aid: building solidarity during this crisis (and the next)* (london, brooklyn, and new york: verso, 2020).

16 "tools of relation" is a collaborative field research project by naira nigrelli and lila bullen-smith about the gerrit rietveld academie and sandberg instituut. the project aims to harvest the unofficial work of past and present members of the academy (grass-roots initiatives), as well as to create an alternative institutional lexicon. the project researches methods to open-source the historical lineage of work that largely goes without memory, like that of students and/or tutor unions which would cease to exist if new members stop joining.

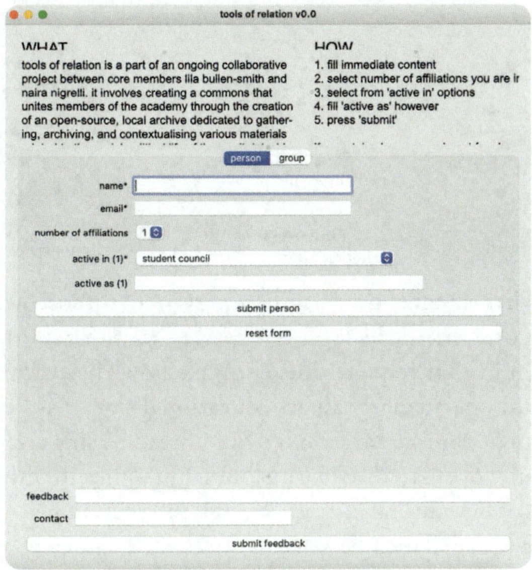

the database, has been developed with the support of the extra-intra departmental fund in 2021 and has been careful in storing data of our institutional colleagues. it is also a map that proposes a network as a biome in which place for experimentation can exist with greater consciousness while improving the logic of a static museum as we know it. we imagine it as the place where all human beings affiliated and operating within these walls, own the right to access, research, affirm, confirm, question, store, compare, learn, unlearn, position, argue, confront, exhibit, juxtapose, comment, reference, challenge, evaluate, acquire, translate, embrace, bury, unveil, dissent, trust, reciprocate, locate, unionise, collectivise, strengthen, overcome, relate, and, ultimately, remember all forms of the cultural inheritance of that institutional, cultural education.

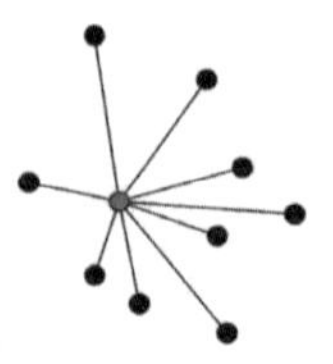

centralised

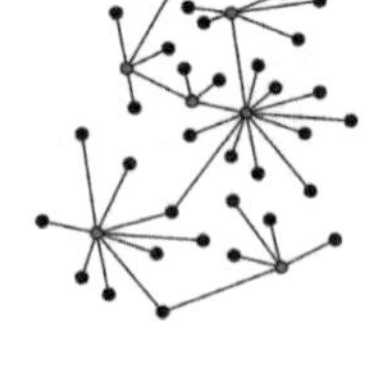

de-centralised

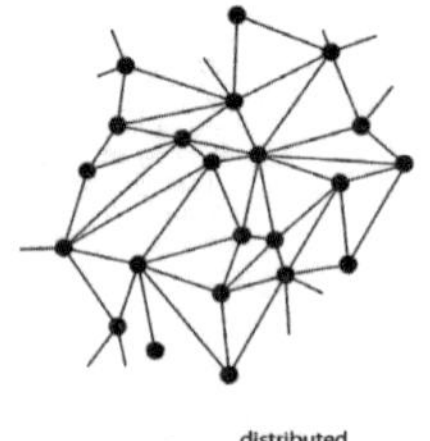

distributed
the centre is the production of culture

but to what extent should – if necessary at all – those who carry cultures other than the local be expected to integrate? the level of racism in that request thus enquires how the culture of an institution, particularly an art educational (local) system, that hosts, can be contrary to a *storage*, but instead a living archive that will acquire open-archive-like qualities. but unlike for established curators of big cultural institutions, this internal archive would be in the hands of all members of this multicultural society. it would be open sourced and hence would not only be about uploading and discussing documents, but also about methods of curation in displaying the cultural history hosted at rietveld and sandberg. it is the idea that established systems will reach a mutually beneficial agreement with their members in the hopes that they may always refer to it as an effort for a sustainable form of infrastructural maintenance. it is an internal museum of common work that shows that the sandberg and rietveld is more than its formal institutional set-up, but an expansive network of activities and engagements.

A GLOSSARY TO COMMON THE ART ACADEMY

the importance of new vocabulary, following the counter-mapping

"the twentieth-century linguist revolution," says boston university anthropologist misia landau, "is the recognition that language is not merely a device for communicating ideas about the world, but rather a tool for bringing the world into existence in the first place. reality is not simply 'experienced' or 'reflected' in language, but is actually produced by language."[17]

if we start overlooking terminology that is contractually binding, our relationship to these practices becomes identified in material assets, rather than educational resources. we can start using "overworked" instead of "underpaid", "crafts expert" instead of "workshop staff", council of surveillance instead of "supervisory board". what would happen to our cultural, institutional practices when we stop adopting suppressed terminology? what happens to our interrelations? and ultimately to our lineage? a radical re-thinking of the institutional glossary is encouraged. hereby, i would like to propose a new vocabulary that would follow the parallel mapping of the art academy. the building of our social institutional memory starts from its languages and the politics of translation is something we should all be careful of. below is a list of terms that have helped lila and i deepen our institutional relationship, and find one that is better suited, more human.

17 roger lewin, *in the age of mankind* (new york: smithsonian institution, 1988), 180.

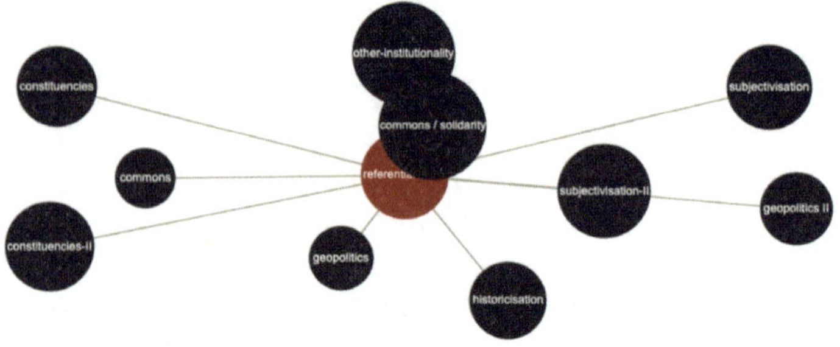

glossary of common knowledge, website: glossary.mg-lj.si

APPENDIX

the appendix includes further readings and supporting internal references annexed to the gerrit rietveld academie and sandberg instituut. together they provide depth when describing the institutional archive, the "museum of common work". particularly, you will find a joint archival proposal for "tools of relation", aimed at the director of sandberg as a concrete plan of how this could evolve in the upcoming year, urgently starting now: how lila and i envision our collaboration on institutional work to continue beyond our time respectively as students or coordinator.

in the appendix i have also highlighted definitive "bac profiles" for the chair of the cvb and profile descriptions, with the implementations brought forward as sandberg student representative in yellow are crucial points that have been raised as a sandberg student representative, and in red, the more formal implementations of bac, rvt, or mr members.

included are references relating to methodologies of informal mapping in "tools of relation": a text describing the project and its relation to the database and relevance to the institution, as well as models of alternative mapping and self-governing (distributed systems, vertical vs horizontal hierarchy). finally, a glossary of terminology used formally that could benefit from revitalisation.

INTERNAL REFERENCES

bullen-smith, l., and naira nigrelli. "lila bullen-smith – sandberg graduation exhibitions and events." sandberg.nl. 2021. sandberg.nl/graduation2021/final/lila-bullen-smith.

nu.nl. "directeur koninklijke academie stapt op na kritisch rapport over bedrijfscultuur." march 23, 2021. www.nu.nl/cultuur-overig/6123551/directeur-koninklijke-academie-stapt-op-na-kritisch-rapport-over-bedrijfscultuur. html.

gerrit rietveld academie. undefined, unsolicited, unsettling: institutional plan 2020–2025. amsterdam: gerrit rietveld academie, 2019. rietveldacademie.nl/en/media/inline/2020/7/3/gerrit_rietveld_academie_institutional_plan_2020_2025.pdf.

g. rietveld academie (2019). institutional plan 2020-2025. [online] available at: rietveldacademie.nl/en/media/inline/2020/7/3/gerrit_rietveld_academie_institutional_plan_2020_2025.pdf.

EXTERNAL REFERENCES

arendt, hannah. *the human condition*. chicago, london: university of chicago press, 1958.

bollier, d. and silke helfrich. *free, fair, and alive: the insurgent power of the commons*. gabriola island, bc: new society publishers.

documenta15. "glossary." accessed december 7, 2021. documenta-fifteen.de/en/glossary/.

european parliamentary research service. "blockchain voting." september 19, 2018. video, 3:12. www.youtube.com/watch?v=2rgbOv_ab4c.

gramsci, a., *lettere dal carcere*. palermo, sellerio, 1996.

kropotkin, peter. *mutual aid: a factor of evolution*. new york: mcclure phillips & co., 1902.

lewin, roger., *in the age of mankind* (new york smithsonian institution, 1988).

lima, m. *the book of circles: visualizing spheres of knowledge*. new york: princeton architectural press, 2017.

madoff, steven. h. editor, *what about activism?* berlin: sternberg press, 2019.

merriam-webster.com. "definition of decentralization." online] available at: www.merriam-webster.com/dictionary/decentralization.

mckenna, t., *food of the gods : the search for the original tree of knowledge : a radical history of plants, drugs and human evolution*. london: rider, 1999.

network, *building distributed systems with blockchain technology*. medium. cere-network.medium.com/building-distributed-systems-with-blockchain-technology-277c402eff94.

papastergiadis, n., *museum of the commons : l'internationale and the crisis of europe.*, new york, routledge, 2020.

rousseau, jean-jacques, *on the social contract*. indianapolis: hackett publishing company, inc, 2019.

spade, dean, *mutual aid : building solidarity during this crisis (and the next).* london brooklyn, new york, verso, 2020.

srivastava, nitish, "what is blockchain technology, and how does it work?" blockchain council, october 23 2020, www.blockchain-council.org/blockchain/what-is-blockchain-technology-and-how-does-it-work/.

treccani.it. "interrégno" in vocabolario - treccani. www.treccani.it/vocabolario/interregno/.

treccani.it. (n.d.). "curare" in vocabolario - treccani, www.treccani.it/vocabolario/curare/.

ukeles, , mierle laderman. *manifesto: for maintenance art 1969! proposal for an exhibition "care."*

Karmel Sabri

Celebration as Resistance

Enveloped in a collective rhythm of love, we proudly occupy Cedar Ave. Our voices, powered with indignation, echo one another. *Beeeeeb beeeeeb beeb beeb beeb*! Each honk by a passerby drives our energy levels even higher. *Whoooooo whoooooo*! We respond. Our hands are numb and tingly from clapping. It is a hot summer day in Minneapolis and the first week of Ramadan. I overhear middle-aged lesbian couples coordinating *iftar* plans with conservative Muslim men. I see more unfamiliar faces than familiar ones but I feel protected by the embrace of a community.

Minnesota is the place where my eldest uncle Azzam Sabri came on a student visa from Palestine in the 1970s. He then finessed the American immigration system to bring his parents and five of his siblings to join him over the next several years. Recently I learned that my youngest uncle, Hamoudi, came to the US through Canada on a visa sent to him in the mail with the face and name of one of his brothers, my father Basim. Things were simpler then I guess, but that's a story for another time. Anyway, my family's determination to survive is what ultimately led to me being born and raised in Minnesota.

The Palestinian community in Minnesota is small and, like other communities, not without differences that keep us fragmented. There are a handful of large Palestinian families, each with their own reputations and similarly fragmented within themselves, one of which is the Abu Khdeir family. On July 2, 2014, sixteen-year-old Mohammed Abu Khdeir, a Palestinian from the Shu'fat neighbourhood of East Jerusalem, was kidnapped, beaten, and burned alive by Israeli settlers in East Jerusalem. On July 3, his cousin, fifteen-year-old Tariq Abu Khdeir, a Palestinian American from Tampa, Florida, who was visiting his family in Palestine that summer, attended a demonstration in honour of Mohammed, where he was detained by Israeli forces and brutally beaten. The image of his swollen and disfigured face is forever burned in my mind.

The Abu Khdeir family didn't ask the community to come together and hold photos of Tariq's face in the streets. It happened spontaneously. In Minnesota, the community that composed these assemblies was not made up only of Palestinians but also other groups with long histories and experience of antiwar resistance, including feminists, Jewish voices for peace, Black Lives Matter activists, anarchists, socialists, and LGBTQ activists, as well as those who found themselves joining these activist communities for perhaps the first time, young children, families, high school and university students, Muslims, East Africans, other Arab communities.

The summer of 2014 was explosive in every way possible. We felt heartbroken and horrified by the images and stories that reached us by way of news from Gaza. Simultaneously, however, our actions made us feel powerful, righteous, excited, valid, and loved. The protests became a social and political classroom for me. My assumptions were challenged by the generosity and understanding I observed that summer. Over the course of those sixty days we claimed the streets across major cities as one collective voice and body. We screamed with intensity and force until our voices became scratchy. Of course with the intention to be heard, but also as a cathartic release to express our shared emotions of anger and pain. Activating our bodies in demonstration was a physical embodiment of our desires and frustrations. The event of coming together demanded an infrastructure to which intimacy and trust were integral. For instance, trusting that if I fell, a caring stranger would help me up, or if I was arrested, the community would quickly raise funds for my bail.

Eventually, as the intensity of the attacks on Gaza dwindled, so did the momentum that drove the protests. The desire to dismantle oppressive systems stayed with me but so did the intense longing for the elation I felt during the protests. I joined long-standing activist communities and regularly attended protests. In a moment of self-reflection, I realised that my desire to relive the feeling of collective power had developed into an unhealthy pattern of waiting or even searching for a terrible injustice to occur to catalyse collective action. After this difficult realisation, I began to question the purpose of a protest and oppressed communities' emotional proximities to anger and pain as a motivating force. I know my motivation was driven by three core factors: a genuine desire to spur political change, an innate longing to shorten the gaps of proximity between myself and Palestine, and the desire to feel lifted by the collective energy of a community. A community that for the first time gave me a sense of belonging.

My lived reality as a first generation Palestinian being raised in the West was one where my culture was not represented, let alone celebrated, in discursive or material spaces outside my own family. I can confidently say that hegemonic cultures of racism went so far as to delegitimise our existence and demonise our culture. Not to mention, most people around me didn't even know what or where Palestine was in the first place. The only time I would find my culture represented in mainstream discourse was in relation to violence, conflict, and controversy, which almost always supported a pro-Zionist agenda, casting Palestinians in the role of terrorists.

I know for Palestinian communities, diaspora and oppression is an ongoing and historical reality. But did it have to be what defined my culture? Did I have to wait for a horrific event to take place to provoke a ripple of pain and anger in order to feel justified in taking space? That was the case in the events of 2014, which triggered widespread insurgencies. An emotional contingency of coming together, however, was joy. It felt good to take public space and to feel celebrated. There were even moments inside the protests that felt like a street festival. Together, we proudly celebrated solidarity and Palestinian culture and simultaneously celebrated and honoured feelings of sadness and anger.

I thought of the notion of the oppressed that states existence as a valid means of resistance. I felt freedom in the realisation that gathering to celebrate was an unrepressed declaration of existence, which in itself held the means for political resistance. It was my desires and this realisation that led me to work within the community to organise parties and festivals to honour Palestine from 2014–2019 in Minneapolis and Chicago, where I was living at the time. In many ways the parties were similar to the protests. They both called for a gathering of communities of solidarity and both interrupted and occupied public space to honour a celebration of Palestine. While the response was overwhelmingly positive, like with most protests, the parties were met with some resistance. There were local businesses, for example, who despite basing their marketing strategies around a progressive identity, declined to support our events for fear that the topic of Palestine might be "too polarising" to be publicly associated with. And, on the occasion of one high-profile event, we even attracted a small Zionist mob. The public element of hosting the parties in the street did leave space for serendipitous encounters, however one major difference between the parties and the protests was that the parties were not spontaneous occurrences but rather planned and permitted. This does not cancel out the potential powers of celebration, but does dilute the sticky atmosphere that is intensified in instances where the object of a political event is so binding that it provokes an unchosen adherence. Where the act of assembling is a unanimous reaction.

Through the lens of events in Palestine, I seek to explore the relationship between celebration and power. By referencing contemporary social political examples and personal experiences, I will elaborate on how celebration and the culture of celebration builds infrastructures that disrupt and subvert hegemonic discourses, social inequalities, and authoritarian regimes. I will address two different but integral aspects of this power. The first pertains to the energetic power and affect that is conjured during moments of celebration. This power is sustained by the mutual object of honour and the enduring effect of a collective body, which validates emotions such as but not limited to love, pain, grief, and joy. The second aspect I wish to address is the material and gestural power of bodies in celebration to create physical representations of unity and resistance. In analysing the impact of events in Palestine I will refer to Deleuzian interpretations of the event, which:

> *... begin from the domain of affect and the virtual (temporal) but are only actualized in space. Consequently, space (not time, the void, or anything transcendent) is intimately linked, if not composite with revolution, with change and challenge. Meaning events not only manifest in space, but through their spatiality also change and reconfigure material reality ... these events spur change;*

they reshape the conceptual and material fabric of connectivity, relationships, path-ways and institutions.[1]

I will also reference Henri Lefebvre and Michel Foucault's theories of spatiality (conceived, perceived, and lived space) in order to unpack how events and discursive cultures of resistance (mental and social space) erupt into celebrations that claim physical, social, and mental space. Furthermore, I will show, through interpretive spatial analysis, how celebrations can be used as a tool to shorten gaps of proximity present within displaced communities.

It is useful to note that the etymology of celebration comes from the mid-fifteenth century Latin word *celebrare*, meaning "assemble to honour", originally "to frequent in great numbers", from *celeber*; "frequented, populous, crowded", with transferred senses of "well-attended; famous; often-repeated". The general association of "a celebration to commemorate or honour with demonstrations of joy comes from the 1550s; formerly it also could be with demonstrations of sorrow or regret".[2] In my interpretation of celebration as it relates to socio-political contexts I refer to the pre-1550s context. This understanding does not limit celebration only to attachments of joy but also sorrow, regret, anger, grief, etc., for example a funeral being a celebration of the life of the deceased.

While the event and object of emotion fluctuates, the foundation of celebration is maintained: to celebrate is to assemble in a demonstration of honour. Dissident powers of celebration are

1 Christian Beck and François-Xavier Gleyzon, "Deleuze and the event(s)," *Journal for Cultural Research* 20, no. 4 (2016): 329–333, dx.doi.org/10.1080/14797585.2016.1264770.

2 "Celebrated," Online Etymology Dictionary, Douglas Harper, accessed December, 5th, 2021 www.etymonline.com/word/Celebrated.

activated so long as a discursive regime of truth is recognised within the members of the assembly, the agreement of truth within the collective body being the unanimous desire to dismantle oppressive and discriminatory systems. I do not wish to proclaim that celebrations possess supernatural energies that make all our differences disappear. To assume that individuals in celebration operate under the same exact ideologies or have the same emotional relations to the object is to assume the impossible. This is to say,

> *... emotions in their very intensity involve miscommunication, such that even when we feel we have the same feeling, we don't necessarily have the same relationship to the feeling. Given that shared feelings are not about feeling the same feeling, or feeling-in-common, Ahmed suggests that it is the objects of emotion that circulate, rather than emotions as such.*[3]

Lived experiences shape our relation to the object of emotion. For example, if the object of emotion is an event of police brutality, someone who has been a victim of police brutality may feel a closer emotional proximity to the object than someone who has never lived that experience or known anyone who has lived that experience. A closeness in proximity, however, should not be confused with a desire to be close to those emotions of pain, but rather indicates a reality of trauma. There lies a contradiction in political events, in that they address the general public, but also possess reverberating effects that intimately touch individuals. The touch of tragedies and victories alike move humans to assemble. This movement stems

3 Sara Ahmed, *The Cultural Politics of Emotion* (Oxford: Routledge, 2015), 10–11.

from an innate need to process emotions together. The perceived stickiness I mentioned earlier creates social spaces of understanding, which are actualised in lived space during the moment of coming together. In other words,

> *... the shock waves of anger that occur in a single location vibrate and resonate on the international stage, and the rest of the world, 'the great globe itself' never ceases to register those fractures, tensions, resistances, ruptures, mutations and discontinuities, crises and catastrophes. As these spatial ruptures, these disturbances in and on space occur, the rumblings and changes of geographical, as well as ideological space can be tracked and understood through a seismography that measures not just intensity, but also the rippling effect that follows. This collection, then, becomes an important and necessary evaluation of shifting spaces and changing places.*[4]

4 Beck and Gleyzon, "Deleuze and the event(s)," 330.

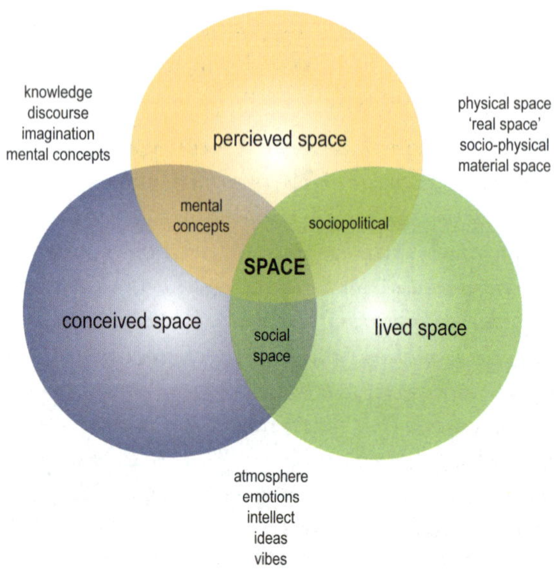

The most intense and recent ripples felt from Palestine were ignited in the spring of 2021. A viral Instagram video posted by Palestinian activist Muna Al-Kurd showed a candid confrontation in East Jerusalem, Sheikh Jarrah, between herself and a Jewish settler from New York, who calls himself Yaacov. In a calm but firm tone Muna says to him, "Yaakob, you know this is not your house", to which he replies in a surprisingly frank and unsurprisingly defensive manner, "But if I go, you don't go back. So what's the problem?" "What are you yelling at me for?" "I didn't do this! I didn't do this!" She raises her voice to tell him "You. Are. Stealing. My. House!", to which he replies, "And if I don't steal it someone else is gonna steal it." I can only speculate as to why some captured moments explode more than others. Perhaps it was the shockingly nonchalant manner in which Yaacov acknowledged his complicit involvement in the ongoing and existing systems of settler colonialism. Or perhaps it was the rare chance to witness a transparent exchange between an indigenous Palestinian and a settler from New York. Or maybe it was because Yaacov possessed an undeniably goofy demeanour, which made the picture of the settler enemy into a laughable character, especially in juxtaposition to Muna's charming and grounded demeanour. The video of Muna and Yaacov began a dialogue around apartheid, ethnic cleansing, and settler colonialism. Soon #SaveSheikhJarrah began to gain major traction. Discursive emancipatory knowledge/power resources flooded social media and rapidly materialised into demonstrations in every major city across the globe. The demonstrations demanded that Palestinians be seen. Once again, I felt the events from Palestine ripple across the globe through cyberspace, social space, and physical space.

Music is an integral tool of celebration. Its viscous quality effortlessly transcends vibes and spreads secret messages that penetrate physical boundaries. It possesses a power to touch, move, and connect the masses through atmospheric waves. In the 2021 uprising, the song "Inn Ann" by Daboor featuring Shabjdeed was released at just the moment to spontaneously become the contemporary anthem of Palestinian resistance. Sharp and unapologetic lyrics became a call for action and a part of the proud culture of resistance. It repeated across the world and was imposed onto countless videos of resistance on social media. The song captures the candid and cool way Palestinians living under occupation approach the complicated ongoing reality of chaos, injustice, and generational trauma, and an unwavering culture of courage and dignity that stems from the belief that we are fighting a noble fight on the right side of history. A culture that is rooted in a fear and faith in God. In the song, Daboor says:

chill	اهدى
because everything shows in crisis	ما هو كلشي باين في المحنة
God witnesses who we are	الله بيشهد مين إحنا

The profound lyrics rang true and for those months of chaotic uprising we felt seen on the world stage. And although we are nowhere near being a liberated people, we celebrated as though we were. The power that was cultivated in the event of celebration made freedom feel closer than ever. It was the frustration and pain felt by Palestinian families who experienced their physical space being stolen from them that spread through webs of emotions and power to activate spatial practices with rippling effects. The mission of the state of Israel to establish a majority Jewish land on top of a majority non-Jewish land created in an ongoing ethnic cleansing. The aim of settler colonialism to silence, displace, disappear, and slowly push out the subjects of oppression until they are eventually lost and forgotten. Celebration refuses these aims. Oppressive attempts to shrink and remove families in Sheikh Jarrah catalysed a counter of expansive global celebrations, which amplified the existence of Palestinians.

Objects of emotion develop in conversation with evolving events and social cultures within the discursive social spaces of celebration. They hold symbolic value and signal emotions that often become circulated throughout unfolding and connected events. A video by Muna El-Kurd captured a joyful Palestinian celebration in the streets of Sheikh Jarrah, where joyful singing and dancing was met with armed Israeli forces on horses. They assaulted and arrested primarily female attendees and effectively interrupted the joyful, celebratory atmosphere. However, a flamboyant celebratory symbol remained. A decorative bouquet of balloons in the colours of the Palestinian flag (red, white, green, and black) stayed tangled in the electric wires above, despite forceful attempts to yank them down. Their unwavering boldness represented Palestinian pride and joy, a persistent thorn in the side of the occupation. In a comedic spectacle, six fully armed individuals plus a ladder worked to accomplish the task of arresting the balloons with the same importance that might be used to detonate a bomb. In a symbolic bubble-bursting, they publicly popped each balloon with a clear intent to kill the celebratory spirits. The image of the lighthearted balloons next to the buzzkill armed forces circulated as objects of emotion, highlighting play and joy as weapons of resistance.

> *A good atmosphere may be generated by the connection 'buzz' or 'vibe' of a group or crowd, but the setting must be conductive; ambience arises from a mix of social and environmental forces. The concept of an environment as the aggregate of surrounding things encompasses both the physical and atmospheric, though we rarely discuss the interdependence of social atmosphere and the biosphere that underpins it.*[5]

5 Jill Bennett, *Practical Aesthetics: Events, Affects and Art after 9/11* (London and New York: I.B. Tauris, 2012), 56.

The affect that moves throughout the space of a celebration holds the essence of energetic power. It's June 2021; I watch live captured moments on the Instagram story of Mohammed El-Kurd (twin brother of Muna El-Kurd). I watch social and environmental forces unfold through the events of a solidarity march, which starts in Sheik Jarrah and ends in the neighbouring village of Silwan. Bodies mobilise and unite, coasting on the current momentum of the ongoing uprisings. *Lilililililiiiiiiiiiiiii* the high pitch ululation known as *zaghārīt*, most famously performed at weddings, is projected by women in the streets and echoed by the whistling and chanting of people who send their support down from staircases and homes above. They sing patriotic songs that are known by all. Collective singing and clapping establishes a rhythm; it is a fun and familiar rhythm but the lyrics hold a deeper meaning. At the edges, the celebration is surveilled by the physical presence of Israeli Occupation Forces. Some participants in the march directly acknowledge the soldiers and patronise them further by documenting the stern and irritated looks on their faces against the foreground of the lively and cheerful atmosphere. Once again the celebration turns the enemy into the object of the joke. They become the uninvited party poopers.

As the march begins to gain momentum, grenades and rubber coated bullets are fired to break up the celebration. It's clear from their reactions that this is a common form of collective punishment. The participants momentarily scatter to take shelter but soon unite again. This time even stronger. "*Hata narak janna, hata narak janna*", "even your hell is heaven", they continue to sing in proud resistance while intermittently being interrupted by more grenades. Despite safety being breached, more and more people including children are drawn out of their homes and into a dense celebration. The rhythm intensifies. Smiles quickly return to their faces and the march ends in a party at the end of the street, arms raised and clapping the air, men lifting one another on each other's shoulders and creating a dabke circle. People bring Palestinian flags, an oud, and loudspeakers. Suddenly, stun grenades and rubber bullets shower into the crowd, injuring some. The Israeli forces randomly arrest individuals and, of course, arrest the loud speakers. My mind immediately plays Kendrick Lamar's lyrics:

Bitch don't kill my vibe
Bitch don't kill my vibe
Bitch don't kill my vibe

The community automatically snaps into action, caring for those who are injured and yelling out to ask the names of people as they are being arrested in order to notify their families. As I followed on the Instagram trail I saw 'ahlanpalestien' share a video of a random family who provided sanctuary for the marchers, inviting them into their home in loving and generous spirits to prepare *maqluba* for them. I couldn't help but feel emotionally overwhelmed by the intense affectual shifts from joy to fear to anger to excitement. Despite the shifts, however, it was clear that love, care, and a will to exist remained at the core of the social sphere.

The physical distribution of space in these celebrations places the sea of demonstrators at the centre in a long and mobile movement, and the Israeli forces who surveil on the margins. In this way the celebration succeeds in creating spaces for subversive power infrastructures. At the core the celebration holds energising and healing powers, which are projected outward by the multitude of bodies mobilised in space to uphold the vibe or atmosphere. This unshakable declaration has, intentionally or unintentionally, a multipurpose effect such as that of fireworks, which are a visually and audibly loud proclamation of celebration. They are simultaneously disruptive, obnoxious, beautiful, and overwhelming. Celebrations in their unbothered and zealous nature are productive in creating a sense of distraction and annoyance for the enemy. Mikhail Bakhtin describes carnivalesque laughter as a festive laughter where: "The entire world is seen in its droll aspect, in its gay relativity ... this laughter is ambivalent: it is gay, triumphant, and at the same time mocking, deriding, it asserts and denies, it buries and revives, such is the laughter of the carnival."[6] The power of celebration lives in us and is grounded in truth and determination for liberation. Though the celebrations have a side effect of disturbing an enemy the most essential aspect is the emotional value conceived within a culture of celebration. It is the validity and safety that is manifested within the space of celebration.

I cannot speak about recent celebrations without mentioning the events that erupted in response to news of the six Palestinian prisoners who escaped from the maximum-security Gilboa prison in northern Israel on September 6, 2021, by digging a tunnel in the ground of their prison cell over the period of several months. On social media the hole at the top of the tunnel became synonymous with self-determined liberation and a slap in the face to Israeli security intelligence. From northern Israel to Gaza, cars filled with smiling faces and honking horns piled in the street proudly waving Palestinian flags while cheering and screaming in honour of the

6 Mikhail Bakhtin, *Rabelais and His World*, trans. Helene Iswolsky (Cambridge, Mass.: MIT Press, 1968), 11–12.

six heroes who made the impossible possible. Jubilant children in Gaza weaved between the cars passing out sweets to savour the sweet feeling of victory. Palestinians basked in the ephemeral feeling of victory despite knowing the occupying forces would stop short of nothing to take their vengeance on the six prisoners who humiliated them. For a short moment they indulged in a feeling of liberation. The spoon that was rumoured to be the digging device became a national symbol of resistance. Protesters in Washington D.C. even threw spoons at the Israeli Embassy to send a message of solidarity with the prisoners. Celebrations of joy quickly shifted to celebrations of frustration when the escaped prisoners were detained once again. In solidarity, the community rushed to the court in Nazareth where the prisoners were detained, to demand their freedom. In other celebrations men sang to the leaders of Hamas to ask for a prisoner exchange.

An unseen dimension of energy that informed the climate of the street parties and protests was the collective knowing that their celebration was echoed by thousands of adjacent celebrations circulating throughout the world. The shared perception that these punitive sanctions and collective punishments are unjust leads to conceived ideas of how to resist the occupation in order to achieve equality and liberation. The perceived and conceived ideologies create a shared discursive space which becomes actualised in social/physical spaces during the moment of celebration. Informed by existing culture and unfolding events, these celebrations contain much of the same gestures; such as dabke dance, *zaghārīt*, singing, clapping, chanting, etc., and symbolic objects of emotion, for example the balloons. The celebrations, which take space from Jerusalem to Gaza, from Amsterdam to Minneapolis, and so on, manifest spatial connections that successfully shorten the gaps of proximity and resist the oppressive policies that limit the physical unification of Palestinians with each other and to their ancestral land.

As we know, waves of momentum such as the ones that took place in 2014 and 2021 are exactly that; tides that ebb and flow but don't always remain at a peak. The tide is influenced by unforeseen political events, which at the surface result in spontaneous asemblance. Much like the huge wave that was caused by the Gilboa prison escape, the image that became glamourised was the top of the hole at the surface. However, it was a lifetime of faith and longing for freedom, and consistent digging that literally took place underground over the course of months that resulted in that beautiful hole. The image of the litteral surface, surfaced across the world as an emotional object of liberation and hope. While these spontaneous semblances seem to be the epitome of celebration, the true catalysts of celebration are unseen infrastructures that transcend time and physical space. A power that is endured by our emotional infrastructure and affectual vibes. Once we access this liberating power, feelings of celebration remain with us far beyond a particular moment or event. The power of celebration is sustained from the start of a perception of a desire until it inevitably explodes in collective illumination.

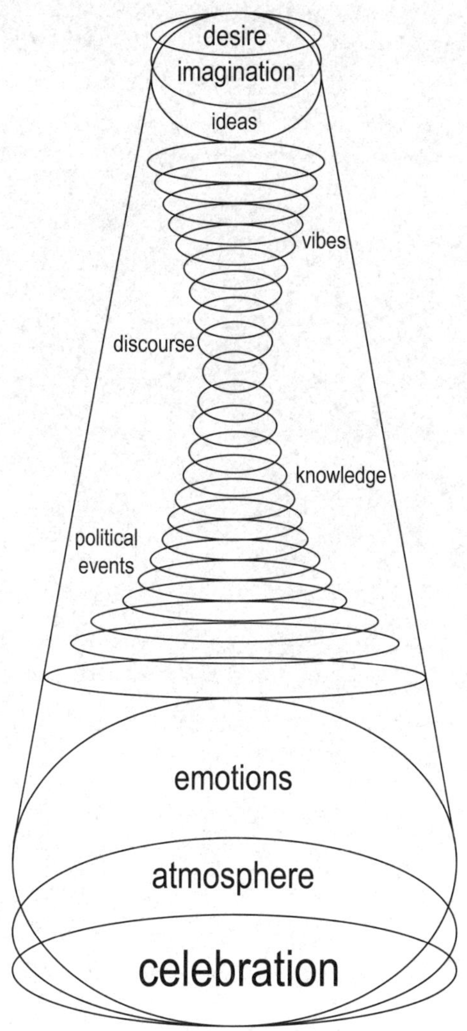
desire
imagination
ideas
vibes
discourse
knowledge
political
events
emotions
atmosphere
celebration

Ayman Hassan

dear reader,
the level of attachment i ask of you
is less severe than ....

the following is a conversation with myself:

what am i writing about?
i find it easier to answer this by first listing
what i am not writing about:
i am not writing about the relevance
of the references we use
i am not writing about why i do
not want to write in english
i am not writing about queer language
i am not writing about translation
i am not writing why this format of typing on a laptop
is a hindrance to the writing process itself
i am not writing about the disconnection i feel
towards my own words in what
they sound and look like
and i am not writing about why this is important.

the following is an imaginary
conversation with Ra'na:

i am narrating.
i am narrating key moments, often collective,
constantly in dialogue.
i am writing an essay on an essay that ~~does not yet exist~~ i have been writing in my notebooks, in our collective space in fafu, on the walls, on the ground, in a glass box at mediamatic, in amsterdam.

i am practising, applying, reflecting on –
and now writing about – my work process.
i am going back and editing my writing as i am writing ~~i do not do this when i write by hand~~ that was a lie; or a misinterpreted thought. sometimes i find myself misreading myself.

i am showing you what i see.
i see the creative processes as inherently intertwined.
i see that within every function we perform,
or role we play, we find ways to art* in it.

*the verb "to art"
from lebanese: "titfannan"

تتفنّن غير تبرع غير تحب أو ترغب عملك
تتفنن يعني تمارس مهنتك بأسلوبك الخاص
ومن خلاله تعيش وتفكر وتكون، بشكل مريح لك ولمحيطك
وبمسؤولية - هي مش دايما فيك تدركها، بس اكيد بتكتشفها،
وبتتعامل معها.

if i am to cook dinner, or design, or write, or drive, or build a stone wall, or have sex, i would like to imagine that i have the capacity to labour and care enough, within my knowledge (and with the will to learn and evolve what i think i know), to fully, or as much as possible, enjoy and respect myself during the process of making. i also see some value in "good" output and in "success", but (and however different these two things may be) they both somehow remain miniscule in comparison to what you gain along the way. "arting" the process

translating/trans-creating from my notebook:

i am sitting at the corner desk in my temporary home in amsterdam. i am sitting in the design department studio at my temporary, time-shared space in sandberg, in amsterdam.

i am researching, and trying to form an argument on what queering a language is. or at the very least, i am grappling with trying to explain to myself what queering a language might mean to a queer arab (identity politics alert) that is exposed to the verb initially in arabic as: "takweer" تكوير

a verb that already exists in arabic,
that already has (a) different meaning(s)

{warning, tangent topic} takweer could mean "to make something into a ball". imagine grabbing some soil, or mud, not too wet, but just enough to bring all the different elements into a heterogeneous group. the water, a binding element, some slug-slime, perhaps another. the soil; the cat hair; the stringy, crinkled blade of grass; the tiny living creatures who just experienced a violent reshaping of their habitat.

takweer is also the title of the eighty-first soura of the quraan. the first verse of which is

إِذَا الشَّمْسُ كُوِّرَتْ

"if the sun were to be snuffed out"

{{{tangents on political correctness and the relevance of translations of the quraan}}}

كُوِّرَت kuwwirat, well, to explain this we
have to go into a nested tangent.

> {{warning, nested tangent – explanatory for non-arabic speakers}} arabic has the capacity to arabise words that do not exist in arabic. this is not a modern evolution of the language – the word for essence in arabic is a direct arabisation of the persian word جوهر jawhar.

so, back to كُوِّرَت kuwwirat.
and back to identity.
if i am speaking as a queer arab that was exposed to the word takweer in arabic in the context of queering, kuwwirat, in this very context, would mean "has been queered", rendering the meaning of the verse: "if the sun were to be queered" – so, do we have a homonym here? one that was created on the basis of a phonetic coincidence?
who decided this? popular use? linguists?

> if relevance/authenticity comes from use, and the word is already in use and understood across speakers of different arabic{s}, then it has accomplished its prime objective to communicate a meaning (or a partial meaning) or to refer to something, a concept or idea.

back to the context of the quraan. كُوِّرَت kuwwirat being used to refer to the snuffing out, or the choking of the sun. almost as if a giant hand reached out to it and performed the same action that one would perform when balling up the bits and pieces of earth and mud. the bringing together of the fingers into the palm to create this non-space in between. a space with an unfixed form or volume.

so, we see one verb,
two contexts, and two meanings,
balling the mud, snuffing out the sun.

however both meanings are linked to the action,
or the motion inspired by the verb itself:
this bringing together of the fingers,
forming a fist around something
choking it in one, shaping it in the other
but still the same action.

تَكوير takweer, as queering, however,
has a historical, political relevance/mission:
aligning queer arabic speakers with the international queer movement. or, at the very least, linking to the international queer movement by arabising and correctly (according to arabic grammar) conjugating the word "queer"كوير.

so again:

i am sitting at the corner desk in my temporary home in amsterdam. i am sitting in the design department studio at my temporary, time-shared space in sandberg, in amsterdam. i am researching, and trying to form an argument on –
i am interrupted by siko

شو؟ ولعانة عندكم!
what do you mean?
haven't you seen the news?

i am sitting in the design department studio at my temporary, time-shared space in sandberg, in amsterdam. i open two new tabs on my browser.

aljazeera live and almanar live

to see/hear, at least two, but two prominent points of view. the two points of view are uttered by the usa and its allies on the one hand, and iran and its allies on the other.

what am i doing here?
i am escaping. i am abandoning.

> {tangent topic warning}{the process(es) of emotionally and mentally dealing with these facts (not feelings) have an effect on my thought process. they also have an effect on my relationships towards the institution that accepted me, and brought me here; towards my families (birth and chosen ones), and towards myself. towards an alternate self that chose to stay. towards my future selves that i have eliminated through the privilege of choice}

i am sitting in the design department studio at my temporary, time-shared space in sandberg, in amsterdam. i plug in my earphones and unmute almanar:

"... القرار الخارجي بإفلات الشارع اللبناني."

the external decision to unleash the lebanese street*
*loosen the leashes and allow for social and economic frustration to manifest in public in the form of mob fights.

i am sitting at the corner desk in my temporary home in amsterdam. i am writing this document – i am interrupted by siko

"come eat"

this mundane interruption allows space to ask myself: why am i writing the above? why is my assessment of the language used on the different channels according to the desires of their funding bodies relevant to my essay topic(s)?

because we talk about the relevance
of language in shaping our lives,
because i understand that these events shape my life,
despite my physical distance, in their immediate and long-term
effects. on my work, on my thought process and my mental
wellbeing, and on everyone and their work and their thought
process and their mental (and physical) wellbeing.

{nested tangent warning}{on economic and hybrid wars;
the sphere of influence of these events cannot be measured
by geographical proximity to the epicentre(s), rather by
the ties and links between the events and global
(or at the very least, regional) economy}

"... الدعوة للهدوء وعدم الانجرار إلى الفتنة."

the small phrases i note down from the live news broadcasts echo in my head as i read them.

a call for a calm to avoid getting towed to the conflict*

*the almost explicitly clear threat of civil war and the
implicit restructuring of the governance system –
an invitation to calmly accept a new form of fascism
backed by the *defender against israel* argument.

of course it is easy to criticise hizballah, and just as easy, if not easier, to criticise every other faction of the lebanese and regional major political players
perhaps with the exception of hamas, it
would be difficult to criticise them –

what an egocentric maniac,
who the fuck do you think you are to try to imagine
what it takes to be in the position of anyone else?
let alone criticise them?

we* are not criticising,
we are trying to position ourselves.

*we, it seems quite fashionable these days for one to be a we, a they, a them.

again we are not criticising, we are positioning.

perhaps it is not important that i share with you the "language analysis" i performed on what i heard. i go on with different references from both news channels, i write and think about it, it occupies my head it is like watching one's future hell being planned out for them.

in moments like this i am reminded of my scale. my distance. my capacity to choose. my allotted quota of freedom.

i want to organise a march to gaza, and to kashmir.
i want to break the siege.
i want –
i want to ask them what they
want when i meet them face to face.
i want them to be able to choose
if they would like continue walking with me.
i want us (people – human beings – living beings)
to be able to choose to live anywhere walk on any land
i want us (people – human beings – living beings)
to be able to choose to live anywhere walk on any land

i want us (people – human beings – living beings)
to be able to choose to live anywhere walk on any land

i want to not think of impossible missions
i went to talk to jeanne van heeswijk – we will do something.
something will happen – there is a "we" now.
we will meet regularly
we have initiated something

i am sitting at the corner desk
in my temporary home in amsterdam.
i extract myself from the first wormhole
and back to siko's first interruption.
i am sitting at my desk
in my temporary home in amsterdam.
i am trans-creating from my notebook.
i am interrupted by siko regarding the street battles currently happening in beirut.

later that day, i think about my relationship to "home" – i realise of course that it would change, but i see and feel it now. i see it in my work. i feel the privilege i have, to choose to know what is going on in a place that used to be the shape of my mundane daily life.

what a privilege it is to take the time to think and write about the translation, or rather arabisation, of the word "queer" and its (the translation process') effect on our (arabic-speaking queer communities) understanding of global political movements and alliances. what a privilege it is to take the time to consider and write about the possible new meanings of takweer from the perspective of the arabic language speaker.

this particular privilege of taking the time to consider and think and write is extremely temporal. it doesn't have a clear tempo though.
i have to force myself to write, due to many factors, some of which i highlight in the list of things that i am not writing about in the beginning of this document.

i am in tempelhofer feld (tempelhof airfield/airport) in berlin. the light rain does not stop my friend's birthday barbecue. i am introduced to mohammed abdallah. a ~~researcher and curator~~ cultural worker now based in berlin. i remember i had met him on a couple of occasions in beirut. i talk to him about our programme at school. i narrate the details of the acrobatics we (most members of our class; students and educators) had to go through in order to extract, to almost squeeze out of them, a decent statement in solidarity with Palestine.

> We want to speak out against violence and oppression, and condemn all actions that violate human rights. We stand in solidarity with our Palestinian students and the people of Palestine in their fight for freedom, self-determination, equality, and justice against forced dispossession, settler-colonialism and apartheid.

the first paragraph of this statement was composed by the class. the second and third were an addition made by the institute*

> As an educational institute, we are ethically bound to taking care of our students' well-being and their rights. We take responsibility for our part in creating a humane and liveable world by striving for a conscious relationship with each other.

*the class saw the need to write the statement ourselves as we had been presented with a statement that was no less than shameful – considering the circumstances and the nature of our programme.

that statement was not shared beyond one member of the executive board reading it out shyly to the class in a closed meeting. regardless, my focus now is on the third paragraph. one that was conceived of and composed entirely by the board.

> We acknowledge that as an institution we have to play our role in educating ourselves about the human rights issues in Palestine and elsewhere; and how broader political concerns play a role in art education. Over the next weeks, we will be using the avenue of art and art education to create an open space for learning and dialogue, mobilising voices within the academy on this matter, in order to truly embody being a place for decolonial discourse and practice. We feel responsible for an open culture within our institute, in which all students, instructors and staff can feel safe, heard, and supported.

they (the institute) made claims and gave themselves a deadline to accomplish goals. we (the class) were flabbergasted for a second, and then began the expected wait for nothing. not an inactive waiting, rather a time during which one mobilises voices and energy for the upcoming battle – the question.

the question is one posed to the board at the start of our second year: has the institute initiated/put into motion any of the actions it* claimed it* shall do (within the time period it* has set for itself)

* i was very clear in my email invitation to jurgen bey to participate in a conversation at mediamatic in public (within a glass box):

...

jurgen, i extend this invitation to you primarily as an expression of gratitude to your follow-up and willingness to engage during the last attacks by the zionist regime on the palestinian people and nation, which coincided with last semester's assessments.

the circumstances back then urged us (as a class) to take several steps to extract a solidarity statement from the institute. and here, i must clarify that i am also extending this invitation to you as an active member of the executive board of the rietveld and sandberg.

...

in short, i would require your engaged conversation and note-taking/drawing/expression on paper for any time between an hour or two, as part of the disarming design exhibition to be communicated soon.

topic: last year's solidarity statement, and this year's solidarity in practice

but that's a story for a bit later.

we almost forgot about mohammed abdallah.
the kind gentleman who took the time to listen to my
story under the rain in tempelhof. listened, engaged, but
did not say much. i felt i was going on a rant. echoing
voices from the studio:
"... they want to liberate everything except palestine ..."
"... this school is a lie ..."
"this programme is a fake"
"i'm not sure i want to graduate from here"
"i'm not sure i want to enrol in the second year"
"collective drop out?"
"i do not want to partake in a lie"
"i do not want to be an ethnic token"
"i am not wasting my time"
"i need to do this"
"i am not doing what i want"
"no one should have to justify why they deserve to exist"

i am in tempelhofer feld (tempelhof airfield/airport) in berlin. the light rain gets heavier, we interrupt our conversation to help pack up and head out of the park before it closes – we are already wet. mohammed turns to pack, then turns back and says (i paraphrase):

let's talk more about this, but i just want you to know one thing:

you see all those people around you?

i look around, some are old friends, some are new acquaintances, some i didn't even meet. together, they look like a group of happy friends packing up and enjoying the irony of a barbecue in the rain.

all these people are going through what you are going through. none of them came here to talk about or try to practise "decoloniality". all of them had other interests.

i look around, some are old friends, some are new acquaintances, some i didn't even meet. together, they look like a group of happy friends packing up and enjoying the irony of a barbecue in the rain. all of them (at least those who were still there towards the heaviest rain, and circumstantial end of the party) were from the global south.

i am on hermannstrasse, walking to my temporary home on karl-marx-strasse. the feeling of wet socks squishing under my freezing feet is just as present and bothersome as the idea that this is what i have come to sandberg to do.

this: to attempt to theorise within international* academic standards. or to "art" within the global** market.
*anglo-saxon
**western european

this: to attempt to convince a dutch institute of why bds is a legal obligation according to international law

this: to attempt to understand how it is possible for an educational institution of european standard to be so full of shit.

is this what i came to do?
while i was practising de-privatisation in beirut?
while i was witnessing one of beirut's phoenix* moments? and the possible dissolution of my country?
isn't that worth witnessing? experiencing? living through?

am i already fetishising? so quickly? despite the fact that i visit my homeland several times a year?

i am not.

i want to be in beirut because of how i practised my daily life, because i was happier there than i am here. not because i want to experience one of the downfalls of my country.

the downfall of capitalism, perhaps. but not the daily slow disintegration of society in an imaginary absurd world waiting to be reborn.

*the idea of creative destruction is not foreign to lebanon, it is how a lot of beirut's "old" centre was rebuilt. why wouldn't they willingly blow up the port and half the city? {warning: paranoia takeover – conspiracy theory alert}{will keep this conversation for another moment perhaps, and take this as an opportunity to realign}

fragments
transcription
sitting on my corner desk in my temporary home in amsterdam.

i’m interrupted by samira, “we are more fun” “we are always glitching” “my brain is working” “you think you are in the same sphere as another elevator step” “no glitch is like, no i swear”
“ok ... i forgot, you were saying something about the glitch,
are we now on the same , like w et alka about tglitches,
we done with the glitches
we done done”

“look look, what”

fragments
in conversation with abdallah
are you ready for the next glitch?

the breaking of the theatrical realm
the moment the white sheep and black figure appear.
the comedic moment of breaking with “reality”
the collapse of both realms, the fictive in
the theatrical puppet show
and the constructed reality/imagination

i am constructing a memory
i am in the car
i am being driven to a puppet show with my friend, my best friend
i am constructing a memory
it is very clear

i am in the car, i look past her face in the back seat
i see the tunnel entrance
the lights in the tunnel flicker rapidly
i move my attention to the tunnel walls

i have always been fascinated by them
i am constructing a memory

i am constructing a memory
memory
the puppeteer runs in the wrong direction or something happens
the point is
the realm of fantasy created on stage is broken
broken comedic-ally
smashing reality into the constructed set
almost literally

the stage is dark
the sheep are scared
the wolf draws near
the harsh light blares as the wolf pounces
the actor runs in the wrong direction
i am constructing a memory
the actor, the puppeteer acting through the almost life-sized puppet
the stage is dark
the sheep are scared
the wolf draws near
the harsh light blares* as the wolf pounces

*the harsh light: the spotlight? not so much, just a harsh light, like a flash, like the flash from an older camera, not so much like the controlled clear slow flash from your phone, the sharp bang flash that cuts.

the sharp bang flash that creates a temporary rift
a space for the realities to collapse on to each other, in my understanding of that moment

i am constructing a memory
i am escaping reality

i am constructing a memory of a sheep that runs in the wrong direction

the flash bang effect of reality hitting you
the moment where you realise that you always knew there was someone controlling the sheep, but you chose to believe otherwise. we allow for imagination.

i am sitting at my corner desk in amsterdam,
i am trying to recount my conversation with abdallah.

the identity of the queer arab as constant unresolved fragments
the identity of the arab as constant unresolved fragments
the identity as constant unresolved fragments

this does not make sense
edit: the identity as constantly
requestioned fragments, repositioned
as per circumstance

circumstantially,
somehow, someone, perhaps i
uploaded a .doc format of my essay onto
the google drive folder shared by ra'na.

i had indeed uploaded a pdf document (titled dec10_edit1.0.pdf). but in addition to that, there appeared a google drive document with that very text (titled dec10_edit1.0)

with one key difference
the words were laid out in an incorrect order, almost backward, or as if someone wrote english with an arabic writing direction. what an interesting glitch!

here i wish to take the chance to introduce the concept of the celebration of a “mistake” or a “glitch”

يعني الإحتفال بالخرية
مش بس بتتقبل الظروف، بتتفاعل معها، مثل الممثل بحلبة الإرتجال.

:myself with conversation a is following The

?about writing I am What
:about writing not am I what listing first by this answer to easier it find I
.use we references the of relevance the about writing not am I
English in write to want not do i why about writing not am I
language queer about writing not am I
translation about writing not am I
laptop a on typing of format this why writing not am I
.itself process writing the to hindrance a is
feel I disconnection the about writing not am I
like look and sound they what in words own my towards
.important is this why about writing not am I And

:na’ra with conversation imaginary an is following The

.narrating am I
.dialogue in constantly, collective often, moments key narrating am I
~~been have I~~ ~~exist yet not does that essay an on essay an writing am I~~
on walls the on, fafu in space collective our in, notebooks my in writing
.amsterdam in, mediamatic at box glass a in, ground the
,now - and on reflecting, applying, practicing am I
.process work my about writing
~~do not do I writing am I as writing my editing and back going am I~~
~~.though misinterpreted a or; lie a was that hand by write I when this~~
.myself misreading myself find I sometimes

.see I what you showing am I
intertwined inherently as processes creative the see I
,play we role or, do we function every within that see I
.it in* art to ways find we
“art to “verb the*
“titfannan: “Lebanese from

also circumstantially, i will not go back to writing in a word document, and will probably not correct my linguistic mistakes here in indesign
(i ended up doing so in another word document. one i had to share with my classmates for the sake of publishing)

karmel brought this "mistake" to light.
and this "mistake" brought forth the question:
what does a text say to the reader when it is irrationally ordered according to some logic, a glitch, but nonetheless a traceable, understandable glitch, a glitch that brings forth to the "author" of the text a different understanding of how they use the order of words in conveying meaning.
circumstantially,
i take this space not to edit my text,
but to expand based on conversations and feedback.
this text says nothing.

the installation at mediamatic says nothing.

they merely portray circumstance. through my perspective. a rendering of my being for the last year and a half, executed by the tools at my disposal and within my reach (mentally and materially) and within the limits of my time and skills.

circumstantially, i am sitting at the corner
desk of my temporary home in amsterdam.
i am listing my references.

this mistake that karmel brought forward, the mis-alignment of the text, and the requestioning of meaning.

this mistake made it very clear that this text does exactly this: it refuses to be a (single) text.

references and contexts:
(ask me for the pdfs)
ayman.z.hassan@gmail.com

القرآن الكريم - سورة التكوير
takweer - taqueer : in the holy quraan
context:
in a debate with moe on the process of knowledge production as a method of cultural / academic hegemony.

جسد وسطور
anna hetzer, *körper und zeilen* (berlin: falschrum, 2021)
context:
in conversation with anna hetzer on the translation of her text, on the translation of the word “queering”
in conversation(s) with abdallah, moe, siko, saja, karmel, ra’na ++ on the same topic and on the arabic تكوير takweer – taqueer. a homonym. origins in arabic. arabic grammar and noun “arabisation” logic. the evolution of language through use. language as an evolving tool – language as a museum piece

on pondering the political implications of understanding تَكوير taqueer with its international* context.
*anglo-saxon

where does this position the queer arab identity?

can we imagine identity politics outside the little boxes of categories and defined meanings?

may we propose identity as the voice(s) you wish to speak near to, or strive to speak with, or climax upon exchanging with.

أحمد فؤاد نجم
ahmad fouad najem
interview link:
www.youtube.com/watch?v=-uHZoTb8BzI&t=2s
01:53:00 - "البتاع، وعبقرية العاميّة المصرية"

context:
in conversation with abdallah and moe
after macron's visit to beirut in 2020
in conversation with siwar, saja, siko, farah, gaber,
sari, abdallah, moe ++ on the relevance and meaning of knowledge
production in (using) local dialects
and reference methods
in conversation with rana on writing
my thesis in "arabic"

Speaking Nearby
A Conversation with Trinh T. Minh-ha.pdf

مسرحيتانن لزياد الرحباني:
بخصوص الكرامي والشعب العنيد
(من ناحية هيكلة المسرحية)
وفيلم أميركي طويل
(حديث رشيد والحكيم: مخه معكوف وبيفرد)
2 plays by ziad al rahbani:
bikhsous elkarameh wil sha3b il 3aneed
and film ameriki taweel

Ahmed, S, Orientation Matters.pdf
Vijay Prashad
www.youtube.com/watch?v=EmF7kbscD6s&t=3s

Microtonality and the struggle for fretlessness in the digital age
ctm_2019_mag_allami.pdf

Mohamed Gaber

The Evolution of Arabic Letterforms

From the Humanist Origin to the Digital Era

ABSTRACT

This essay investigates the evolution of Arabic letterforms throughout history under the influence of changing technologies. It highlights the key moments in the history of Arabic script, from the artistic essence of medieval calligraphy all the way to the digital age.

Informed by archival research and manuscripts, this essay analyses the principal factors that influenced the evolution of Arabic letterforms. It highlights the sophistication of calligraphy and the sociopolitical role that Arabic calligraphy played at a certain point in history. It also looks into the technical constraints of machinery originally conceived for Latin script, and its impact on the development of Arabic letterforms in modern times.

The essay celebrates a new era for Arabic type-making. The text is backed by rigorous discipline-specific research in order to develop a better sense of responsibility towards quality standards and better representation of the art, history, and culture of the Arabic script.

INTRODUCTION

Understanding how Arabic script evolved into its current letterforms is an important step in securing its future. Arabic script's open interaction with its surrounding environment throughout history is inspiring and useful in grasping a better understanding of its value and role beyond a script's main role to inform.

For the last three years, I've been part of an international team of type-designers, engineers, and researchers working on composing the new typeface for the Google brand. The project is unprecedented not only in terms of technological innovation, but also in that it works with sixteen scripts, fifteen of them formerly grouped as "non-Latin", with the design and research tasks for these assigned to native speakers. During the project, I experienced first-hand the lack of a common disciplinary knowledge that would support the development of a contemporary typeface and answer the needs of digital media while maintaining authenticity.

Inspired by this lack of disciplinary knowledge, I initiated a study of the letterforms of modern Arabic typefaces. While the study at first focused on the development of Arabic letterforms across the past five decades, the research led me to more influential events over the past fifteen centuries, where Arabic calligraphy and typography played a sociopolitical role in its environment, and was received by readers as having capacity beyond being only a tool for informing.

In this essay, I will not attempt to study each influential event in detail, since this cannot be covered in one brief text. However, I will illustrate a historical map of events that played a role in the evolution of changes in the Arabic letterforms that can inform practising type-makers through the process of designing the future of the Arabic letterforms.

THE HUMANIST ORIGIN

Over the past fourteen centuries, Arabic letterforms have undergone many developments catalysed by various functional, aesthetic, and geopolitical circumstances. Having developed profound social, religious, and political bearing over time – straddling calculated sophistication and mystic spirituality – Arabic calligraphy is much more than an art form; it's a culture. According to the Swiss scholar Titus Burckhardt, "The noblest, most extensive art in the world of Islam is calligraphy, and the Quran is called the holy art. The calligraphy in Islam plays the same role as iconography in Christian art because it represents the Divine Word."[1]

During the early days of Islam, Arabic script contained neither dots nor diacritics.[2] A word with neither of these orthographic features had multiple meanings, leaving readers to rely on intuition, memory, and context to understand which of these meanings is more adequate. During the fourth caliphate (656–661 AD), with Arabic becoming the lingua franca of many native non-Arab converts, the misreading of words became a nuisance. Deemed hideous, primarily when reciting the divine word, the problem had to be urgently remedied. New rules had to be put in place to articulate words correctly, rid them of ambiguity, and improve their comprehensibility among new Muslims. The caliph Ali ibn Abi Talib assigned the task to his companion Abu al-Aswad al-Du'ali, a poet and linguist who devised the first dotting system. Al-Du'ali's system looked nothing like modern Arabic script, however it was the first building block towards the *Harakat*[3] system (short vowel marks) which is still in use today.

1 Titus Burckhardt, *Art of Islam: Language and Meaning* (Indiana: World Wisdom, 2009).

2 Early Arabic writing included no dots. The dots found today in Arabic writing were one of the first innovations that came after the spread of Arabic (after Islam). These dots make it clear which consonant is to be pronounced.

3 The Arabic script has numerous diacritics, including i'jam (إِعْجَام, 'Iʿjām), consonant pointing, tashkil (تَشْكِيل, tashkīl), and supplementary diacritics. The latter include the ḥarakāt (حَرَكَات) vowel marks–singular: ḥarakah (حَرَكَة).

After dotting and diacritics	Prior to dotting and diacritics
بَيت، بِنْت، نَبْتٌ، ثَبَتَ، يَبِثُّ، يَثِبُ	ٮٮ
ثَابَ، ثَابَ، بَاتَ، بَابٌ، نَابَ، نَابٌ	ٮاٮ
يَجِرُّ، يَحِرُّ، بَحْرٌ، يَخِرُّ، نَحْرٌ، نَخَرَ	ٮحر

Table 1: Showcasing how one word in Arabic without dots or diacritics can have endless meanings depending on the context.

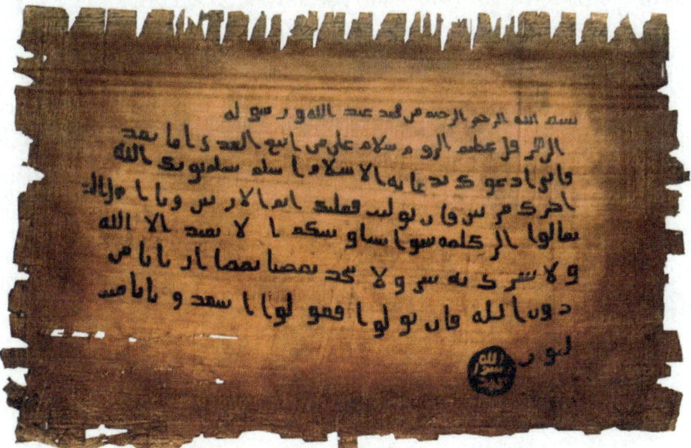

Figure 1: A photograph of an original copy of Prophet Muhammad's letter to the Byzantine emperor, Heraclius, who was stationing in Damascus at that time. Featuring the Jazm style of writing Arabic letterforms. This copy is owned by a Yemeni family and dates back to the second or third Hijrī calendar (eighth to ninth century).

CALLIGRAPHY IN THE COURT OF THE CALIPHATE

Major developments, however, were not all that new to Arabic calligraphy. Only a decade before al-Du'ali started his holy mission, Arabic calligraphy witnessed one of its major developments as the first complete version of the Quran was compiled during the caliphate of Uthman Ibn Affan (644–656 AD). This version was written using Jazm[4] script, an early predecessor of Kufic[5] script (named after the city of Kufa) and one of the first universal scripts to dominate Arabic calligraphy for centuries. Jazm itself would see a major systematisation during the "Golden Age" of calligraphy, which spanned a succession of three great calligraphers: Ibn Muqla (886–940 AD), Ibn al-Bawwab (961–1022 AD), and Yakut al-Musta'simi of Amasya (d. 1298 AD).

4 The earliest style of the modern Arabic script, historically known as al-Jazm, was used by the early Muslims during the time of the prophet Muhammad.

5 Kufic script is a style of Arabic script that gained prominence early on as a preferred script for Quran transcription and architectural decoration, and has since become a reference and an archetype for a number of other Arabic scripts.

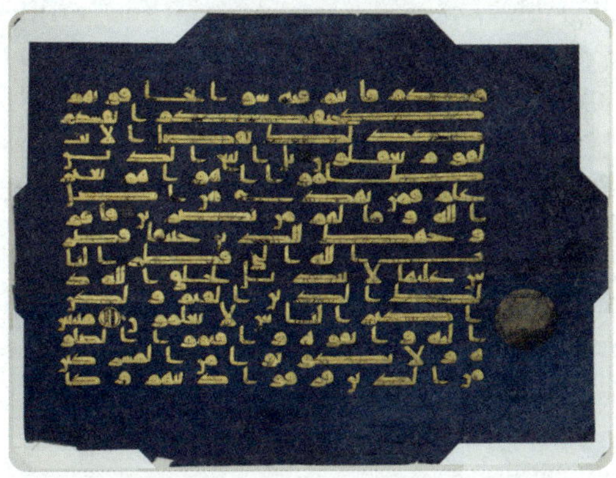

Figure 2: Folio from the "Blue Quran", from the second half of the ninth to the mid-tenth century. Stolen from Tunis in the nineteenth century, it can now be found in The Metropolitan Museum of Art. This folio comes from a sumptuous, multivolume Quran with indigo pages and silver verse markers that was probably copied in North Africa. Its palette is thought to refer to the purple-dyed, gilded manuscripts made in the neighbouring Byzantine empire. The manuscript is written in early Kufic, showing an inconsistent absence of diacritics in most of the text despite the introduction of diacritics in the eighth century.

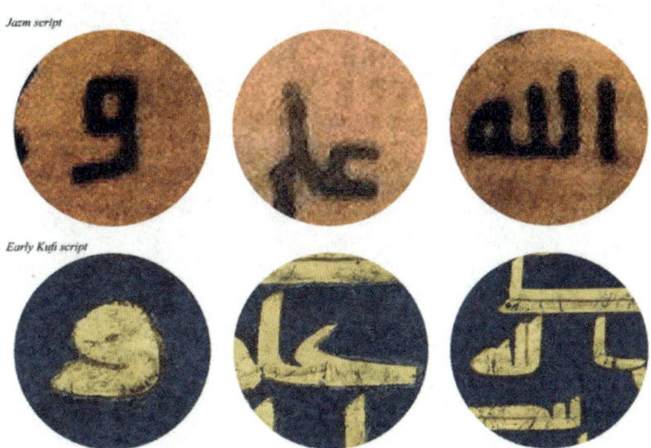

Figure 3: An analogy between the copy of Prophet Muhammad's letter to the Byzantine emperor (eighth to ninth century) (top row) and "Blue Quran" (ninth to tenth century) (bottom row), showing the difference in the development in the letterforms between the pre-islamic Jazm script and early Kufi script.

These calligraphers were also state officials and courtiers of the caliphate, working most of the time with direct orders from the caliph himself. In fact, Ibn Muqla – credited for establishing the rhomboid dot and the length of the *alif* stroke as modular measurement units for all letters in a particular script, which is known as the theory of proportion and is still used to this day – served as a vizier in the court of al-Muqtadir (908–929 AD). Thus, it was not uncommon for Muslim rulers to practise calligraphy and to become accomplished calligraphers themselves. Stories such as that of sultan Bayezid II holding the inkstand for the legendary calligrapher Shaykh Hamdullah populate the history of Arabic calligraphy.

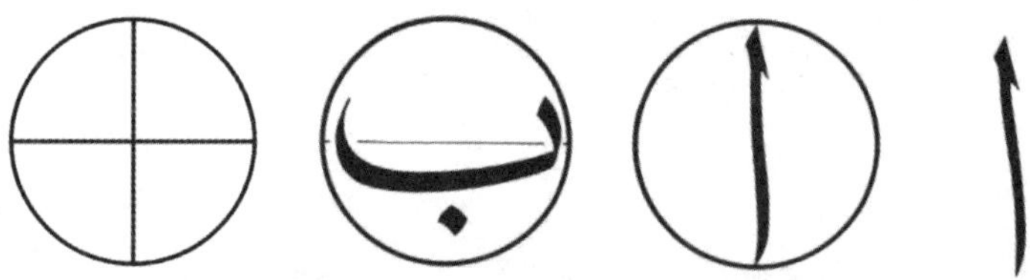

Figure 4: Ibn Muqla's "virtual circle", an intuitively drawn alif determines the height of the vertical diameter, which in turn determines the horizontal dimensions of a final bā'.

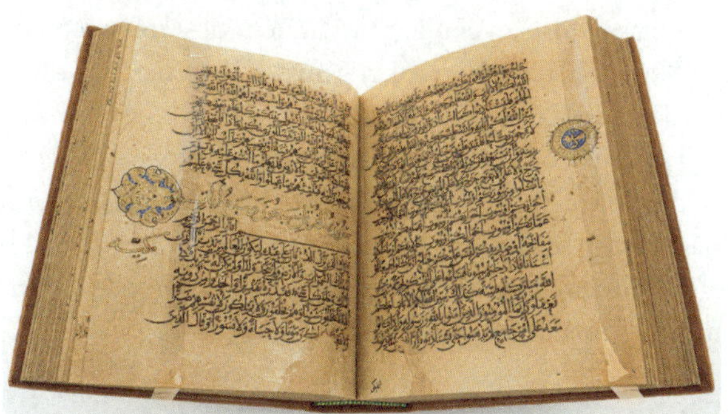

Figure 5: The Ibn al-Bawwab Quran, 1000–1001, gift of the Ottoman Sultan Selim I (1470–1512), The Chester Beatty Library in Dublin, Ireland.

Even during the reign of the mamluk warriors, who were, with a few exceptions, near-analphabets, calligraphy retained a great symbolic power, quite often in reference to mamluk philistinism and barbarity. As such, Arabic calligraphy turned into a site of diplomatic hostility between mamluks and the Marinids of Morocco, when the Moroccan sultan, Abu al-Hasan, gifted the city of Jerusalem, then under mamluk rule, a Quran written in his own hand, insinuating the mamluk lack of calligraphic sensibility. A similar offence was spurred when the mamluk sultan al-Nasir Muhammad had substituted the name of his enemy Öljaytü, the famed Ilkhanid sultan, with his own, on an exquisite version of the Quran dedicated to the latter. The political weight of calligraphy was further intensified under the Safavid and Ottoman empires, whose ideology of *ilm l huruf* (the belief that Arabic letters possess elemental and astrological values that can summon divine intervention when used in specific combinations) was at the basis of their conception of political and military power.

Calligraphy was also an explicit instrument of state sovereignty. In the late 800s, master calligrapher Youssef al-Shajary, at the orders of Al Ma'mun, developed the style known as *al-ijazah* (lit. "the license") to be used in official documents. The style was exclusively practised by the calligraphers of the court, and could not be copied or forged easily. In the late 1300s, it was further developed by the master calligrapher Mir Ali Tabrizi and became the style of Ottoman bureaucracy until the early 1900s.

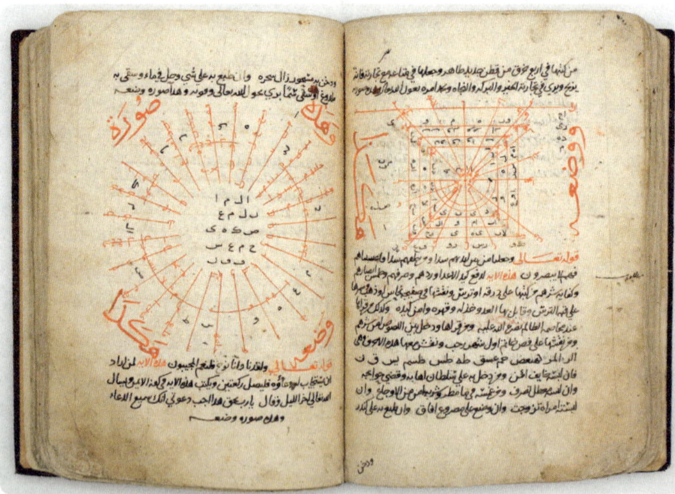

Figure 6: Folio from Abu'l-'Abbas al-Buni (d 622 AH/1225 AD), "ilm al-huruf" on the Magical Uses of the Ninety-nine Names of God and the magical power of the Arabic letters.

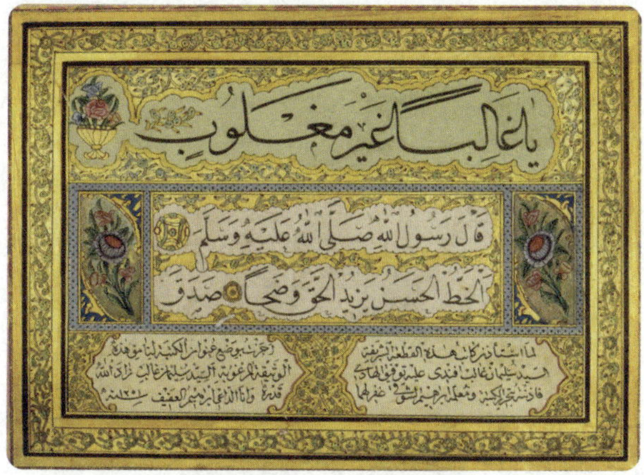

Figure 7: A Calligrapher's Diploma (Ijazah), approved by Ibrahim Afif Ef endi and Ibrahim Shevki Ef endi, Turkey, Dated 1251 AH/1835 AD. Penned in Naskh, Ijaze, and Thuluth scripts.

THE INDUSTRIALISATION OF ARABIC

Early European Attempts

According to Karl Schaefer,[6] block printing was a common practice in the Arab world long before it found its way to Europe. The technique was long used to produce miniature texts consisting of prayers, incantations, and Quranic verses.[7] These were kept in amulets and worn close to the body, or attached to a weapon to ward off the evil eye and confer protection upon its possessor. An

6 Karl R. Schaefer, "Enigmatic Charms; Medieval Arabic Block Printed Amulets in American and European Libraries and Museums," *Handbook of Oriental Studies*, section one, Near and Middle East, vol. 82 (2006): 201–205, ill. pl. 49.

7 Schaefer, "Enigmatic Charms".

eleventh-century scroll manuscript (fig. 4) from Fatimid Egypt shows the maker's knowledge of Arabic letterforms and its humanist calligraphic nature. The print follows the rules of Fatimid Kufic style with its letter variations and ligature compositions, something that would not be available on Gutenberg's movable-type press before the 1800s.

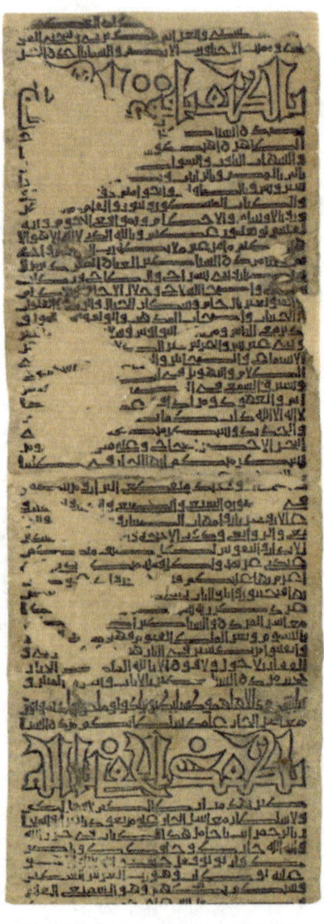

Figure 8: Kufic scroll Fatimid, eleventh century, 24.9 cm X 7.9 cm, The Metropolitan Museum of Art NYC, NY, USA.

When Gutenberg's movable-type press was first introduced in the 1400s, the idea of mechanised printing was not completely foreign to Arabic. However, in 1483 AD, Bayezid II issued a ban punishable by death on using Gutenberg's machine to print Arabic,[8] which was later confirmed by Selim I (1512–1520 AD). The ban was celebrated by booksellers in Istanbul who believed that "manuscript copyists deserved to go to paradise", and that "the printing press was made of the poisonous oleander".[9] While the reason behind the ban was never historically confirmed, it was exclusive to Arabic script. In fact, Istanbul print shops have commonly used Gutenberg's machine since 1493, but for printing in languages other than Arabic.

Early on, simplifying Arabic manuscript forms proved inevitable if Arabic was ever to be printed on Gutenberg's machine, which is perhaps one of the reasons why statesmen as well as printmakers were fearful of using the new technology to print Arabic. Unlike the Latin script, where the one-to-one relationship between letterforms can work, Arabic, by its humanist nature, requires a lot of alternation. Projecting the static one-to-one relationship on to Arabic letters would have harmed their dynamism; a dynamism that would require the calligrapher and manuscript copyist to synchronise their breathing with the movement of the calligraphy nib.

8 Christoph K. Neumann, "Book and newspaper printing in Turkish, 18th-20th century", in: *Middle Eastern Languages and the Print Revolution*, ed. Eva Hanebutt-Benz, Dagmar Glass, Geoffrey Roper (Westhofen: WVA-Verlag Skulima, 2002) 227–248.

9 According to Orlin Sabev (Orhan Salih), "A virgin deserving paradise or a whore deserving poison: manuscript tradition and printed books in Ottoman Turkish society," in *The History of the Book in the Middle East*, ed. Geoffrey Roper (Oxford: Routledge, 2013), 389.

In Arabic, letters have four main forms: an isolated form ف , an initial form ﻓ , a medial form ﻔ, and a terminal form ﻒ . Based on its relative position in a given word, each letter might incur alternations and ligatures like in في , فى , فئ . These alternations hinge on many factors, such as the printer's and punchcutter's knowledge of Arabic, their artisanship, the model on which the type is based, the size to which the type is cut, and, crucially, the physical properties of the metal type itself. Despite posing a major challenge to the then Latin-only machines, European printers continued to experiment with the Arabic type.

The first book to be printed in Arabic using movable type[10] was *kitāb ṣalāt al-sawā'i (The Book of Hours)* in 1514 by Gregorio di Gregorio, commissioned by Pope Julius II for Arabic-speaking Christians.[11] The book featured a very beautiful floral border – initially copied from the Latin version – and a malformed and broken Arabic type. Following Gregorio's steps, Alessandro Paganino, an Italian printer and publisher from Venice, experimented with printing the first Quran in Europe in 1537. A similar experiment was carried out later by Officina Schultzio-Schilleriana in Hamburg in 1694. Both experiments came out quite poorly, featuring awkward spacing, broken compositions, and inconsistent proportions, which was shocking to the Arabic readership at the time, especially when compared to the perfected proportions of the calligraphers and manuscript copyists. The Iraqi-American scholar Muhsin Mahdi

10 Movable type is the system and technology of printing typography that uses movable components to reproduce the elements of a document (usually individual alphanumeric characters or punctuation marks).

11 Miroslav Krek, "The Enigma of the First Arabic Book Printed from Movable Type," *Journal of Near Eastern Studies* 38, no. 3 (July 1979): 203–212.

explains: "*It must have made Muslim readers of the Quran think that only the Devil himself could have produced such an ugly and faulty version of their Holy Book.*"[12]

It must be noted, however, that these prints were not simply faulty manuscripts written by some ignorant scribe. Rather, they were organised, orderly, expensive, and most importantly widely distributed editions, making it a lot more difficult to dismiss them as inconsequential incidents in the history of Arabic calligraphy.[13]

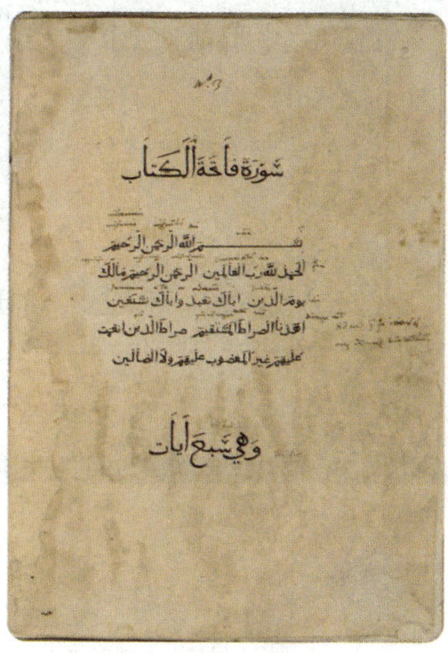
سورة فاتحة الكتاب

بسم الله الرحمن الرحيم
الحمد لله رب العالمين الرحمن الرحيم مالك
يوم الدين اياك نعبد واياك نستعين
اهدنا الصراط المستقيم صراط الذين انعمت
عليهم غير المغضوب عليهم ولا الضالين

وهي سبع ايات

Figure 9: Kitāb ṣalāt al-sawā'i., 1514, featuring a very beautiful floral border – initially copied from the Latin version – and a malformed and broken Arabic type.

12 Muhsin Mahdi, "From the Manuscript Age to the Age of Printed Books," in *The Book in the Islamic World: The Written Word and Communication in the Middle East*, ed. George Nicholas Atiyeh (New York: SUNY Press, 1995).

13 Mahdi, "From the Manuscript Age".

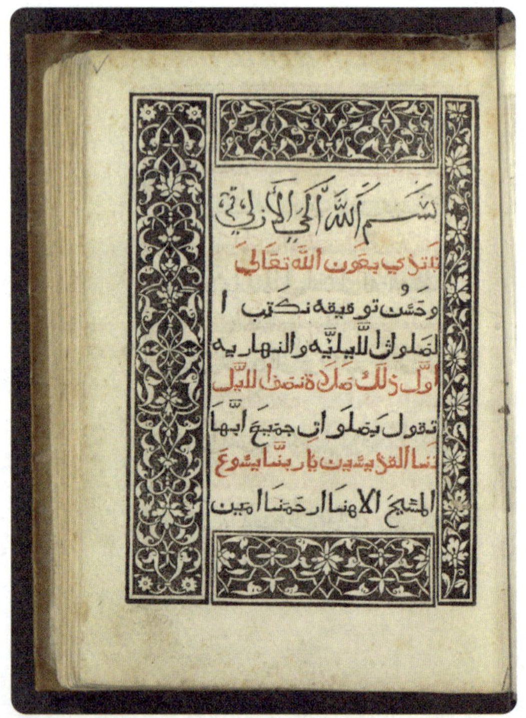

Figure 10: Paganino Quran, between August 9, 1537, and August 9, 1538.

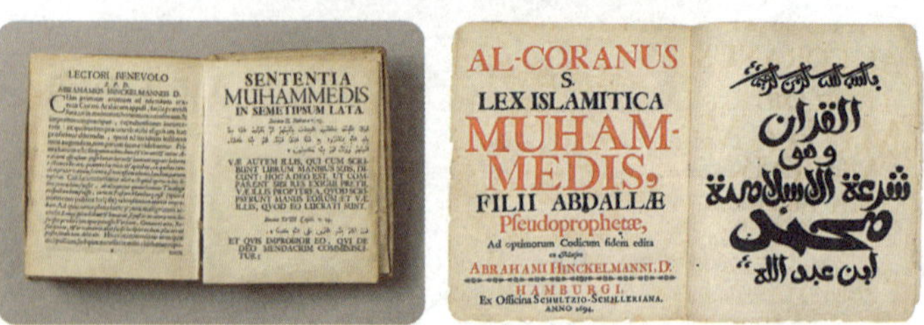

Figure 11 & 12: Abraham Hinckelmann Quraan 1694.

Introduction of Movable Type to the Islamic Empire

It was not until the 1700s that Ahmed III abolished the Sublime Porte's ban on movable type printing in Arabic. Persuaded by Ibrahim Müteferrika,[14] a former Hungarian Ottoman taken prisoner by the Turks and one of the most influential publishers in Istanbul at the time, Ahmed III ratified the *fatwā*[15] to establish the first official Arabic press in Istanbul. Since printing religious texts meant that thousands of manuscript copyists would lose their jobs, the press was exclusively limited to secular books and maps that would have been too difficult or costly to copy. Demand for printed books was largely curtailed by a conservative readership that preferred bespoke manuscript works. Between 1728 and 1745, the press produced only seventeen books on lexicography, geography, and history.

Yet the fundamental evolution of the Arabic press came with Muhamed Ali's rise to power in 1805. Ali started his career as a ruler of Egypt by sending a delegation to Europe to collect books on a wide range of subjects. A few years later, he commissioned Nicolas Massabki to study type-founding and printing in Rome and Milan.[16] He also shipped three presses from Milan, along with the necessary paper and ink from Leghorn and Trieste. When Massabki

14 Müteferrika was also the first to produce copperplate engravings in Istanbul, according to Janet Starkey, "James Rennell and his Scientific World of Observation", in: *Knowledge is Light: Travelers in the Near East*, ed. Katherine Salahi (Oxford: Oxbow Books, 2011), 48.

15 A legal opinion or decree handed down by an Islamic religious leader.

16 Syliva G. Haim and Elie Kedourie, eds., *Modern Egypt: Studies in Politics and Society* (Oxford: Routledge, 1980).

returned from his mission in 1819, he was appointed manager of the Egyptian Government's first press in the district of Bulaq, which lent the new institution its name. Between 1822 and 1842, the Bulaq press was at the forefront of the then-nascent printing industry in the region with 243 titles, paving Egypt's way into the cultural awakening movement, *alnahḍa*.[17]

In the beginning, the press worked with three Arabic typesets made in Italy under the supervision of Massabki. These were used in its first publication, an Arabic-to-Italian dictionary. In his study on the subject, scholar Radwan Abu al-Futuh noted that Arab readers were dismayed by Bulaq press' early publications due to their quirky and oversized letterforms.[18] In response, Mohamed Ali approached the Persian calligrapher known as Sinkelakh al-Hindi and requested that a proper Arabic type be designed for the press.[19] Sinkelakh worked on two Arabic sets, one in the style of *Naskh* and another in *Nastaliq*. The latter was particularly notable for making an exceptionally dynamic calligraphic style work within a rather rigid system.

This achievement was of great significance to the Pasha.[20] He was closely following the progress of the new type throughout, and upon inspecting the first publication he rewarded both the calligrapher and the punchcutter for their great work.[21] This was, however, only

17 Albert Hourani, *Arabic Thought in the Liberal Age 1789–1939* (London, New York, Toronto: Oxford University Press, 1962).

18 Radwan Abu Al-Futuh, *History of Bulak Press*, 1953, 90.

19 Radwan Aby Al-Futuh, *History of Bulak Press*.

20 *Pasha* or *Paşa*, in older works sometimes anglicised as "bashaw", was a higher rank in the Ottoman political and military system.

21 Radwan Abu Al-Futuh *History of Bulak Press*, 90.

one step of many on a long journey to overcoming the rigidity of the letterpress when working with Arabic letterforms. It was not until the 1870s that printing the *Harakat* characters, an essential development for printing copies of the Quran, became possible.

While Sinkelakh's type was very aesthetically successful, it was composed of over 800 pieces (not including *Harakat* characters). With such a huge set, typesetting was an extremely daunting task, with each page consuming a whole day of work. Immense skill and speed was required of the typesetters. In terms of productivity, the new Arabic type made printing a rather slower and financially inefficient process.

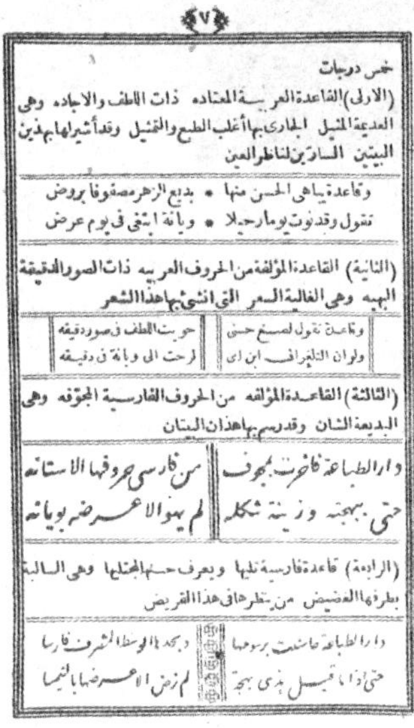

٧

خمس درجات

(الاولى) القاعدة العربية المعتاده ذات اللطف والاجاده وهى البديعة المثيل الجارى بها أغلب الطبع والتمثيل وقد أشير اليها بهذين البيتين السارين لناظر العين

وقاعدة يباهى الحسن منها * بديع الزهر مصفوفا بروض
تقول وقد نوت يوما رحيلا * وبانة ابتغى فى يوم عرض

(الثانية) القاعدة المؤلفة من الحروف العربيه ذات الصور الدقيقة البهيه وهى الغالية السعر التى انشى بها هذا الشعر

(الثالثة) القاعدة المؤلفه من الحروف الفارسية المجوفه وهى البديعة الشان وقد رسم بها هذان البيتان

دار الطباعة فاخرت بمجوف * من فارسى حروفها الاستانه
حتى ببهجته وزينة شكله * لم يهوا الا عرضه وبيانه

(الرابعة) قاعدة فارسية تليها ويعرف حسنها لجتليها وهى السالبة بطرفها الغضيض من نظرها فى هذا القريض

Figure 13: The four Arabic types developed at Bulaq Press, 1873, featuring two of Sinkelakh's Nastaliq types.

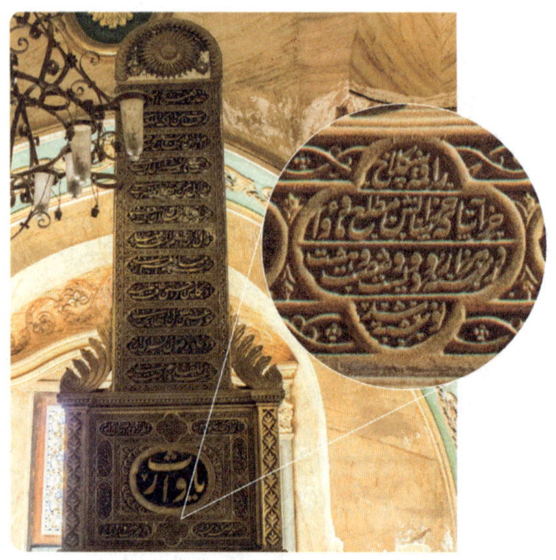

Figure 14: Tomb of Ibrahim Pasha (1805–1848), Cemetery of the Family of Muhammad 'Ali in Cairo. Featuring engravings in Nastaliq script signed by Sinkelakh al-Khurasani.

The Era of Mechanical Composition

By the turn of the century, and as Arab publishers were still struggling with the movable letterpress, the industry in the west was already moving towards mass production with the advent of typesetting machines: the Linotype, the Intertype, and the Monotype system. These new mechanical systems reduced production time and labour significantly.

In February 1898, *al-Hoda*, an Arabic weekly newspaper founded by Naoum Antoun Moukarzel, a Lebanese immigrant in Pennsylvania, was the first to adapt an Arabic type for a Linotype machine. Naoum first imported the Arabic sets of the Bulak press from

Egypt,[22] before his brother, Salloum Moukarzel, would adapt them for the first Arabic Linotype in 1912.[23] While mechanical typesetting was a breakthrough for Arabic mass publishing, it ushered in further technical challenges. While the lack of kerning was a minor aesthetic shortcoming in Latin type, it amounted to a severe design and legibility problem in Arabic. Arabic letterforms frequently protrude into the space above or below adjacent letters, and therefore require kerning for an appropriate typographical representation.

These challenges hinted at the need for a change, not only in how the industry worked, but also in the ways that Arabs conceived of their own letterforms. Throughout the 1900s, many initiatives – heavily supported by western companies and fundraisers – would set their aim at developing simplified Arabic letterforms, from the discussions on script reform at the Academy of the Arabic Language in Cairo in 1936,[24] to the work of Nasri Khattar (1911–1998) on simplifying letterforms,[25] and Ahmed Lakhdar Ghazal and the ASV Codar type.[26] These initiatives were largely driven by western aesthetic ideals. Under the guise of modernisation, they shared a common tendency to walk away from the humanist

22 Naoum Mokarzel and Salloum A Mokarzel, *Al-Hoda 1898-1968: The Story of Lebanon and Its Emigrants Taken From the Newspaper Al-Hoda*, (New York: Al-Hoda Press, 1968), 1.

23 Mokarzel, *Al-Hoda*.

24 Hans Jürg Hunziker, “Aspects of Arabic Script Reform”, *Typographische Monatsblätter* 4 (1985): 15–16.

25 Yara Khoury Nammour, “Fighting Illiteracy With Typography,” *Works That Work*, no. 6, worksthatwork.com/6/unified-arabic.

26 “ASV Codar, Arabe Standard Voyellé, Codage Arabe” (Institut d’Etudes et de Recherches pour l’Arabisation, Rabat, n.d.), Box Simplified Arabic, DTGC.

tradition of Arabic script. The results were often inclined towards fitting Arabic to the mandates of a machine, initially designed for Latin script, at the expense of legibility. Type designer Walter Tracy explains: In practice, the Khattar characters produce a result comparable in impact to what we would experience if we were asked to accept a single Roman alphabet made up partly of capitals, partly of lowercase and partly of letters which were neither one nor the other."[27]

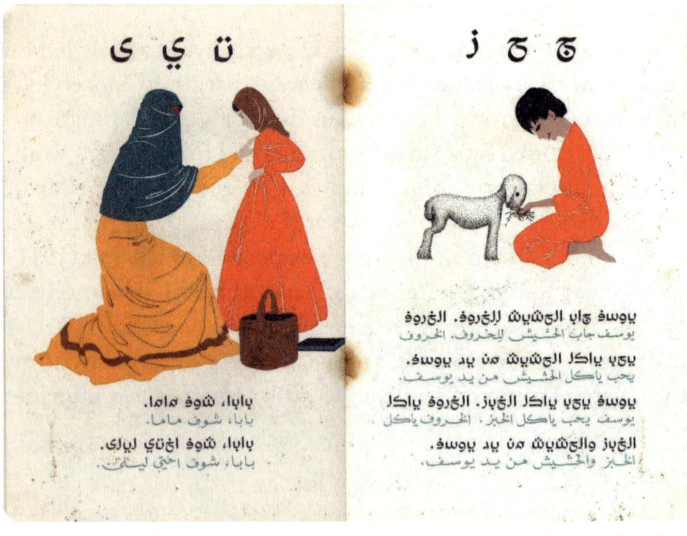

Figure 15: Unified Arabic (UA) by Nasri Khattar. Sample pages from the children's book Shouf Baba Shouf *published in 1955. The UA forms are placed next to the traditional ones for direct comparison and learning.*

27 137 Walter Tracy to Raleigh Christie, Letter, 18 June 1957, Box P3640, NMAH.

THE DIGITAL ARABIC TYPE

Arabic type entered the digital era inheriting former delays from the machine age. Technological advances for Arabic script commonly found their way into practice years after they had been soundly established for Latin script, sometimes even towards the end of their life cycle. This became more evident in the late 1980s as personal computers became accessible on a commercial scale. Operating systems like Mac (system 4.1) and Microsoft Windows CE became a dual interface for Arabic and Latin scripts, rendering obvious the difference in development between the two.

Arial	خط آريال عربي
Times New Roman	خط تايمز نيو رومان
Traditional Arabic	خط تراديشونال عربي
Tahoma	خط تاهوما عربي

Figure 16: Sample setting of Microsoft fonts Arial, Times New Roman, Simplified Arabic, Traditional Arabic, and Tahoma (top to bottom). A slight improvement can be seen in Traditional Arabic that happened over time in comparison to Arial and Times New Roman, yet Tahoma arrived following that with misshapen letterforms, such as the Yeh-Fina in the image taking the shape of a final tooth yaa'ligature.

Back in the machine age, not only did Latin-centric machinery have an influence on Arabic letterforms, but also the design and manufacturing of these machines often reflected the western origin of typesetting technology. Companies at the forefront of technological innovation back then lacked cultural and language-specific competence when it came to Arabic. Therefore, they had to make do with whatever they had, very often at the expense of Arabic calligraphy's original aesthetics.

Arabic script has been treated so far in typesetting as the sequential putting together of single graphic forms instead of an unbroken stream of joined characters as they are produced by a calligrapher's reed. The technical constraints of typesetting have forced so many Arabic readers to accept poor typefaces and unaccented texts and resulted in a noticeable degeneration of the former elegance of Arabic script.[28]

This deficit in the proper development of Arabic type not only stifled the aesthetic development of the original humanist calligraphic writing system as it entered the digital age, but also choked the very possibility of a contemporary discourse on Arabic calligraphy, leaving unanswered many questions on the present and future of Arabic type. This may explain why the history of Arabic type and typography remains an understudied subject. Reliable published resources are rare, and primary research about Arabic typography is desperately lacking. Students and practitioners often rely on a few publications whose accessibility and academic rigour are always a matter of question. This is particularly the case with literature aimed at a general design audience, where scrutiny and depth are often sacrificed for exceedingly simplified narratives.

28 Gerhard Lieser, "Production of High-Quality Arabic Texts on a CRT Filmsetting Machine," *Advances in computer-aided literary and linguistic research: proceedings of the Fifth International Symposium on Computers in Literary and Linguistic Research held at the University of Aston in Birmingham, UK from 3–7 April 1978*, Department of Modern Languages, University of Aston in Birmingham,1979:1, 4.

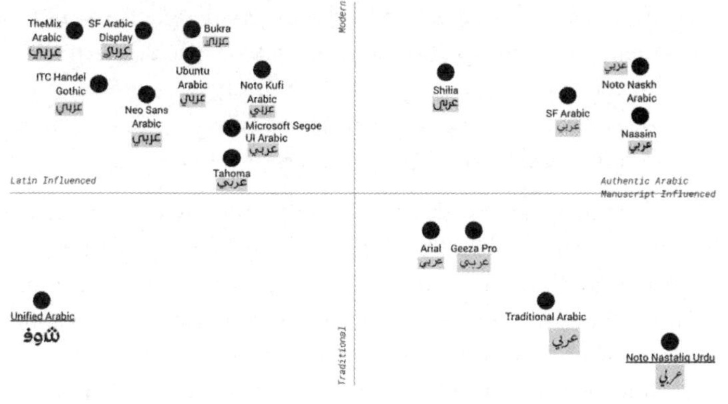

Figure 17: Diagram visualising the Latin influence in a group of famous modern typefaces.

THE STATUS QUO

We can evaluate the maturity of a field of knowledge by considering four questions: first, are the boundaries of its focus, and – consequently – its positioning and relationships with other fields, clear and well understood? Second, is there a body of knowledge that is accepted as foundational for all activity by the community active in the field? Third, are there established routes for learning and participating in the field? And fourth, are there established paths for research, reflection, knowledge generation, and correction in the field?[29]

29 Gerry Leonidas, "Foreword," in *Theory of Type Design*, Gerard Unger (Rotterdam: nai010, 2018) 7.

Despite the continuous effort by Arab type-designers to fill the aforementioned knowledge gap, the lack of discipline-specific study remains as a major obstacle. Such study will not only serve as a space to learn the craft, but will also facilitate access to archives and literature and improve practitioners' research skills.

In a recent discussion[30] with Gerry Leonidas, professor of typography at the University of Reading, UK, as part of the ongoing seminar organised by The Type Platform,[31] Leonidas noted that the more we learn about typography, the more we realise that it is a discipline on its own, and probably one of the best entry points to fathom the complexity of cultures. However, we have not yet figured out how to do this.

According to Leonidas, when looking at typography as a discipline, design comes at the top of a pyramid that combines the history of technology, sites of labour, histories of resources, finance, trade, and the politics of everything. This demands us to slow down, think, reflect, read, question everything, and then contribute a little perspective into a rapidly evolving narrative.

30 TypePlatform X Gerry Leonidas, "The Role of Individuals and Institutions in Sustainable Knowledge Production", January 3, 2022, recorded discussion, 01:42:20, youtu.be/XYDtiHH8eco.

31 The Type Platform is a research space for type designers and underrepresented scripts from the Global South, with a focus on Arabic script. Thought as a laboratory of embedded knowledge, it aims to open a dialogue around type-design discourse and to question the status quo of knowledge production through a series of open live discussions with type designers and scholars from the SWANA region and the Global South. See:typeplatform.design

CALLING FOR A NEW ERA

> *It is time for a new era in Arabic Type Design. An era in which the script is the source of typographic information. What we ask for may sound obvious and it is. Understanding the script then moving to type is nowhere near innovative. In Arabic however – contrary to popular belief, this bridge has not yet been made.*[32]

Throughout the past five decades, the accelerated regression of aesthetics and the heavy westernisation of Arabic letterforms has been indisputable. More than ever, the need for research in type and script history is essential for developing a sense of responsibility towards quality standards and better representation of the art, history, and culture of the Arabic script.

Particular geographies – namely the west coast of the United States – dominate over a commanding share of global technology and capital. This often translates into a global bias towards some of the most simplistic writing forms, straitjacketing all other complex scripts to work from within a particular framework. However, the technical knowledge necessary for overcoming this limitation is becoming more accessible than ever. More native designers can participate in the making of types that are more adequate for Arabic script. Yet, technical accessibility has not been met by an equivalent body of knowledge.

32 Lara Captan, Kristyan Sarkis, "Arabic script to Type: A Manifesto (v.1)", tptq arabic, June 17, 2017, tptq-arabic.com/articles/arabic_script_to_type_a_manifesto_v1.

We have a desperate need to lay foundations for the design of typefaces, ones that embody the essence of the script. We need to observe, deconstruct and relay the mechanisms that dictate script behavior. We need theories of proportional systems, contrast behavior, what is constant and what is style-specific in script grammar, where optical compensations take place, how to handle proportions and contrast in general, as well as when moving from hairline to bold, to black ... We must experiment with postures, document the effect of extension, condensation, and weight change on the letters in diverse settings. The list is endless, the experiments are endless, so why are we not exploring them?[33]

What are the features of a contemporary Arabic letterform? How much can we push the matchmaking process between Arabic and Latin scripts? How far can we simplify Arabic letterforms before they lose their characteristics? These questions, and many others, are rising as Arabic type continues to evolve on digital media. Many of them remain unanswered in the present body of knowledge, highlighting the need for further research and study of Arabic letterforms.

33 Captan and Sarkis, "Arabic script to Type".

Qusai Al Saify

Orbits / Madarat
مدارات

This text consists of:

- Introduction – Praising the Margin –
- Orbits
- Scenes

The Introduction – Praising the Margin – is a key to open this text. The Introduction is a moment to place your seat, ground it on a cloud.

After opening the text you find yourself floating between six orbits: each one resembles a journey on an island.

From the movement back and forth between those islands, eight scenes were born.

Those scenes were written in order to be illustrated, so the illustrations that are scattered all over this text can be considered as the scenes' imagination.

Orbits:

- Al Nakba / Diaspora Orbit
- Sun Ra and Afrofuturism Orbit
- Pal-futurism Orbit
- Joy and Pain Orbit
- Transformation Orbit
- Mythology Orbit

INTRODUCTION
– PRAISING THE MARGIN –

To the other Palestinian.
The Palestinian who lives in the margin of the Palestinians.
And each of us is marginal, relative to the others.
And there are many others.

To the Palestinians I failed to recognise at our
first meeting
and second meeting
and third meeting
and I'm failing to recognise until now.

To the Palestinian who goes through life as an outsider.
To the Palestinian who lives in the edge and on it.
And the edge is a sharp knife that is survivable by dancing.

We heal together.

AL NAKBA / DIASPORA ORBIT

We are one and we are many.

I keep asking myself, what makes a Palestinian Palestinian? As everyone is scattered throughout the world?

What are those connections that make us Palestinians?

How do Palestinian people connect?

How can we live and use the Palestinian diaspora as a way to connect with ourselves, with each other, and with the world, in an endless process of transformation? How do I/we give the diaspora a different meaning, a different feeling? How to experience the diaspora?

We lack the basics; a homeland, a country, a place to get back to when there is no other place to hold us. Like an orphan, we go on in life like something is missing, we keep looking for a home, and wherever we are we feel that here is not the final destination.

Al Nakba is a constant circumstance that we are forced to live by and in until now, wherever we are.

The city of the purple moon
was turning into liquid
Everything was floating
The moon was becoming more
and more purple.

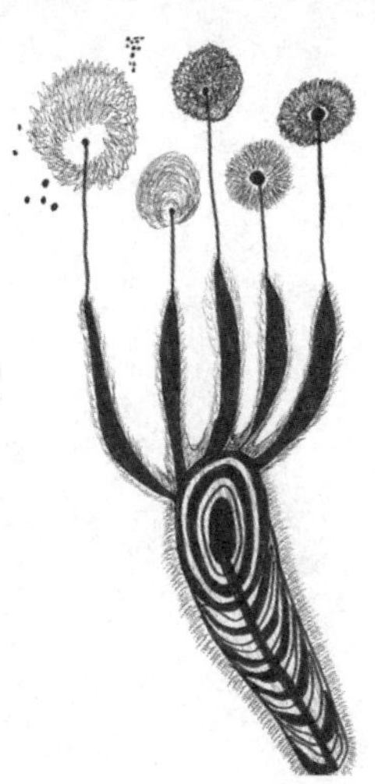

And in this circumstance we have:

- The Palestinians who are forced to live outside the country, the one who is dreaming to come back, the one who is still remembering, the one who is forgotten.
- The Palestinian who is forced to dream to live outside the country, each year hundreds, if not thousands of us, give up the country and look for an imaginary salvation 'outside', I live in this dream/illusion. Once moved elsewhere, we discover that there is no place for us in this world, and we discover that we are not the problem, we understand that we are the problem and the solution.
- We live in an optical illusion that we have options to choose from.
- In this situation, I personally find my salvation outside of planet Earth, in outer space, by looking at Al Nakba as a metaphor for an extraterrestrial diaspora, and asking how this extraterrestrial diaspora can act as a bridge to bring joy for Palestinians who are part of and affected by it.

Our bodies are instruments
Our only choice is to own our bodies
to own the vibrations
our bodies are the instruments
we will become what we want to be by
knowing what kind of music we are
here to play.

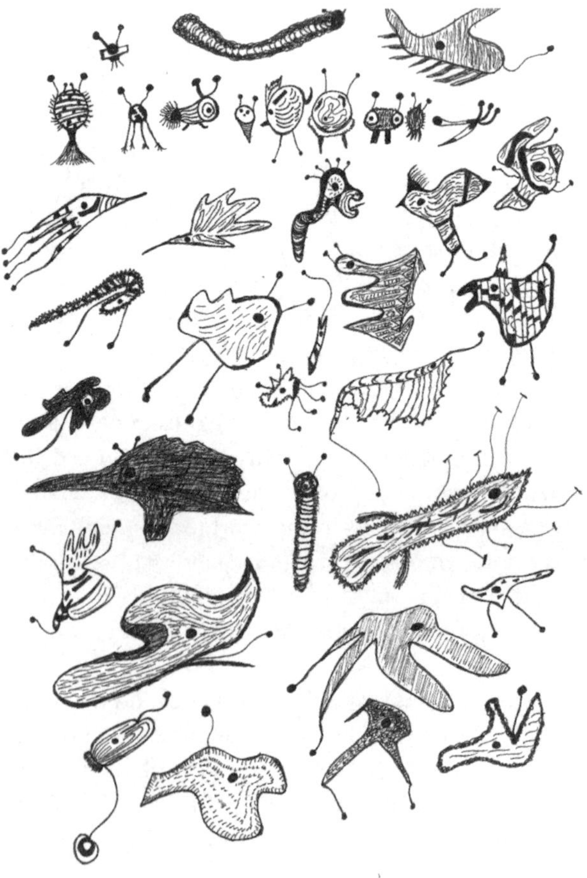

TRANSFORMATION ORBIT

God is Change
All that you touch
You Change.
All that you Change
Changes you.
The only lasting truth
Is Change.
God
Is Change.
$\infty = \Delta$
Octavia Butler

We battle our existence through life to transform it into a better place for us and for the others, and in this fight we are transforming things and being transformed, in this process we are living in a constant state of transformation, until we become transformation itself.

It's like we are a square piece of paper, that can be transformed (folded) into anything you can want or imagine, but no matter what shape, model, state, or forms the paper is transformed into, the paper is in essence still paper. No matter what form we are transforming into, our essence, too, stays the same, and we keep transforming from one shape into another in a constant process.

SUN RA AND AFRO-FUTURISM ORBIT

When I started listening to Sun Ra, I had no idea what world I was entering. It was nice jazz music with a bit of weirdness. I didn't know that this music would transform and shape the way I think, feel, write, and express myself, and it feels that I'm on the surface of what is there.

While listening to the Arkestra or watching one of their concerts, I feel that they are the future, or the past, and how their play has its own time and space, how they live in and create an altered universe and destiny, how they move from space, to planet Earth, and back to black ancient Egypt, all the way to the transatlantic slave trade, and again back to space, to the aliens, and how their music cleanses the air, and transforms the atmosphere, how they create joy, or as Sun Ra calls it "Joyful Noise".

The Arkestra created their own world. They were designing it, playing in that realm, imagining that their world would keep growing, and at some point their world would become larger and larger until it would swallow this world – reality – and then we would all become citizens in their world.

It's like they undid a spell that was cast upon me, they liberated me from the unpleasant conditions I face, and whispered to me: look at what we are doing!

After years and years of listening and digesting I came across the term Afrofuturism, and from there another journey started for me that I'm trying to unpack.

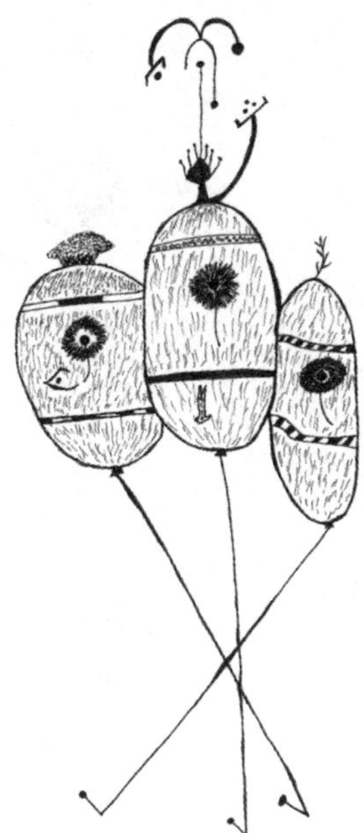

Jabaliyeh el Merameyeh
(This sage is from mountain)

suddenly he found himself holding
a dried branch
and heading to his spot in the mountain
he built the rocks together and started the fire
he put the tea pot on waiting for the water
to boil
he added plenty of sugar
when the water boiled he added
a bit of black tea
he picked two sage stems from a plant near
him and added it to the pot
and let it boil for around a minute
he took the pot off the fire and let it settle for
another minute
he poured the tea in his glass cup
and poured it in a second cup
and in a third
and in a fourth
and in a fifth
and in a sixth
and in a seventh
and whenever he poured into a cup
a member of his friends and family
appeared from nowhere.

Synchronicity: meaningful coincidence

she found herself caught up in a fight
she still doesn't know when and how she was
part of this fight
holding our breaths
holding waiting for the signal
a friction created a familiar smell
sniff sniff, what is this smell?
it's zaatar
yes it's green zaatar plant
it was her first time seeing and
smelling the plant
but for her it was so easy to recognise
the smell of the zaatar teleported her into an
altered timeline
in that space there was nothing but the smell
This was her first time visiting Palestine.

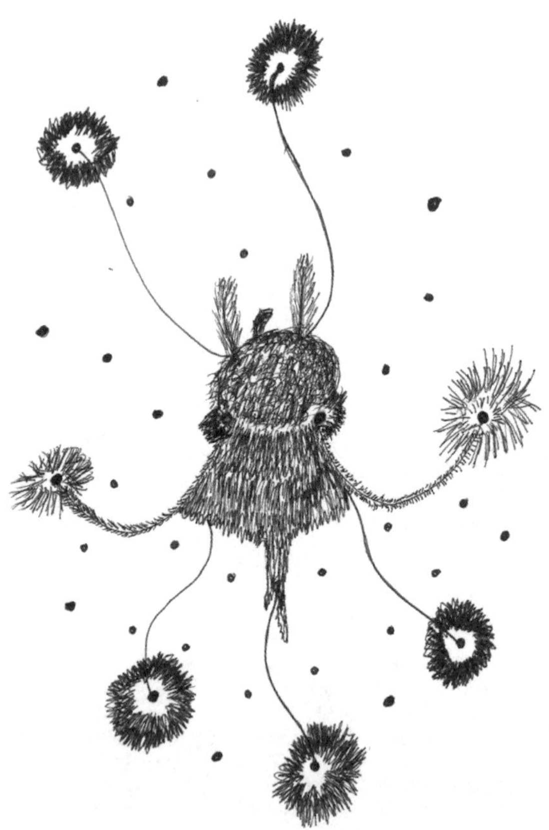

Empty space is not empty
Hussein Al Barghouthi wrote that
he was the emptiness in the flute
not the flute
his form is created by the flute
player / by his breath
The wind is playing him
And he is the wind transforming
into a human.
Why does it feel sad?

MYTHOLOGY ORBIT:

*"If we're nothing, if we're just myths, why not make that literal, why not make it material? Why not create, why not become, glittering black matter?"**

*"When people live under oppression for years and years, people develop alternative ways to exist alongside and outside of these oppression, under oppression life is unpredictable, nothing makes sense but power."***

Survival instinct becomes sharp and in a way becomes part of our state of being. In these situations resistance takes different forms and has variant components; playfulness can save us when things are at stake, humour makes us sane and gives us solutions for unpleasant and traumatising conditions. Imagination and improvisation are a way to master our day-to-day life.

In this state of mind, when nothing makes sense at all, we question reality and what is real, we question if the real can save us or provide a solution for anything. In this process myth becomes something that is far more effective than the real, myth and its potential seem to nurture life with unlimited abilities to tell stories, or our story, maybe that's why we keep looking for the myth as a space and a story.

* Namwali Serpell "Sun Ra: 'I'm Everything and Nothing'", The New York Review, July 23, 2020, www.nybooks.com/articles/2020/07/23/sun-ra-everything-nothing/.

** Ytasha L. Womack, *Afrofuturism: The World of Black Sci-Fi and Fantasy Culture* (Chicago: Lawrence Hill Books, 2013), 13.

JOY AND PAIN ORBIT

From the ashes we will keep rising, we will burn ourselves to open space for our utmost potential, we will cleanse our existence, and then we will rise, we will rise to celebrate our joy and our pain.

Joy is a core component in dealing with our struggle in our day-to-day life, sometimes it feels that we've lost it, but it's there waiting for us to own it.

The more painful our life is, the more joy becomes a revolutionary act in our struggle.

I find joy in creating a different narrative.
A different narrative to experince the Palestinian time,
to follow the traces of joy in what seems natural and random,
the search for a power.

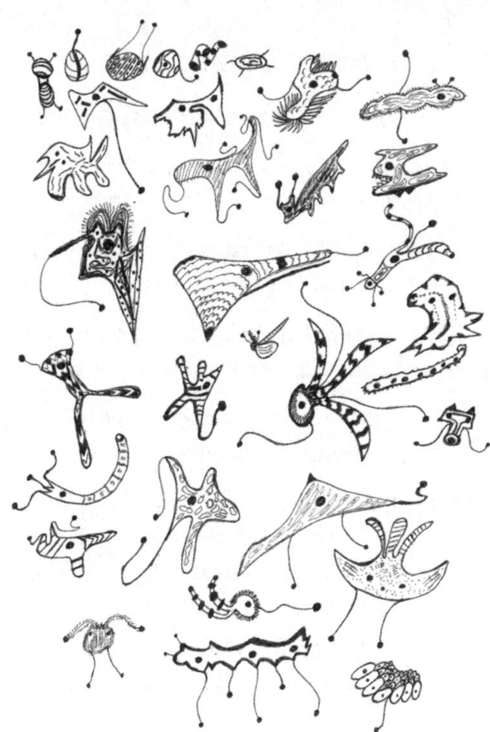

Grape leaf as papyrus

Rolling grape leaves
the family gathered around the table
we were eating them
while turning into mythological beings by the taste and the atmosphere
one leaf stood in the middle of the dining table, looked at all the satisfied faces and stopped the time flow
as she was taking a picture for that moment
to capture the essence of that moment
and saving it into our collective memory
This image is still transferred between all generations.

A garden with no home

From the depths of the Earth
He brought the rain
in spring and summer times
he watered the fields
the God whose home was stolen
still lives in our garden
until he announces to his brothers that he is back to his home.

PAL-FUTURISM ORBIT

"Imagination is the magic carpet"

– Sun Ra.

How to define or explain Pal-futurism*?

It's inspired by Afrofuturism, it's a trial to adopt Afrofuturistic imagination into our own struggle.

It's a wormhole that we use to transform while moving between the imagination and what we call reality.

It's to use our own magic carpet to imagine life outside all the systems of oppression.

Pal-futurism is a memory box. In this box, memories communicate with each other, and they have their own lives and awareness of themselves. They keep growing and becoming more complex until their awareness starts to leak outside of the box, and then the borders between the imaginary and the real are no longer recognisable.

It's to experience how we are becoming more powerful, generation after generation, even though our circumstances are getting worse.

It's a way to have the ownership of our own lives, and to have the confidence to hope and dream.

It's to live and act in the now, and in this space we can create or recreate the past and the future, as our imagination is our limit.

Pal-futurism is a way to connect the oppressed in a joyful context, and to bring things back on track; time, space, nature, people, and joy.

It's to expand the borders of the possibilities for Palestinian life, and to shed light on the Palestinians who live in the margins of the Palestinians, and to place them in their right position.

It's to imagine an altered destiny and a future where the Palestinian is centered, is appreciated, is creative, is creator, is joyful, and is transformative.

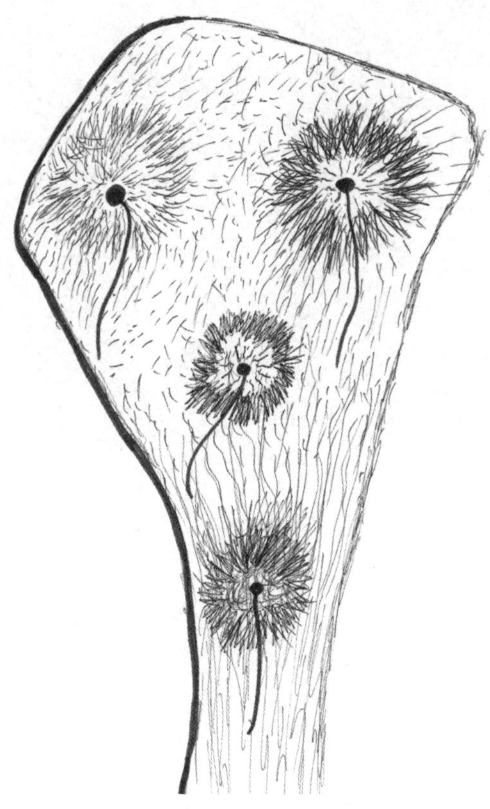

Samira Vogel

GATHERING, ON WEAVING

dear reader,
dear fellow weaver, gatherer, and trace maker,

I invite you to think along with me and different actors through different processes of making and being. What are the threads we pick up and pass on in our process of becoming?

Weaving as a practice, form, and method structures this essay. Fabric is made through the interlocking of two sets of threads at right angles; the warp and the weft.

A loom is needed: an apparatus or a frame that holds the warp under tension as long as the weaving proceeds. Into this structure, the weft threads are introduced by passing them over and under those of the warp.

Once the weaving is complete and removed from the loom, the fabric holds together only by the interlocking of its threads and fibers.

> "*Weaving has long been a metaphor for the creation of something other than cloth, whether a story, a plot, or a world.*"[1]

This essay is a frame; I bring together experiences of material encounters, collective ways of making and tracing processes. Different voices and concepts find each other, woven into each other and patched together. How can processes of making help us attune to rhythms of material, nature, and different forms of relating?

1 Kathryn Sullivan Kruger, *Weaving the Word* (London: Associated University Presses, 2001), 23.

My words and those of others invite you to spin your own threads of thought; from unraveling the coming-into-being of a linen thread interlocking its ways with other filaments to weavings in spaces building a fabric of the social.

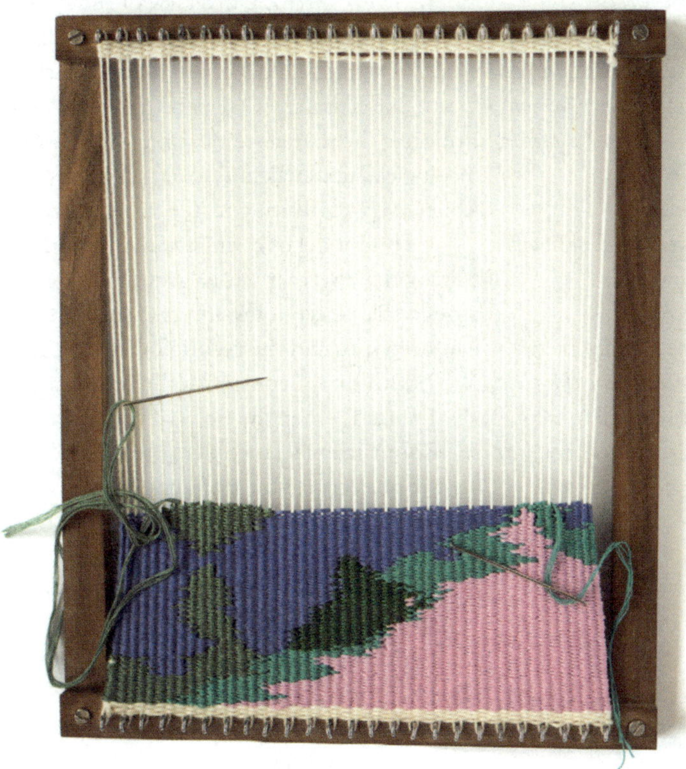

BECOMING LINE BECOMING THREAD

Planting seeds, preservation.
Stored information.
Something to grow
and nurture.
An invitation to care.
To sustain, and create life.
Shape environment.
The seed of a plant,
of a tree.
An idea.
Roots and networks
to grow.
Seeds as
travel companions,
meeting on the fields
one by one in a row.
Planting as resistance.

In May 2021 I joined The Linen Project, a project initiated by the masters program Practice Held in Common at ArtEZ University of the Arts. The project works towards reactivating small-scale flax production in the Netherlands. One part of The Linen Project is the shared stewardship, where the ecological, material, and social processes of collectively cultivating textile are explored. This model of caring for the field and growing flax together with a group of people through shared economy and responsibilities had been initiated the year before. Together with Liza, Leonie, Carolie, and Maria Franca I joined the stewardship. After a Zoom call where we were introduced to the project and the different steps in the process we realized that we had joined late, after the flaxseeds had already been planted. The seeds had been put into the soil, with a 'Zaaimachine', a tool that furrows the soil and distributes the seeds evenly. Row by row, combing the soil and feeding it with seeds, with enough space in between them for the flax plants to grow, at the same time dense enough so not too many weeds would find their way to the sunlight.

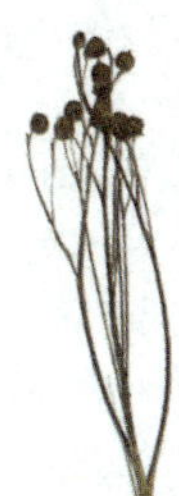

Taking care of the linen field brings us close to soil, rain, and other weather. I would like to think of this project as a way of rooting ourselves, finding a way back to analogue techniques and acts of caring for nature and one another. Committing to the year-long process from planting the seed to spinning and weaving the linen allows us to experience and attune ourselves to the timing of flax. Growing textiles is a slow process and stands in stark contrast to capitalist modes of production. There is a shift in focus from a material outcome to learning and adjusting to the flax field and its environmental and organizational conditions.

The organization of the linen stewardship, caring for the field and visiting the barn where the flax plants are stored, happens mostly through online communication; Zoom meetings, e-mails, and a Signal group chat. We send short notice updates and photos for those who can't be part of a certain step in the process. I remember the days when the plants were blooming, and the pain of not being able to go and see them. There were messages in the group chat about when the flax was probably going to bloom; later a lot of photos of the lovely blueish-purple small flowers. I would have loved to go and see, it just didn't fit in to my schedule.

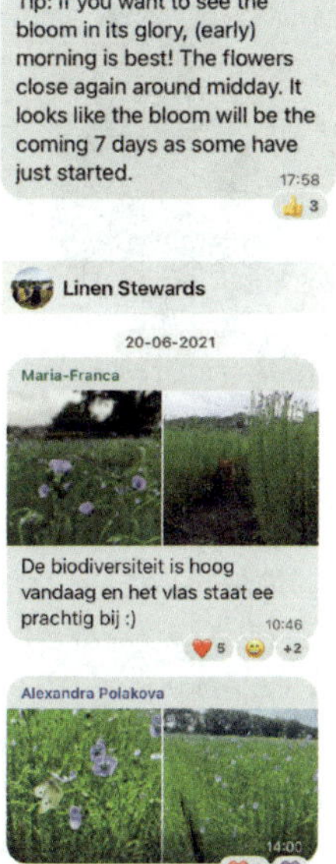

Meeting the spinning wheel indicates a moment of transition; Our fibrous form, twisted into thread. Resting in the vlasstok, the wooden stick we reside around in a draped manner, we get pulled out, bit by bit. Out into the force field of the spinning wheel. That's when we become thread. Us, fibers > hand that pulls > I, thread. Flax > hand > linen. A transition in wording.

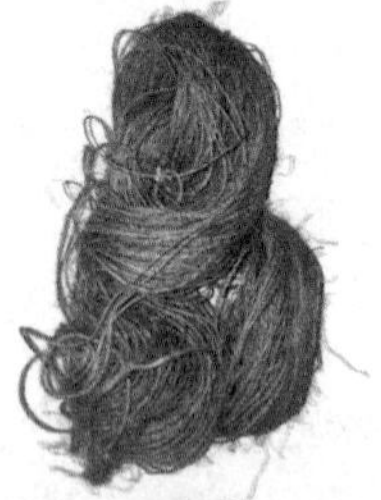

Fibers twisted into the single element of a thread. Through force, tension, and the circular movement of the spinning wheel. Short fibers are poking out, not fully engaging in the thread-event. Poky fibers, still

The word "line" comes from the Latin word *linea*, meaning linen thread, referring in particular to the longer fiber of flax. Before the concept of the line, there was the thread.

Narration, in drawn or written form, starts from a line; with the forming of letters, the line became a building block for texts. The line as a row of letters and words extending across a page or computer screen. The striation of nature into the thread, and from there as a building element to weave fabric, or as a binding element to stitch and patch things together. The line as a path through two or more points, derived from the event of a thread.

I hold one end of the thread in my hand, with the other hand I'm pulling it off the bobbin and I wrap it from my hand to my elbow and back. Around and around, until my arm is wrapped in linen. A loop of spun fiber. I take it off my arm, holding the strand with

carrying soil or dust, or hard wooden pieces; leftovers from the process beforehand.

one hand. It curls into a funny shape, into multiple twirls and twists, as if the threads wanted to wrap themselves around the bobbin they were just taken off. It's the fibers twirling into their new shape, the thread remembering.

Remembering what was before, going back to a source of alternatives hosted in the past. How to trace a memory?

Comparing the chain and the knot, I have already noted that the chain has no memory. When you release the tension in a chain and let it fall to the ground, it comes to rest in a disordered heap. But if you untie a knotted rope, however much you try to straighten it, the rope will retain kinks and bends and will want, given the chance, to curl up into similar conformations as before. The memory is suffused into the very material of the rope, in the torsions and flexions of its constituent fibres. So it is, too, with timbers that have been joined. They may be pulled apart, and used in other structures, but will nevertheless always retain a memory of their former association.[3]

The act of remembering, the task of listening. To the possibility of breaking open the linear continuity of history.[2]

For Donna Haraway, string figures are about a companion practice. They help us draw lines of our interconnected relations. Following threads and finding out where they lead to, string figuring serves as a method of tracing entanglements and patterns of becoming-with each other. Of picking up threads, passing them on and dropping them, receiving patterns that are crucial for staying with the trouble.

100 days after the seeds had been planted, we travel to harvest the flax. It's rainy and quite cold for a day in July.

2 Rolando Vázquez, "Towards a Decolonial Critique of Modernity: Buen Vivir, Relationality and the Task of Listening", In *Capital, Poverty, Development, Denktraditionen im Dialog: Studien zur Befreiung und interkulturalität* 33, edited by Raúl Fornet-Betancourt, 241–252 (Aachen: Wissenschaftsverlag Mainz, 2012), 9.

3 Tim Ingold, *The Life of Lines* (London and New York: Routledge, 2015), 25.

SF is a sign for science fiction, speculative feminism, science fantasy, speculative fabulation, science fact, and also, string figures. Playing games of string figures is about giving and receiving patterns, dropping threads and failing but sometimes finding something that works, something consequential and maybe even beautiful, that wasn't there before, of relaying connections that matter, of telling stories in hand upon hand, digit upon digit, attachment site upon attachment site, to craft conditions for finite flourishing on terra, on earth. String figures require holding still in order to receive and pass on. String figures can be played by many, on all sorts of limbs, as long as the rhythm of accepting and giving is sustained. Scholarship and politics are like that too—passing on in twists and skeins that require passion and action, holding still and moving, anchoring and launching. 4

On the field, pulling the flax. Alongside many other hands we grab a bundle of plants, pull them straight up, so the plant does not break. Wet from the rain, us and the plants. We shake off clumps of soil sticking to the roots. Wet plants on our skin, soil under our nails. The tractor passing through the field is an event that lies in the past, an event prior to the picture being sent to the linen stewards' group chat, and prior to the flax seeds being planted. However, the flax plants connect that past event with the present, through their uneven growth they reveal the imprints the tractor left in the soil. The rows the flax plants have been planted in can be seen similarly to the lines of a text; in the analogy between trace-making and writing, the field equals the writing surface and the flax plants the writers or translators of the traces left by the tractor.

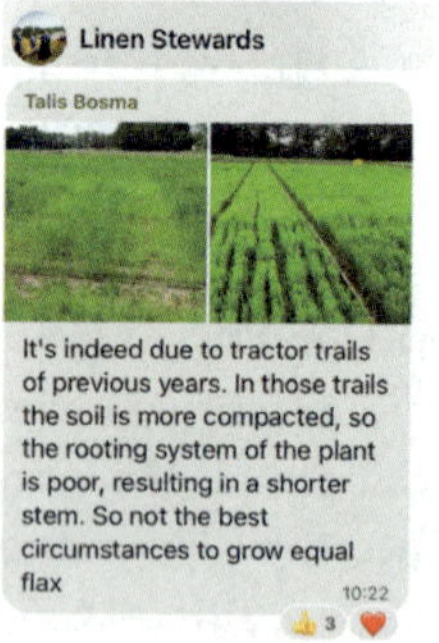

Linen Stewards

Talis Bosma

It's indeed due to tractor trails of previous years. In those trails the soil is more compacted, so the rooting system of the plant is poor, resulting in a shorter stem. So not the best circumstances to grow equal flax

10:22

4 Donna J. Haraway, *Staying with the Trouble: Making Kin in the Chthulucene* (Durham and London: Duke University Press, 2016), 10.

WEAVING A HOME

The nest building of weaverbirds, made from long strips torn from the leaves of grasses. A transformation of nature.

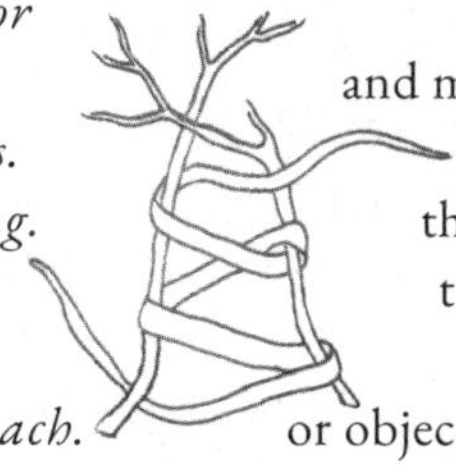

Anthropologist Tim Ingold suggests to think of making as a way of weaving, rather than the other way around. "To emphasize making is to regard the object as the expression of an idea; to emphasize weaving is to regard it as the embodiment of a rhythmic movement."[5] Inverting making and weaving can therefore be seen as inverting idea and movement. Weaving focuses on the process by which the worked material takes shape; a form or object comes into being.

The beak as a tool, like a needle in sewing or darning, creating loops and knots. Then poking and pulling.

Patterns of movement, as far as its beak will reach. Passing strips over and under strips already laid. Over, under, and through. Practice. Over and over again. Weaving as making, not restricted to human beings.

According to Ingold, the "standard view" on giving form and making implies the presence of a surface to be worked and transformed; the carpenter transforms the surface of wood, the potter shapes the surface of clay.

In the process of weaving, there is no surface to be transformed, the surface is being built while making. Thread by thread, inserting threads over and under

5 Tim Ingold, "Making culture and weaving the world," in *Matter, Materiality and Modern Culture*, ed. Paul Graves-Brown (London: Routledge, 2000), 64.

Future building, gradually taking shape. The nest and the basket. The weaverbird. Practice and experience, a process of world-weaving.

a set of other threads, the surface is growing. The rhythmic movement, leading threads back and forth, building up row after row, then applying force on the interlocking of threads; through these actions, movement becomes the generator of what comes into existence.

It starts with a strip of grass, it should be fresh. We go find them on a grass patch nearby. I grab it with my beak close to the ground and then fly straight up. Zack! With the strip in my beak I fly to the branch that will eventually hold my nest. The first and most important step is to tie the leaf strip onto the twig.

The notion of making – as an activity that forms certain objects of material culture – is generally defined as human labor, while the objects made are seen as products of that human labor. Weaving as a way of making is then understood as a uniquely human activity. This relation inverted: to think of making as a modality of weaving. The activity of weaving is not restricted to human beings.

I hold on to the strip with one foot, then tie the knot with my beak. All work depends on this knot. Knotting takes practice. Next, I weave a ring. It has to be big enough to sit through. The knot and the ring. I depend on them, they carry me throughout the building of the nest.

Patterns of movement. Passing strips over and under strips already laid. Over, under, and through. Practice. Over and over again. Weaving as making.

Future building, gradually taking shape. Over, under, and through. Over and over again. A process of world-weaving.

I grew up with craft surrounding me. My father is a carpenter, my uncle a potter, both my grandmothers work with textiles, knitting, and weaving. Being surrounded by objects and living in a house that was renovated and partly built by my family, many everyday objects in my life came with a story. Knowing that the time of my family members went into the making of these objects made me relate to them. I could touch the objects, imagine, remember, and listen to how they were made.

My uncle's pottery workshop: glazed vases, cups, and bowls in the front of the shop. Vessels, traveling from his hands to others, to be filled with food and beverages. In the back of his working space: objects of wet clay drying, others ready to be fired, others coming-into-being on the throwing wheel.

Making, being, and weaving. Weaving the world. Transforming – forming, giving form to material, surface, nature, threads. Shape-maker and shape-taker. Making in process, the experience of time in making, growing, feeling, shaping, listening, attuning oneself to that time. Set by the matter, the weaving, the process.

I always loved spending time in the wood workshop of my father, being surrounded by tools and the smell of wood. The experience of seeing, hearing, smelling, and feeling the processes of production in my close surroundings made it natural for me to connect to objects through where and how they were made.
I grew up in a house where objects held memories.

Objects meet in the kitchen my father built: tea towels handwoven by my grandmother, bowls, cups, and jugs from my uncle.

I see the traces my uncle's fingers left in the clay.

Soft lines, traces of his body, while he was throwing the jug on his pottery wheel. It's the jug my father and I used to make black tea in the morning. Black tea with milk and a bit of agave sweetener – our daily ritual. In the evening we would negotiate who had to wake up first in the morning to prepare the tea.

I think of the wood my
father works with that
grows on our family land.
A pear tree – it grows,
it dies, it dries.

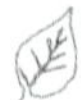

My history is revealed
by growth rings.
Formed by the cycle of
the seasons. In spring, when
my buds detect

In *The Craftsman*, Richard Sennett writes about the metamorphosis of tools and principles of a craft across time. How they develop and can be applied in making processes with other materials.

the lengthening of the days,
my cells start to grow wide
tubes to carry the abundant
water leafward.[6]
Water, soil, roots, leaves,
growth of lines.
Lines of large vessels counted
to determine my age.
My lifecycle alongside
different cycles of time.
Cycles that go beyond
my existence.

Weaving, the joining of cloth in
weft threads across warp threads
at a right angle, shifted domains
to the mortise-and-tenon joint in
carpentry. As far as we know, it
occurred first in
shipbuilding, when
Greek cities colonized
settlements far from home.
The mortise-and-tenon
joint is a way of weaving:
two pieces of wood are locked
together, the end of
one cut into the side of the other.
Weaver and carpenter are joined
through the making of tight right-
angle joints.

This metamorphosis proceeded into a further domain, as the locked orthogonal joints of both cloth and wood suggested a way to lay out streets. Older grid-plans had connected individual buildings, but the Greek city of Selinous, for instance, founded in Sicily in 627 BCE, was pure warp and woof; the corner itself was emphasized as the major design element. The image of an "urban fabric" was not here a casual metaphor, rather a direct description; similarly, Selinous had the tightness and compactness of a ship.

7

6 Robin Wall Kimmerer, *Braiding Sweetgrass: Indigenous Wisdom, Scientific Knowledge, and the Teachings of Plants* (Minnesota: Milkweed editions, 2013), 144.

7 Richard Sennett, *The Craftsman* (New Haven: Yale University Press 2008), 128.

SHARING THREAD SPACE

I invite you to sit with me on either side of my twisted appearance. You choose to sit or stand. My threads reach up high, to the wooden beam, higher than you can reach. If you choose to interact with me in a seated position there are five cushions, arranged around my thread space, in different heights and shapes. Make yourself comfortable.

From the wooden beam high up there, my threads reach down, to another wooden beam attached to the train tracks, they're not in use anymore. My threads, 300 in number, reaching from up to down in a ninety-degree twist. I ask you to sit with me, for a moment in time and space.

We're in the barn of Mediamatic, where we have our exhibition *Disclosing Discomforts* with the class. The loom I built – I call it thread space rather than a frame – stretches its warp threads up to a wooden beam, responding to the architecture of the space. On the night of the opening we start weaving. I choose a cushion to sit on and start to weave from the bottom, in white cotton threads, the same material as the warp. I decide to restrict myself to only that material, the white cotton thread; it seems to me like a skeleton, building the main structure of this weaving in space. I want my woven swatches to be invitations for fellow weavers to interweave with them, extend, and respond to what I started.

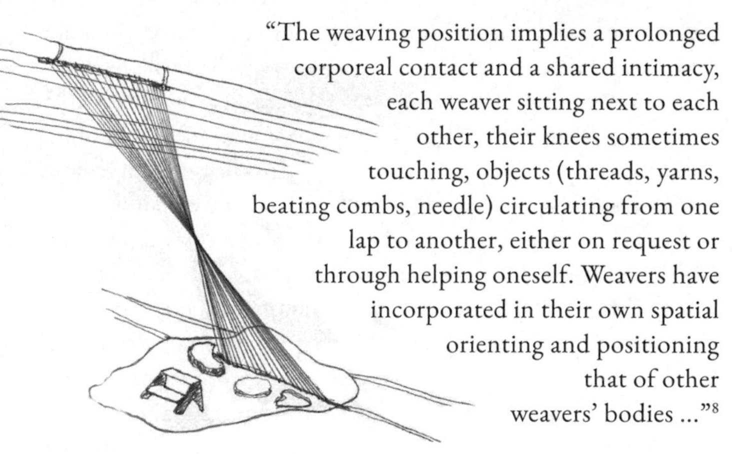

"The weaving position implies a prolonged corporeal contact and a shared intimacy, each weaver sitting next to each other, their knees sometimes touching, objects (threads, yarns, beating combs, needle) circulating from one lap to another, either on request or through helping oneself. Weavers have incorporated in their own spatial orienting and positioning that of other weavers' bodies ..."[8]

The wooden beams,
the threads stretched across space in tension,
the sitting area, the weaving coming-into-being,
the density of the air, the temperature
and the light, your body and those
of other weavers.

I invite you to touch me and leave your traces,
alongside others. The thread you choose; its color,
materiality, and length. Where you start to pass it
through, over, and under. Your thread passing
through me; we draw, we build structure.

8 Myriem Naji, "Gender and Materiality In-the-Making: The Manufacture of Sirwan Femininities Through Weaving in Southern Morocco," *Journal of Material Culture* 14, no. 1 (March 2009): 55.

An arm length, or two.
Picked out by the weavers,
unraveled, then stretched out
from their hand to their
shoulder.
Then cut off.
Led by the weavers'
hands we find our way
into the weave.
Interlocked with
other threads
we build structure.
Some weave us fully,
some leave us halfway.
We hang there,
our length an indicator of time.
Of time in relation to bodies.
We might get picked up
by other weavers,
arm lengths continued
by other hands.

Rana sits across from me, Maureen to my left. Choose a thread in any color you like, cut off a piece of one or two arm lengths. Hold your thread in one hand and pass it through the warp threads, alternating, over one thread, under the next one, and so on. If you like, you can already pull the warp threads with your other hand, with your index finger you pick the threads and create a gap where you can pass your thread through more easily.

I try to keep my instructions minimal, and leave space for experimentation, exploration, and learning while making. Aram joins the thread space; she sits on Rana's right side. "I can show you how it works, it's very simple," Rana says. This moment stays with me, the introduction to weaving can be so simple, a technique that is easily picked up and passed on. And from that first introduction, the weave and the materiality take over, and teach us about their characteristics and techniques.

A wooden frame: painted black, around
1.5 meters square. It was in
the studio space before we
moved in. After making
the corners more stable and putting
on a warp with the help of Farah
and Ayman, it became our
frame for collective weaving.

Traces of spaces.
The frame loom. The big
collective weaving in our studio,
changing places in space.
Hanging on the wall,
now suspended from
the ceiling.
It's double-sided.
We spend an afternoon weaving,
at times just ten minutes
to calm down.
To keep our hands busy.
To escape a conversation.
You pick up a thread and continue
where I started.
Or you choose a new color,
start to draw with threads
in an empty space.

My eyes wander
to the small woven circle
in the middle of the frame.
With a light green cotton thread
Saja wove a small circle,
the thread moved through
the warp like a spiral.
It's upper border has an
additional orange thread.
The warp threads involved
come together in
the circle,
as if they're pointing
towards it.
Around the circle there are
gaps, negative spaces
that evolved through the
condensed circle.
Three warp threads stretch

Saja tells me about the circle
she wove: "I was thinking of
a traditional type of weaving that
people used to make baskets with.
It starts small and while weaving
around it gets big. It's a very specific
woven shape that my mum
and my grandma knew.
The idea of the circle was
inspired by that. I was trying
to find a way to do it, I remember

from the green circle to a
patch I wove in light blue,
on the circle's
lower-right side.

"Could you unweave
your part a bit so I can use
more warp threads?"

I started by making a cross
with the threads and trying
to weave around it. But somehow
the warp threads were loose, or the circle
got too dense. Maybe I should have
done it differently.

It ended up shrinking into
the middle. I was really excited
to make this circle grow, but
I think it came to an end
in an early stage. I mean
it was a very interesting place to
experiment, to try to do something.

Another thing that
was interesting for me,
apart from the circle,
was that the weaving took place where we
were having lectures
or classes.
Using my hands while listening
to the person speaking
helped me to
focus more."

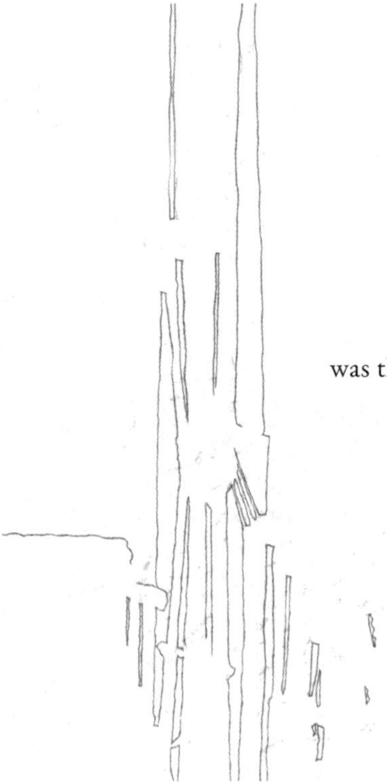

I facilitate:
making, conversations
around it,
I am present in space
and change shape
throughout time.
Woven swatches change
the tension of my threads,
some weavers weave me loose
some dense, collaborating
with threads, with others,
with me coming into being.

I become:
their shapes,
shaped other
than imagined.
Their ideas, crossed by others' threads.
Acceptance.
Their space in the weave, surrounded by gaps.
Bridging the gaps.
Their conversations about authorship.
Decision-making.
Their hands handling material.
Traces of tension.
I remember.

Tension: "a stretched condition" deriving from the French word *tension* or the Latin *tensionem* – "a stretching". A struggle or contest in medieval Latin. Tension as the condition of being held between two or more forces, which are acting in opposition to each other.

The word is used in different contexts, such as a psychological state of being tense, the state of an elastic object stretched to increase its length, or the force transmitted through a rope string or cable in electricity.

Tension, a force needed in many textile processes; in crochet or knitting the yarn is held in tension between two fingers, in weaving the warp threads are stretched and held by the loom or frame. The threads held in tension give us clear sight, help us move the weft through the warp and interlock them into a tight fabric.

My hands remember
working the soil,
pulling the flax,
spinning fibers.
Making and weaving.
I pick up threads, interweave
them with those of others, pass them on. Tracing
processes of tensions in space, of threads as lines.
Threads held by many.

Once the fabric is taken off the loom,
the tension released, what stays is the
interlocking of threads. The fibers carrying
the memory of soil and land, the weaving
telling stories of its becoming.

Glossary of Narrators

flaxfibers 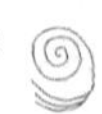 my hands 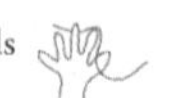 weavebird  tree

threadspace 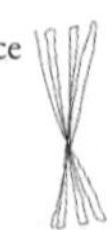 threads 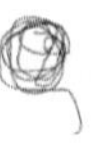 frameloom 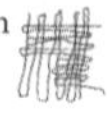

Sarah Saleh

Where Should We Go After the Last Frontier?

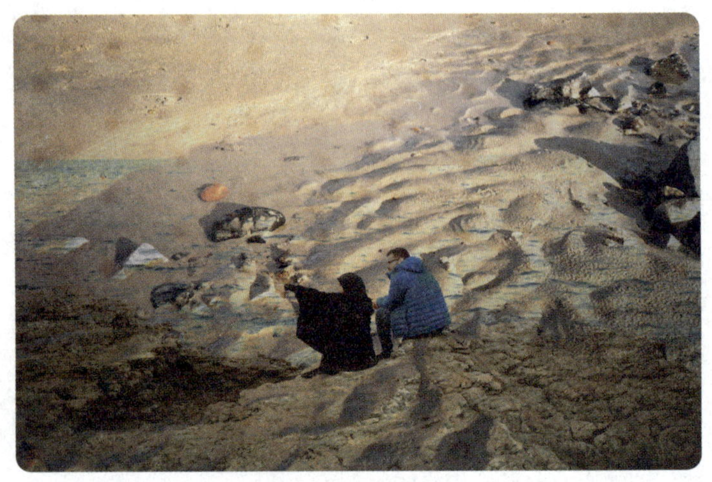

MEMORY AND SOUND

Living in a new city, I was haunted by the fear of forgetting my past, my traditions, and my language. The only way I could go back in time was by looking through my archives, wishing I could relive some memories in the present. In order to bring back these memories, I started to collect sounds and images that could make me feel this sense of "home".

Home is comfort
Home is traffic
Home is chaos
Home is childhood
Home is family
Home is tradition

This sentiment of nostalgia and fear of forgetfulness is due to the sense of loss and displacement, a feeling of going back to a specific space and time. How to get rid of this so-called "historical emotion" that forbids us to move forward when I crave the sound, chaos, and warmth of Lebanon? How to experience my mind and body in the present moment? How to intersect my memory of the past and imagination of the future to come together in the present? Different bodies at different times.

Where is home when you are forced to flee your country due to the failure of a corrupt government, forcing migration among citizens in order to live a so-called "better life" and seek better opportunities? Perhaps there is no final destination when you are in constant movement. Neither on the ground nor in the sky, neither in the past nor in the present, but a constant "in-between" place.

I felt home in the words of professor of Literary Studies Ernst van Alphen, in his text "Imagined Homelands: Re-mapping Cultural identity", as he mentioned:

> *Home is not necessarily located in the past, for it is continuously remembered, lived and imagined in the present. Memory and imagination are no longer two separate things facing in opposite directions. Memory of 'the past' and imagination of the 'future' come together in 'the present' – casting me in 'the now' and casting my life in passing images. These images belong to the 'now' I inhabit.*[1]

1 E.J. van Alphen, "Imagined Homelands: Re-Mapping Cultural Identity," in *Mobilizing Place, Placing Mobility: The Politics of Representation in a Globalized World*, ed. G. Verstraete and T. Cresswell (Amsterdam and New

Amsterdam is the "now" I inhabit; confined between the walls of my room, looking through the window, longing for the sun to appear. Will the sun ever appear again? Will I ever feel the warmth of the sunrise after a feverish and long, cold night the same way I did back "home"? I guess the now has more to it than its polished, flat landscapes and its delusional politics.

Amsterdam doesn't feel like home yet. How can I imagine being 'home' in a city where I have been living for over a year now? Where are the spaces and sounds that would make me experience this sense of "home away from home"?

Thinking back over my past year, I remember the lockdown made it more difficult to travel around, even within the city. This is why I travelled virtually, by listening to songs and creating playlists with my DJ partner Claar, which triggered deep emotions. We called them *Saar and Claar playlists*, and actually we started on them a few months before my move to Amsterdam. I was in Beirut, she was in Amsterdam. We shared a similar taste in music and felt more connected than ever.

// Saar and Claar playlist 3 track list // [2]

- Francis Bebey – Forest Nativity
- May East – Tunel Do Tempo
- Violet Eves – Listen Over The Ocean
- Bullion, Tapes, Wayne Francis, Juliano Fiori – Say Arr Ee
- Bô'vel – Check 4 u
- Anna Domino – Trust, In Love

York: Rodopi, 2002), 53-70.

2 open.spotify.com/playlist/05zSGy29HgVcCbJZHInoT0?si=0157e3e4ce5f4f3e.

- The Freak scene – Rose Of Smiling Faces
- Ryuichi Sakamoto, David Sylvian – Bamboo Houses
- Keysha – Stop It!
- Holger Czukay – Persian Love
- Grauzone – Eisbär
- SAVE, I:Cube – The Darkness
- Frankie Knuckles, Jamie Principle – Your Love
- Jungle Wonz – The Jungle
- Eris Drew – Trascendental Access Point
- Roberto (CA) – When U Come Around
- Gray – The Mysterious Ashley Bickerton
- The Durutti Column – Katherine
- Vanderschrick – Ochtendgrijs
- Dean Blunt & Inga Copeland – 2

We could compare mixing sounds with a double exposure of a cinematic image, or a superimposition of two images; of home and abroad, of past and present, of dreams and everyday life. The moment we try to force it into a single track, it breaks the frame or burns the surface.[3]

Beatmatching, overlapping, ordering, transitioning, assembling, and reassembling pieces together leads to a never-ending track. By overlapping these sounds of the past and present you create an experience of "here" and "there".

3 Svetlana Boym, "Nostalgia and Its Discontents," The Hedgehog Review, *Critical Reflections on Contemporary Culture* 9.2 (Summer 2007), hedgehogreview.com/issues/the-uses-of-the-past/articles/nostalgia-and-its-discontents.

Up until now, my DJ sets consist of reusing existing tracks and collaging them in a way that seems to make sense. Some of these tracks have specific sounds that bring me back to a specific place and time. The fusion of Western and Arabic music reminds me of the spaces and time I inhabited between Beirut, Milan, and Amsterdam. Mixing the Adhan with Dub sounds, for example, in an electronic context reminds me of the past in the present. The Western and Eastern influences I had throughout my experiences of living in different localities, going to clubs and sound festivals, and the people I encountered, expanded my knowledge in terms of communities, cultures, and religions.

By playing music I try to project these experiences into the now that I inhabit, using music as a form of making home, virtually migrating from one place to another. I try to find the similarities in sounds that would be familiar to my sense of place, and I try to capture these 'sonic memories' by recording sounds from "here" and "there" in these in-between places. As if the sounds of the waves here and 'there' evoke a personal emotion that is not necessarily sameness but an attachment to an immaterial object. The Mediterranean Sea is nothing compared to the North Sea but just listening to the sounds of the waves somehow evokes an emotional attachment.

Throughout the different parts of my essay I will be crossing music's borders, flying from one place to another in search of identity by tracing sound trajectories through the lens of migration, identity, and resistance in different non-localities and diasporic spaces. In the following chapter I will explore how we can identify my scattered identities through sounds.

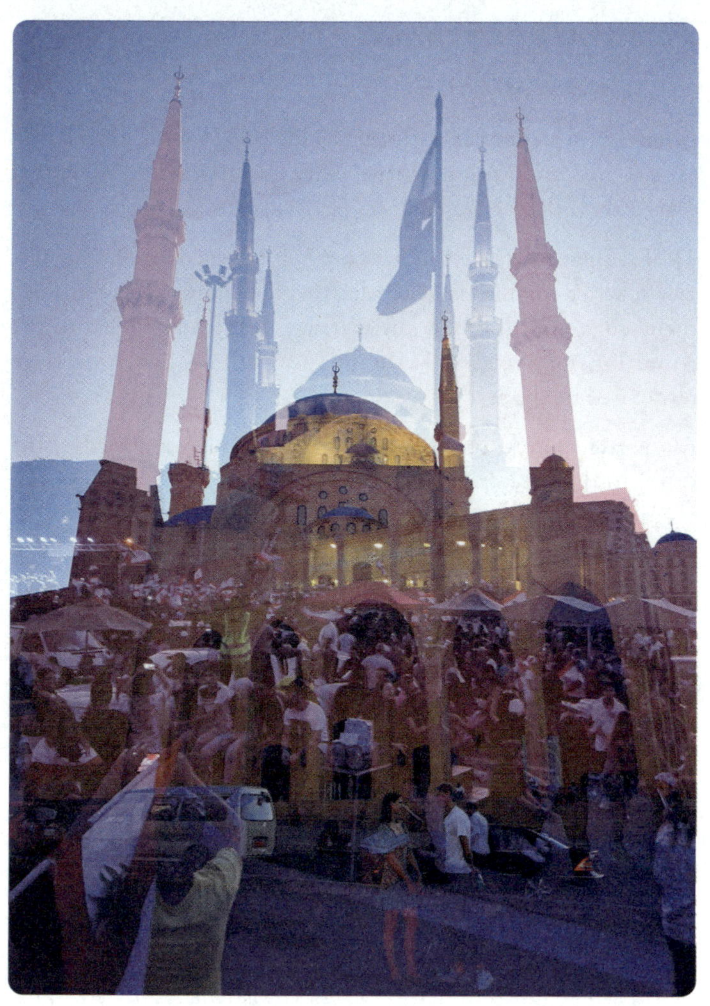

A STATE OF TRANCE

Scattered identities

I come from a complex and avant-garde background considering my parents' interfaith marriage. They got married in 1992, two years after the sectarian civil war (1975–1990).

The Lebanese *sectarian state par excellence* is based on confessionalist views, with a commonly held belief that one should marry "inside" their religion. Still today, any marriage that's not subject to the conditions of social and religious authority is not a marriage recognised by the sect.

All marriages must be recorded (in order to be recognised by the state) in the husband's jurisdiction of birth after having been performed by a religious body, which often obligates one of the partners to convert to the faith of the other for the marriage to be able to take place. For this reason, my parents decided to go through a civil marriage in Greece, without any religious interference.

Because of their decision to get married against their parents' will, I always felt my parents were ahead of their time. They believe in their faiths but never practise them. They raised me without imposing any religious views, hence I was never really interested in reading the Qur'an, nor the Bible.

Most of my French-educated friends from school came from Christian backgrounds and did not understand my position, which meant I always felt like an outsider not knowing where I belonged. Our school was located in Ashghafieh, an area in Eastern Beirut where most French-educated Christians reside. For them to understand your background many questions would arise;

"Where are you from?" or "What is your last name?" Your religion can be determined based on the area you are from. People always felt estranged by my answer, knowing that my mom's family comes from Bkhechtay, a small village in the southern east of Lebanon, and my Dad from Hama in Syria.

My mom is Christian Orthodox and my dad Sunni Muslim, and they got married despite their parents' opposition to their union and the country's opposition to civil marriage. Nevertheless, they flew to Greece and joined in their love.

I've always been grateful for their openness but have nevertheless wondered, where do I belong?

Mom, am I Christian or Muslim?
You are Muslim Shia' on your passport
and baptised at birth
Why Shia' not Sunni?
In order for you to inherit from your dad

My name is Sarah. I am Sunni Muslim converted to Shia' (for inheritance reasons), Christian Orthodox (baptised at birth), Lebanese, and French-educated.

In the name of identity, Amin Maalouf argues that "identity can't be compartmentalised." "You can't divide it up into halves or thirds or any other separate segments. I haven't got several identities:

I've got just one, made up of many components in a mixture that is unique to me, just as other people's identity is unique to them as individuals."[4]

Similarly, one album has one identity; the scattered tracks are made of many components that are woven together to create a single unique album. The sounds that I collect and record make me question my scattered identities but also help me understand and dissect these many components. While listening through my sound archive seeking a familiar sound I came across the Adhan, Islamic call to prayer. Many western artists such as Muslimgauze, Rootsman, Pippa Murphy, and Natasha Atlas, among others, incorporate the Adhan in their production. They carry the listener on a journey and a state of trance, parallel with dub or electronic sounds, which accentuates this in-betweenness and the feeling of being both "there" and "not there". This cross-cultural borrowing makes it interesting in relation to my own scattered identities, my Western and Eastern influences.

That being said, can sound evoke memories in relation to my own identities? As I mentioned earlier, the juxtaposition between Western and Eastern sounds remind me of my own complex, scattered identities and experiences of migrating between one place and another. Can sound fill this in-betweenness that has for so long kept my thoughts in a fret?

4 *In the Name of Identity: Violence and the Need to Belong* is a 1998 book by Amin Maalouf, in which he discusses the identity crisis that Arabs have experienced since the establishment of continuous relationships with the West, adding his personal dimension as a Lebanese Christian.

This void ignited my interest in looking further into the Islamic call to prayer (salat). "Adhan" means to listen, it is recited by the muezzin five times a day during prayer time as a way of calling people to the mosque to pray. In some countries the call to prayer is broadcast through speakers or can be recorded. It is sung by the muezzin several times in a row in different melodious ways based on the variations of the maqam melodic system[5] depending on the time of prayer.

The chant was popularised by Sufi groups and great musicians such as Umm Kulthum and Gamal Abdel Nasser, who were inspired by tape recordings of reciters in the 1960s and use the Arabic system of musical modes, such as maqamat, that bring this emotional expression.

God is the greatest الله أكبر*; intoned four times.*
I testify that there is no God but Allah
أشهد أن لا إله إلا الله *; intoned twice.*
I testify that Mohammed is God's Prophet
لآ إلَهَ إلّا اللهُ مُحَمَّدٌ رَسُوْل اللهُ *; intoned twice.*
Come to prayer حي على الصلاة *; intoned twice.*
Come to security/salvation حي على الفلاح *;*
intoned twice.
God is the greatest الله أكبر*; intoned twice.*
There is no God but Allah لَا إِلَٰهَ إِلَّا ٱللَّٰهُ *; intoned once.*

5 Maqām or maqāmāt (plural) is a system of scales, pitches, melodic elements, and patterns that together form a rich melodic framework and artistic tradition. It can evoke a myriad of emotions and ignite a spiritual experience within people.

Another line is sometimes added to
the first prayer of the day (first light fajr):
Prayer is better than sleep الصلوة خير من النوم *;*
intoned twice.

The five prayer times[6] span from before the sun rises to after the sun sets, and are dictated by the sun, making the timings different daily, and based on geographic location. In this case, if the notion of time is dictated by the sun, how can I tell when it is time to pray if the sun barely appears here?

The sky is a sea of darkness
When there is no sun
The sky is a sea of darkness
When there is no sun to light the way
When there is no sun to light the way
There is no day
There is no day
There's only darkness
Eternal sea of darkness[7]

Drowning in the darkness as if attacked by a snake, descending through the underworld preventing the sun from rising and destroying all life on Earth. Nothing could compare the vibrant sun of Beirut, where the sun rises with the beautiful chant of birds,

6 The five prayer times are known as: Fajr – Dawn (the first appearance of light on the eastern horizon), the early morning prayer (before sunrise); Dhuhr, when the sun begins to descend after reaching its highest point in the sky, the noon time prayer; Asr, when the shadow of an object is the same length as the object itself, plus the shadow length at dhuhr, the late afternoon prayer; Maghrib, the sunset prayer; and Isha, the late evening prayer.

7 The Sky is a Sea of Darkness When There is no Sun – Sun Ra.

and later, with spiritual chants, it sets next to Mohammad Al Amin's mosque. This in-betweenness is like having two residencies, one has purely a practical function, and the other I am emotionally attached to.

Another way to dictate time is by listening to the tone of the Adhan.

"The art of the adhan was developed during the Ottoman Empire, and was a creative way for listeners to be able to tell the time of prayer just by hearing the tone of the adhan," said Shaykh Saad.[8]

In this case, the beautiful chant of muezzin could be compared to a ghost chanting from different non-localities. He is invisible and, moreover, the immateriality of the sound of his voice brings listeners back to a remembrance, which is the time of prayer. "One does not need to understand a language to understand music. Music is a universal language. Music is not material but spiritual. Music is air, a universal existence common to all the living."[9]

Where do we belong?

The repetition and boldness of Koranic lines reminds me of the repetitiveness of chants and slogans of revolutions that are easily transferable across borders. It evokes an uncanny emotion, which is attached to a memory of being between places.

8 Indlieb Farazi Saber, "The art of the adhan: The multiple melodies of the Muslim call to prayer," *Middle East Eye*, May 5, 2021, www.middleeasteye.net/discover/adhan-muslim-call-prayer-melodies-maqams#:~:text=The%20art%20of%20the%20adhan,-Although%20the%20words&text=Based%20on%20variations%20of%20the,call%20can%20evoke%20myriad%20emotions.

9 Sun Ra.

One of the slogans that emerged from the Tunisian Revolution of 2011 has been adopted throughout the Arabic-speaking parts of the Middle East, from Libya to Yemen, passing by Egypt, Bahrain, Syria, Iraq, and Lebanon:

"The people demand the fall of the regime"
الشعب يريد إسقاط النظام
"The people demand the fall of the regime"
الشعب يريد إسقاط النظام
"The people demand the fall of the regime"
الشعب يريد إسقاط النظام
"The people demand the fall of the regime"
الشعب يريد إسقاط النظام
"The people demand the fall of the regime"
الشعب يريد إسقاط النظام
"The people demand the fall of the regime"
الشعب يريد إسقاط النظام
"The people demand the fall of the regime"
الشعب يريد إسقاط النظام
"The people demand the fall of the regime"
الشعب يريد إسقاط النظام

What about the policies in the Netherlands regarding the integration of immigrants? Should we also ask for the fall of the right wing regime? Is the Netherlands a model of "successful" integration? Is coexistence possible at all? If that is so, why are immigrants segregated in specific parts of Amsterdam, such as Nieuw-West, and not "white" residential areas?

When I first moved to Amsterdam, I was not aware that most Turkish and Moroccan residents were concentrated in western sections of the city, particularly in the Nieuw-West area. Is that the Netherlands' idea of "integration"? Or is it a fear of other cultures?[10]

Integration holds different meanings for different people. My idea of integration and belonging is finding spaces and sounds that make me think of home; the chaos and shops of western or eastern areas of Amsterdam and the sounds of the Adhan. The Dutch citizens of Moroccan or Turkish origins, who are concentrated in certain areas and neighbourhoods, might not have this emotional attachment to home as much as their parents did. I wonder if this residential segregation helps towards social and cultural integration. Integration policies in the Netherlands are still complex, and perhaps this in-betweenness is different from mine.

Maybe what we have in common is this nostalgic feeling of living between two worlds and, by going back and forth in our imagination, remembering what it might feel like to belong somewhere.

In this case, can sound fill the role of integration or segregration in certain areas of Amsterdam?

10 The first traces of Islam in the Netherlands date back to the 16th century, followed by the creation of the first mosques in the 17th century as a result of the settlement of Ottoman merchants in the country's port cities. After the Second World War, the second generation of immigrants from Turkey and Morocco settled in the Netherlands due to a need for a larger 'low-skilled' workforce. The share of the different groups in their own ethnic concentrations increased substantially due to family reunification and, increasingly, due to family formation. "Islam in the Netherlands", Wikipedia, en.wikipedia.org/wiki/Islam_in_the_Netherlands#:~:text=The%20early%20history%20of%20Islam,in%20the%20early%2017th%20century..

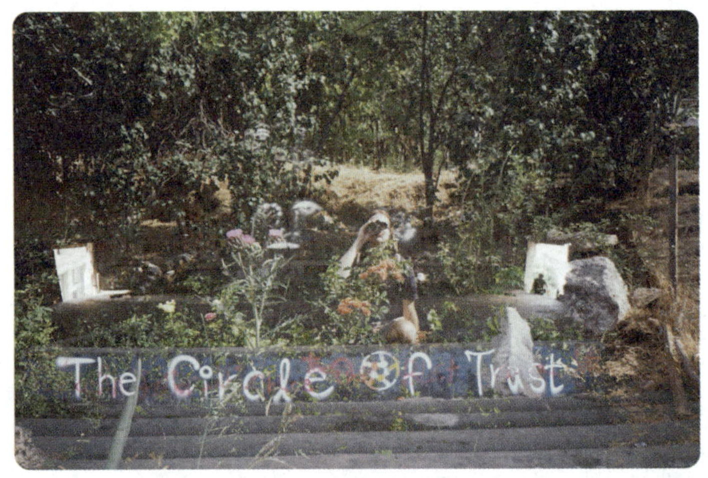

DANY, DANY IS THAT YOU?

Where do we go after the last frontier?

One of the sounds that reminds me of home in Amsterdam is the melodic sounds of birds.

My family home is in Martakla, a residential area ten minutes away from Beirut by car. My mom spent most of her childhood living there with my grandparents, but her memories of home are different from mine. At the time she lived there there were only three buildings, and the rest of the space was full of trees and plants. Now, most of the green spaces have been privatised and replaced by tall buildings.

The only house that has remained the same is 'The Martakla Palace', a villa that used to be owned by the former French ambassador but is now inhabited by a wealthy American family. The house is surrounded by trees, birds, and crickets that we can hear from the balcony. I remember waking up every morning, having a sobhiye[11] with my mom; drinking coffee and listening to the sound of birds.

[pointing at the bird] Mom:
Dany, Dany is that you calling us?

Dany is my very special aunt who passed away more than a year ago due to a 'cancer orphelin' that she had been battling for twenty years. The doctors used to say that it was a miracle that she was still alive after all those years. Dany was not only my aunt but my second mom. Calm, wise, generous, humble, selfless, patient, and loving were just some of her many traits.

They say that the best people always leave first, and Dany was definitely one of them. I can still feel her presence whenever I hear a bird. I can feel her when she appears in my dreams. One of the things that Dany loved was birds. She had a collection of bird figurines and paintings that now remains untouched in the house where she lived with her husband Nabil.

Her absence is always with us like a ghost inhabiting a film, especially when we hear a melody that attaches easily to a memory. In this case, the sound of birds reminds me of the [non]presence of my dear aunt inhabiting my deepest thoughts, always watching over us.

11 A sobhiye in Arabic is sharing a morning coffee with a group of women or men, mainly friends and neighbours.

"Sound is where time and space collide jumping back and forth between the timespaces of the human and the ghostly, past and present, reality, imaginary, and unconscious."[12]

Dany is now one of these migratory birds, flying from one place to another, witnessing what is happening to the world from above. She is travelling through history informing us on what went wrong with humanity. Operating as a protagonist, reflecting on shared realities, and chanting along with all the revolutionaries. The migration call-notes of birds is a way to express the feeling of migration in order to spread it, and to unify all the birds in the same way that revolutions call for unity. Birds are in constant movement, and so are we. In their case, they are forced to migrate from their tropical homes to the north when changes in weather occur. In our case, forced migration is induced by violence, conflict, persecution, climate change, urbanisation, poverty, and economic motivations.

It makes me wonder ...

Where should we go after the last frontiers?
Where should the birds fly after the last sky?
Where should the plants sleep
After the last breath of air?[13]

Where should we go when our own government leaves us with no money, no electricity, no gas, and no hope?

12 Isabella van Elferen, "Chapter 21. Haunted by a Melody: Ghosts, Transgression, and Music in *Twin Peaks,"* in *Popular Ghosts: The Haunted Spaces of Everyday Culture*, eds. María del Pilar Blanco and Esther Peeren (London: Bloomsbury Academic, 2002), 282–295.

13 Mahmoud Darwish, "The Earth is Closing on Us", poem.

Where do we seek better opportunities and a so-called better life?

Where do I belong?

Maybe I should just accept the fact that wherever I go, I will never have this sense of belonging. Just like migratory birds I will be moving from one place to another. Going to these in-between places, from the Mediterranean Sea to the North Sea, hoping to find my place. Deep-thinking whilst listening to Brian Eno's ambient album *Music for Airports* in the hope of finding my place.

In the context of the Middle East, that means traversing routes through transitory forms from the Mediterranean Sea of Greece, Spain, and Turkey, to Europe, including the regions of Iraq, Jordan, Syria, Lebanon, Israel, and Occupied Palestinian Territories (OPT), the Gulf Cooperation Council (GCC) countries, and Turkey.

Cacerolazo

Just like the different melodious ways of the Adhan and its variety of tones, there is a distinction between songs and calls in bird vocalisation. Songs are long and associated with territory and mating, whereas calls are used as an alarm to alert other birds. In comparison, the chants of the revolution alert other countries across borders through different mediums. These slogans and chants of the revolutions are later broadcast in different continents as a political organising tool or force to maintain unity among different factions and to sustain devotion to a common cause. Music works to unify collective public willpower behind protest movements, and its contribution in that respect is different from the role it plays in fostering collective memory.

The most popular, and my personal favourite, version of the slogan is, "*The people demand the fall of the regime*",[14] linking struggles in Lebanon with Sudan, Algeria, Libya, Yemen, Syria, Palestine, Iraq, and Tunisia, including the Libyan ballad by Adel Al Mshiti. For the first time in Lebanese history, people from different sectarian backgrounds would chant in solidarity with each other – from Tripoli where the Sunni majority resides, to Dahieh and Nabatiyeh where the Shia' community is, and vice-versa, fighting for the same goal.

Music was just one form of sound that played a role in the revolutions but the sonic atmosphere included different soundscapes. From hitting the walls with rocks to banging pans and pots as a way to make some loud noise, this effective method is called Cacerolazo, Cacelorado, or Casserole, and is a form of popular protest in order to call for attention.[15]

In the light of the 17 October Revolution for the fall of the sectarian regime, the Cacerolazo was used across different parts of Lebanon, among neighbours, on the street, on the balconies – it felt like a never-ending jam session, a performance of improvising sounds on the spot as a group, a community being together like there was no tomorrow. It was magic.

14 Thawra - Rayess Bek.

15 The Cacerolazo method, meaning stew pot in Spanish, was first used in the 1830s by opponents of Louis Philippe I in France and was followed a century later for the independence of Algeria during the Algerian war in the 1960s. This method then emerged from South American countries, in particular, Argentina, Chile, Venezuela, and Brazil.

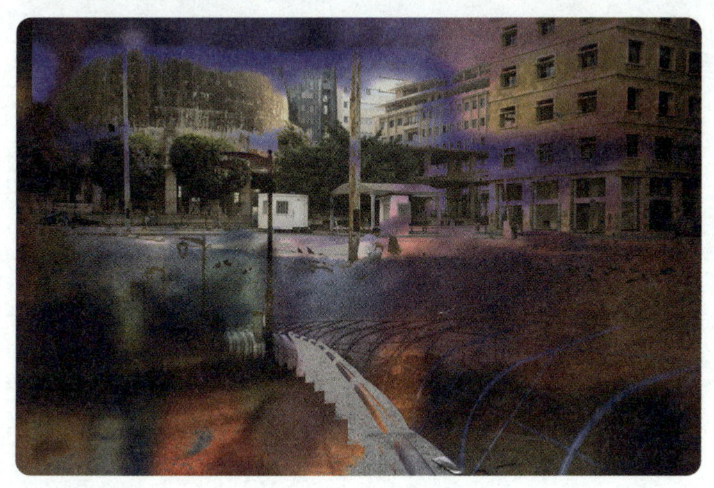

HERE, THERE, AND EVERYTHING IN BETWEEN

Sampling as a political practice

These improvised sounds of Cacerolazo can be used in terms of sampling as a political tool among other sounds. Sounds of revolutions and political speeches have long been used in the history of music as a way to represent marginalised communities. The tradition of the religious sermon or preach had quite an influence on the young generation of music producers that emerged in Chicago and Detroit at the end of the 1980s.[16]

16 Francesco Fusaro, "Ain't Nothing Wrong (With Political Dance Music)," in *Sampling Politics Today,* eds. Hannes Liechti, Thomas Burkhalter, and Philipp Rhensius (Bern: Norient, 2020), Chapter III.

In the beginning, there was Jack, and Jack had a groove.
And from this groove came the groove of all grooves.
And while one day viciously throwing down on his box,
Jack boldly declared, «Let there be House!» and house music was born.
[...]
Jack is the one that can bring nations and nations of all Jackers together under one house.
You may be black, you may be white; you may be Jew or Gentile. It don't make a difference in our house.
And this is fresh![17]

These speeches are not only used as political tools but also as a way to sustain a universal language brought by communities facing discriminitation for musically expressing hybrid identities.

Collage of existing sounds

In the same way that sounds can be sampled, using theories and quotes from other authors in parallel with your own voice is like collaging existing sounds to create something new, or finding my scattered identities in the multiple genres existing in sound. This path guided me in a certain way to face my fears of being stuck in the past. It cured me from "contemporary nostalgia". I found my place through an immaterial medium that helped me cherish my background. What had been unclear finally became clear.

17 Rhythm Controll – My House [sic], released in 1987 on the ephemeral Chicago-based 'Catch A Beat' record label.

By tracing my past and meandering through the non-place of non-linear time, I began to understand my position in the present. It is not about feeling home "here" or "there", but in in-between spaces, navigating through different fragments of memories that were buried in my thoughts for so long. Home is not necessarily a specific space located in the past but can be found in the present. For a while I tried to recreate my past; I was cursed with restorative nostalgia, trying to recreate spaces of my homeland. The pre-packaged "usable past" may be of no use to us if we want to co-create our future. Perhaps dreams of imagined homelands cannot and should not come to life. Sometimes, it is preferable to leave dreams alone, let them be no more and no less than dreams, not guidelines for the future.[18]

18 Boym, "Nostalgia and Its Discontents."

Anna Celda

A Taula

"*A taula*" in Valencian is a phrase used to mean "come to the table, it's time to eat". *A taula* is not normally said softly, it's often pronounced with the urgency and acuteness of hunger. *A taula* is something you hear when you are sitting in your room busy with your own life, more than likely in the voice of an older woman, that claims you back into the world you share with her. It's a phrase I now scream recklessly whenever I cook for people. *A taul*a is a cry of love.

It's almost time to come *a taula*. I'm preparing lunch for us. Come with me to the kitchen as we cook through today's menu: *allioli*, سلطة غزاوية, *potatge*, and *truita*. I want to let you in on a few secrets ...

GHOSTS IN THE KITCHEN

Tools have the potential to become voices in the kitchen, speaking to us of other times and places as they go about the business of preparing our daily fare.[1]

I put garlic and salt inside the mortar. My right hand holds a tubular shape that is round at the end. A mortar and a pestle, a vessel and a weapon. Different iterations of this tool have appeared throughout all the kitchens I've inhabited in my life.

The earliest one I remember is made of clay, yellow with a green stain on each of the four sides. It's so shiny and smooth to the touch, with some rough chipped edges that show the raw clay inside. The pestle is made of wood. In it I see, smell, and taste *picada*, *romesco*, or

1 David Sutton and Michael Hernandez, "Voices in the Kitchen: Cooking Tools as Inalienable Possessions," *Oral History 35, no.2 (Autumn 2007)*: 67–76.

ajoarriero,[2] and of course lots of *allioli*[3]. These foods are physically and metaphorically ingrained in the wood of the pestle.

I learned to cook from my mother, my grandmother, and from the kitchen we cooked in, each of the objects within it telling me different stories and teaching me different recipes. I would grab the *mà de morter*,[4] following the stains on the wood of the hands that have held it before me. The shape and weight of the handle would direct my movements and without thinking, only with feelings, I would make *allioli*.

The next mortar that came into my life is made of stone. It has a rough texture with thousands of small incisions and spaces for food to become infinitely smaller; to break apart and reconfigure. It's cold to the touch. I don't know where the stone came from, and it bears no signs of usage that can teach me of its history. It is, nevertheless, a very efficient tool.

I attack, pum pum pum pum. My hand goes up and smashes down, applying all the force my arm can muster. In my hand through the wood and the stone I feel the coarse salt dissolving the garlic into a paste.

I moved to Amsterdam in September of 2020. More than a year later, I haven't had a place to call home yet; the housing crisis has

2 Three different sauces, typical in the south-east of Spain, made using the *morter*.

3 The Valencian word for a very popular sauce made of garlic and oil. The version of this sauce known around the world was popularised by French cuisine, though it is closer to a mayonnaise with the added egg. The one I know and have grown up with is made with just garlic and oil, and is a lot stronger.

4 Valencian for "*pestle*", literally translates to "*hand of the mortar*".

forced me to move around every three months. What I do have is a very heavy stone mortar and pestle that I bought from an online marketplace when I arrived, and that I painstakingly carry from kitchen to kitchen in the basket of my bike.

This tool, *cobek dan ulekan* in Indonesian, came to the Netherlands through migration. A violent history of colonialism, one that is covered up and conveniently forgotten by the Netherlands[5] but that shaped modern-day Indonesia, brought waves of migrants and with them tools and foods like the *cobek dan ulekan* or the *sambal* that's made in it, which now are even considered part of everyday Dutch cuisine.

When the object first arrived to me, I viewed the tool with curiosity. I experimented with grinding all kinds of different things inside it, little by little getting used to the weight, manoeuvring the heavy stone to tilt freshly ground spices into hot oil. After learning about the history of Dutch colonialism and understanding the fact that this mortar is made of stone not by chance, but as a product of this violent history, I now see the object with a more sober view.

Sometime after the *cobek* entered my kitchen, I asked it to deliver a very familiar taste of home: *allioli*.

5 "For the Netherlands, the year 1945 was not an end to its war history. The country started a ruthless war, lasting almost five years, against Indonesian independence. Dutch colonialism had a façade of decency about it, a façade that has endured long after the so-called 'police actions'. Dutch tolerance extends only so far; there is still no room for issues that question the decency of the establishment." Anne-Lot Hoek, "A façade of decency. How the Netherlands deals with its colonial past," the low countries, May 25, 2020, www.the-low-countries.com/article/a-facade-of-decency-how-the-netherlands-deals-with-its-colonial-past.

The visual clues are helpful, sure, but the knowledge my right hand holds is the ultimate determiner of when enough force has been applied. I can feel the paste's smoothness through the stick in my hand.

When trying to produce this sauce, I truly realised what the materiality of this object meant to me. The outcome wasn't a glossy, bright, yellow *allioli*, it was a runny, greenish-grey, semi-broken sauce. I couldn't stop thinking about the *mà de morter*, the hand of the mortar that lent me its hand so many times before and guided me towards saucy success. The material of this tool was the determining factor in the success of all the *allioli* we made inside it.

Then, my left hand comes into play. It holds a 'setrill': a glass bottle that I tilt just the right amount so that the smallest stream of olive oil is poured into the vessel where the garlic paste is held. Xup, xup, xup, xup. At this point, a dance starts to happen between my left and my right hands. The right is moving in a constant circular motion, feeling the oil become one with the garlic and the salt. It knows when to tell my left hand to tilt the setrill more or less.

As I stir the thick paste, I hear my grandmother saying that if I change the direction of my hand, the sauce will break, though I take this information with a grain of salt nowadays.[6]

6 To make *allioli* (any sauce, really) you have to emulsify at least two components. In this case, oil and garlic. The emulsion in this case is facilitated by the continuous circular motion of the wooden pestle. It's believed that when making it, if you change from a clockwise to a counter-clockwise motion, the sauce will break. Although not completely factual, it does hold some truth, as the stopping of the circular motion can affect the emulsion.

There has to be just the right amount of fat. You can't overwhelm the garlic or it will scream and cry like a small child that misses its mother. It will break and become two separate pieces coexisting in one space as opposed to one whole. My mum repeats the superstition/knowledge that she can't make the *allioli* because she's on her period. Everyone knows this, but I also know I have made *allioli* while bleeding. I think I must be a witch because I've somehow pulled it off.

Twenty-five years of my life I've spent inhabiting these objects. The stone mortar is physically heavier, but the clay and wood weighs more on me. The voices inside them coexist within me, bringing me backward or forward in time whenever I need them to.

A CAU D'ORELLA[7]

After inhabiting the *cobek dan ulekan* for about a year, I engaged in the process of making my own *morter* from wood – hoping to feel closer to home through the material. It started with a big wooden block that originally came from a tree in the Amsterdamse Bos.[8] Before coming into my hands, this block had been standing in a wood shop in the De Pijp neighbourhood for years. Because it was so big, heavy, and hard, it was used as a surface on which to chop other smaller pieces of wood. When it arrived at my work table in the studio, it started giving space, little by little, to the round hole in the middle that would become the vessel. As I chipped away at it, I kept running into knots and gaps in the wood, reminders of

7 Expression in Valencian, meaning to say something very quietly, in a whisper, almost touching the other person's ear ...

8 Park in Amsterdam.

the history of the tree that grew and fell and dried and broke and became *el meu morter*.

We're at Mediamatic, in the group show *Disclosing Discomforts*.[9] I'm sitting on the ground next to the fire, enveloped by a layer of green things grown in the earth. I'm surrounded by plates, knives, fruits, nuts, and spices in what is an impromptu kitchen space. In the middle of it all is the mortar I made. A few friends have joined me, and we're all sitting on a semi-rug that Samira put together so we wouldn't feel the coldness of the concrete beneath us.

There is a tomato sitting on the corner, on the straight surface that surrounds the somewhat round cavity in the middle. Chup, chup, chup. The knife glides across its length, slicing first in half, and then across, and then over and over again until all that is left is small red cubes that fall into the hole in the wooden block.

I had spent the past two days feeding people that sat around the kitchen. On the third day of being here, I feel some kind of resentment towards being "expected" to cook and not getting to enjoy the entirety of the show and walk around as I please. Instead I am confined to my position in front of the mortar, grinding almonds and dill into a paste. As if reading my mind (and probably she did), Saja decides she wants to feed us instead, so I am on the other side of the kitchen waiting to try her [10] سلطة غزاوية. Being in this position, I get to focus a bit more on the conversations happening around me. Some seemingly superficial gossip: "Johanna & Bernard[11]

9 Exhibition organised by the students of DD department together with Hannes Bernard as curator, October 28, 29, 30, and 31, 2021.

10 Palestinian salad from Gaza made of crushed vegetables in a mortar and pestle.

11 Not the real names, but if you know, you know.

were making out last night at the party!", says Farah. Our words get stuck in the nooks and knots of the mortar, its wood absorbing our histories and secrets through our voices and the food we grind in it.

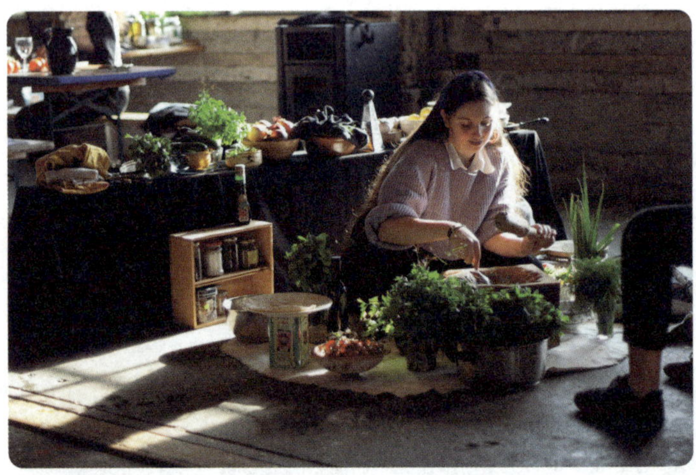

In Valencian, the word for "*gossip*" is "*xafardeig*". It comes from the word "*safareig*", meaning "*lavoir*". In Mediterranean towns, these wash-houses were public buildings located by the river or a similar body of water:

> *The term 'laundry [safareig]', from the Mediterranean tradition, refers not only to the community space where women were going to wash clothes, but also implicitly collectively action that we can hardly understand separately from an extensive network of urban, social relations and policies that, despite their origins and diverse nature, maintain a common denominator: it is*

a space dedicated to a specific way of socialisation, where domesticities break into urban space and intimacy is diluted.[12]

This tradition of communal acts of reproductive work shaped the way women related to one another. Through gossip, they formed networks of care that were integral to their survival. Nowadays, gossip is a vilified act: women chatting away about the lives of others in a demeaning tone meant to ruin reputations. The moralisation and demonisation of gossip has proved to be very useful for a neoliberal capitalist society, in which these networks of care that women form can be a very threatening tool of emancipation and resistance.[13]

Gossip gives power. I'm thinking of my own history of legal abuse, as I'm currently being threatened with fines and jail time after publicly calling out a sexual predator. Thanks to gossip, this man was able to get my personal information in order to file a complaint to the police. But it is also thanks to gossip that I can breathe easily even as this threat looms on the horizon. At the same time we were in

12 Elena Sanmartín, Pau Mendoza & Pau Olmo, "Safareig / L'Apartament," Fundació La Posta, February 29, 2020, fundacionlaposta.org/en/safareig-lapartament/.

13 "... Neither in rural nor urban areas were women dependent on men for their survival; they had their own activities and shared much of their lives and work with other women. Women cooperated with each other in every aspect of their life. They sewed, washed their clothes, and gave birth surrounded by other women, with men rigorously excluded. Their legal status reflected this greater autonomy." Silvia Federici, *Witches, Witch-Hunting, and Women* (California: PM Press, 2018), retrieved from: Emily Janakiram, "Gossip Girls," Verso blog, April 2, 2019, www.versobooks.com/blogs/4290-gossip-girls?fbclid=IwAR0dKM3jn-Q7UBlJU4JU44qwauw-zQYUx0jm7d5X_HnS9k_QIbzmjViV-Q8.

Mediamatic being fed by Saja, back home in València, Antoni and Pau organised a dinner in La Mandràgora[14] to raise money for this legal case. More than one hundred people came that night, even though nobody could publish on social media what the reason for the gathering was, as the case was still ongoing. Had we not told each other the story in confidence, the dinner would never have happened. Instead, I know that as long as we keep gossiping and caring for each other, I can keep relying on this network. I suspect these court dates and letters from lawyers would weigh much more on me if that wasn't the case.

Clonk, clonk, clonk. You hear the pestle hitting the mortar. Inside it, there was already garlic and salt, ground into a paste that clings into the crevices of the wood. A stalk of green onion and a bush of dill join in, first shyly resting on the same surface the tomato was on before the sharp metal of the blade comes down to divide them into more manageable pieces that naturally cascade into the red mess of things inside. Toc, toc, toc, crshhhshshh. The pestle once again comes down with force. The mortar is as much a witness as an active member of this delicious massacre, lending its walls to be the surface upon which the weapon makes contact. No sound, but a visual: a golden stream of liquid gold, pouring like blood from a wound as Saja stirs it into the rest of the food inside.

14 La Mandràgora is a vegan food association located in the old town of València. It functions as a restaurant, serving lunch and dinner every day. It's run cooperatively and horizontally by all the people that work in it, and is frequently used to organise fundraisers and other kinds of events by the community around it. Antoni and Pau are my friend and my brother, and part of the team that runs the restaurant.

Around the world, mortars and pestles in all kinds of different kitchens hold all kinds of different gossip. Wood or marble or clay packed with flavour packed with secrets packed with care. My mortar tastes of disclosing discomforts, it tastes of dill, of secret makeouts that we shouldn't have found out about, and it tastes of Saja making سلطة غزاوية for us.

RAGE AGAINST THE MACHINE

We're in Javi's house, making dinner with Lorenzo. They suggest using the hand blender to make mayonnaise, but I decline, saying I would rather use a fork. They laugh and point out, "With Anna, we don't need electricity to cook, we do it like in the olden days." I'm constantly reminded that I could do a lot of these processes faster with a *minipiver*, a nutribullet, or a magimix.[15] At the canteen, my boss also laughs at me after spending half an hour chopping a box of red onions: "You could have finished in five minutes with the machine!"

I'm sitting down at the table in the living room. It's almost nine pm, and there are hungry children around me waiting for dinner. València CF is playing against some random team on TV. I don't care very much for football, but my husband is enthusiastically watching it.

I'm stuck in the past. Not because it's better there, not actually stuck. I walk in and out of the past; I inhabit it like I inhabit the present. The gestures I make with *la mà de morter* would otherwise

15 Different brands of food processors.

be lost if I were to give up completely on the past,[16] make the mayonnaise with a hand blender, and surrender to the technological loss of control that characterises our present.[17]

I prepare everything I can while sitting here before I go into the kitchen, in the same way my mother would prepare most of the meal in the courtyard outside her kitchen. Toc, toc, toc, chop an onion; plaf! Lightly smash a couple of garlic cloves; crrrsh, crhhjss, crhss, *"espetega un parell de creïlles"*.[18] Once in the kitchen, everything goes smoothly: olive oil goes into the pressure cooker, then onion and garlic go in. While they're browning, I open two jars: one with deliciously ripe summer tomatoes, and one with chickpeas in cooking liquid. I discard the liquid and rinse the chickpeas.

The point of technology is to be efficient, which in the cooking process affects the quality of the final product. In bread-making, for example, advances in technology have allowed us to produce loaves of bread in under two hours, with quick-acting yeasts and stand mixers. During the slow fermentation that is used in sourdough baking, which can be up to twenty-four hours, the yeast has more time to break down the sugars in the flour, making it easier for

16 "Giard analyzes this shift in relation to cooking, noting the loss of many 'ancient gestures' made obsolete by technology and by the pre- processing of foods before they reach the hands of the consumer. She sees this loss of gesture to be both a bodily and a cognitive de-skilling." David E. Sutton, *Remembrance of Repasts* (London: Bloomsbury Publishing, 2001), 134–135.

17 "Giard [wishes] to find room amidst 'frenetic overmodernization' for the 'reasoned differences' that would resist the contagion of conformism implicit in the replacement of all the local variations of gestures and techniques with the hegemonizing force of technological loss of control." David E. Sutton, *Remembrance of Repasts*, 131–132.

18 A very specific way to cut potatoes I learnt from my mother, where you break off pieces rather than making straight cuts.

your body to digest the final product. I don't want to be efficient, I have no interest in active dry yeast that you can buy in a package at a grocery store. I want to make sourdough bread with complex flavours and deep histories stored in the ancient starter that lives in my fridge.

When I started cooking in La Mandràgora, I was still learning how to cook. There, my colleagues and I would spend afternoons getting to know ingredients together, stirring stews like witches making potions in cauldrons. I had no incentive to be efficient, only to be curious. I took my time, I soaked dry chickpeas in the night so I could cook them in the morning.

Between the strong fire and my distraction with cleaning the chickpeas, I start smelling the onions getting almost too brown, I hear them *queixant-se*.[19] As I stir them and lower the fire, I add a spoonful each of smoked paprika and *pebrella*.[20] Next comes the can of tomatoes, fast so the spices won't burn. I mash up the mixture with a wooden spoon. Now a bay leaf from the branch hanging next to the fridge, the rinsed can of chickpeas, the cut potatoes, and enough water to cover everything by a bit. The cover is placed on tightly and the pot is put on a high heat. Pressure starts building up making everything hot and bubbly. I leave it on and go to do some other task.

Back at home, my mum is always taking shortcuts in the kitchen. She did not have the experience I did when learning how to cook.

19 Meaning "complaining". My mother would always say that the food was complaining when it was making noise.

20 Herb that grows in the mountains close to the Mediterranean along the coast of the Valencian country. Closely related to thyme, though with a harsher flavour.

Instead, she would come home from work to start the second shift,[21] in which she had to make dinner while doing laundry and brooming the floor and cleaning up the dishes and and and and. She was tired from being on her feet all day, so whatever food she could prepare sitting down or speed up with the aid of technology was preferred. My mum taught me a lot of things in the kitchen, but most of all how to enter and exit as soon as possible. She did not want me to have to spend more than the strictly necessary amount of time in front of the fire.

In thirty minutes time I hear the familiar ffffffifiiiiiiiiiii of the steam releasing from inside the pot, and I know now it's only a matter of calling the kids "*a parar la taula*"[22] and sitting down to eat a warm deep plate of *potatge de cigrons*.[23]

Cooking in La Mandràgora was some sort of rebellion against the fast and hurried pace that my mother was forced to have in the kitchen. Even at the height of the rush of dinner service, we never lost our calm, never shouted at each other, never did any of the things that characterise a regular restaurant kitchen. We would meditate while washing plates, pots, and pans by hand.

21 In Marxist-feminist theory, the second shift refers to the labour that women had to perform at home in addition to their waged labour.

22 To set the table.

23 Chickpea stew.

SHHHHHHHH, PLEASE BE QUIET

In my right hand there is a small knife, nothing too fancy. In my left I hold a potato, tenderly.

We're in the space known as Fafu, a studio in the Old School Amsterdam building shared by the students of the DD department. It's May of 2021, and we've spent the past couple of weeks organising here in response to the escalating violence of the settler-colonial entity known as Israel against Palestinians. Today we planned a radio show about institutional solidarity, specifically solidarity with the Palestinian people. The idea for this radio show came from DIWAN,[24] and was organised by us, the DIWAN team, and our tutors, teachers, and comrades Francisca Khamis, Rana Ghavami, and Agustina Woodgate.

Samira and Agustina are on the controls, Ayman is speaking to Farah and Rasha live on air, the rest of the guests and DIWAN team are quietly listening. In the background you can hear Julina, Saja, and I cutting onions and potatoes non-stop: chop chop chop chop. Emirhan came in earlier and asked quietly, so as not to be picked up by the microphones: is there something I can do to help? Why yes, you can peel all of these potatoes! Peel peel peel peel. All of these sounds interfere with the radio show. Ideally, we would have a quiet studio in which to do the show and a separate kitchen where we would cook the food, but the architecture of our space doesn't permit such a luxury; all sounds must share the open air.

24 A platform co-initiated by Fadwa Naamna, Hilda Moucharrafieh, Ehsan Fardjadniya, Margarita Osipian, and Emirhakin.

I sink myself into the potato but not all the way through, then I hold it between my thumb and the knife that is now lodged inside it. Pull, not too hard. I don't want to hurt it, but just a little bit should be fine, like a playful hair-tug given at the right moment to a lover willing to receive it. The potato snaps to reveal a beautiful, awkward shape with a sharp and uneven edge. I hear a familiar tak, tak, tak, tak ... At the same time I'm *espetegant* the potatoes, Julina is next to me chopping onions.

We're trying to make as little noise as possible. Somebody shushes us and I frown. Have you ever tried to cut potatoes quietly? It's the most annoying task. But there's no wasting time, just as the radio show is working through their grid, the kitchen is working through our schedule: if these potatoes are not cut right now the *truita* won't be on the table when the show finishes.

Fssssssfsfsssss ... Bits and pieces of veggies hit the hot oil, gradually becoming soft, tender, sweet, and warm (too warm! Ouch, it hurts). Tactac, grgrshhh, plop: out comes an egg from its shell into a bowl.

In this intimate setting of the radio show I can really focus and feel the way that care is exercised within this specific group of people. It's now been almost three weeks dedicated to exercising solidarity with Palestine in whatever ways we know how. These days, the studio smells of the coffee Ayman is constantly making. Agustina, Miquel, and Fran come by in the evening to help us make stencils and spray paint banners for the protests in which we all walk, sing, chant, and scream together. Ott, Gaber, and I work on a website-archive about the events that have been happening.[25] Brent from the silkscreen workshop and Juni from the Asian Union help

25 www.disarm.design

us take over the Rietveld billboard in a week's notice. Agustina tells us her radio station is one of the many mirroring the Sonic Liberation Front broadcast from Radio AlHara.[26] These days, the air feels electric.

Xup xup xuuppp gggszggzgg xup. The egg-potato-onion mixture is now on the fire, complaining and protesting. It hurts to touch hot oil, I understand. The microphones pick up the cries from the food in the pan. We lower the temperature, the radio show doesn't need to hear how badly the hot oil is hurting the *truita*.[27] A plate goes on top of the pan. Julina and I look at each other, we can't talk out loud but our eyes communicate in place of our mouths. I see confidence in her eyes as she gives me a nod as if to say "go ahead, you know how to do this". I do, she's right, but god is it nerve-wracking to flip a *truita*. One swift motion and it's on the plate, no mess left behind. Bravo. Back on the fire it goes, three minutes should suffice now. I think everyone is looking at the clock now that almost three hours of non-stop talking have passed and the distracting delicious smell of love is floating around the room. First one done, we have a few more to go. We start slinging them out non-stop until we're out of potato-egg-onion mixture. We make it just in time.

Back on the radio, they're on the last segment. Ayman is talking about how to implement the cultural boycott we've called for, and what the next steps are beyond a statement of solidarity from the school. Afterwards, Margarita signs us off –

26 The Sonic Liberation Front is an initiative by a group of sound platforms and sound artists who came together to unify their sound for Palestine and protest against the ethnic cleansing of the Palestinian people.

27 Potato and onion omelette.

Of course thank all the people who were present with us here whose voices you heard but also thank all the people whose voices you didn't hear. Agustina and Samira who organised the radio amazingly. This was a big thing to do because we had to have zoom looped in, we had to have all twelve of us be able to hear each other, so big big thank you for that. And thank you to Francisca and Rana from Disarming Design for the amazing organising work and the support work to make this happen, to put it together. All that little connectivity work is, like, really so vital to keeping everyone sane but also supporting one another and really redistributing the kind of labour that it takes to have solidarity to each other. And of course cooking work. So to Anna, Julina, and Saja who are cooking, I watched them flip a tortilla *really beautifully. So, thank you, thank you so much. That's the stuff that really sustains us and these conversations that help us really feel like we have allies and also can be critical with each other and really deal with these complexities that are present and yeah, anyways, complexities in a good way. I mean I think we should embrace the complexities and not use it as a way to refuse so yes just ... Just a lot of love to everyone that's here with us. I know for some of us, well for a lot of us, it's also very personal, for some of you it's really directly personal, and that is also really often quite difficult to process. So just a big thank you for also the kind of emotional work that has been done. And to all the students at Disarming Design, the three of you have been here with us which is amazing, and then I know that you've also been fed by your fellow students as well. So yes, that's what I want to say.*[28]

As she says goodbye, we start hearing the first notes of the music set Sarah has prepared to end the show. And what have we learned?

During these months of political action in our studio, there was always someone cooking, making coffee, someone taking care of the rest. We were lucky enough that, in this group, people have enough sensibility to understand when you have to pick up the task of cooking or the task of cleaning. Silvia Federici tells us that all the work we do that is sustaining and reproductive is devalued and fails to be recognised or properly remunerated under capitalism.[29] In spaces like this radio show, I don't ever feel devalued when doing care-labour. Somehow, though, there is a tendency to blend into the background and become invisible, even when running a noisy kitchen in the middle of a radio show. Reclaiming these spaces, these actions, and this work can teach us so much of what it means to organise, and can help us better understand what it means to care.

... Reproductive work, insofar as it is the material basis of our life and the first terrain on which we can practice our capacity for self-government, is the 'ground zero of revolution'.[30]

28 Goodbye speech from Margarita before we heard the music set by Sarah to dismiss the show: archive.org/details/institutional-solidarity-set.

29 Jordan Kisner, "*The lockdown showed how the economy exploits women. She already knew,*" The New York Times, February 17, 2021, www.nytimes.com/2021/02/17/magazine/waged-housework.html.

30 Silvia Federici, *Re-enchanting the World: Feminism and the Politics of the Commons* (California: PM Press, 2018), 499.

There is a sense of urgency in the air around me, like we are waiting for a cataclysm (a revolution? The collapse? Perhaps the fall of the empire?). Until this bang comes (and probably during, and after), we will have to keep organising and tending to our needs. We will have to keep the people around us fed, safe, clean, and cared for.

A TAULA!

I'm so grateful you came and sat with me to taste all the singularities of this kitchen: the voices inside the tools I use, the gossip that coats the pots and pans in my kitchen like a thick layer of seasoning, the food processor that sits in the corner dusty and mostly untouched, the rustle of lots of people cooking together in a tiny space ...

Just one last thing! I'm missing the dessert: poached pear.

Sweet, soft, romantic. It smells strong from the wine and warm from the spices, when you bite into it you meet almost no resistance, and once your tongue hugs the flesh it's a perfect balance of the sweet fruit and sour alcohol. If you are naughty and love the indulgence as much as I do, perhaps you'll eat it with a hint of flaky sea salt that enhances all the flavours within, and adds a satisfying textural contrast.

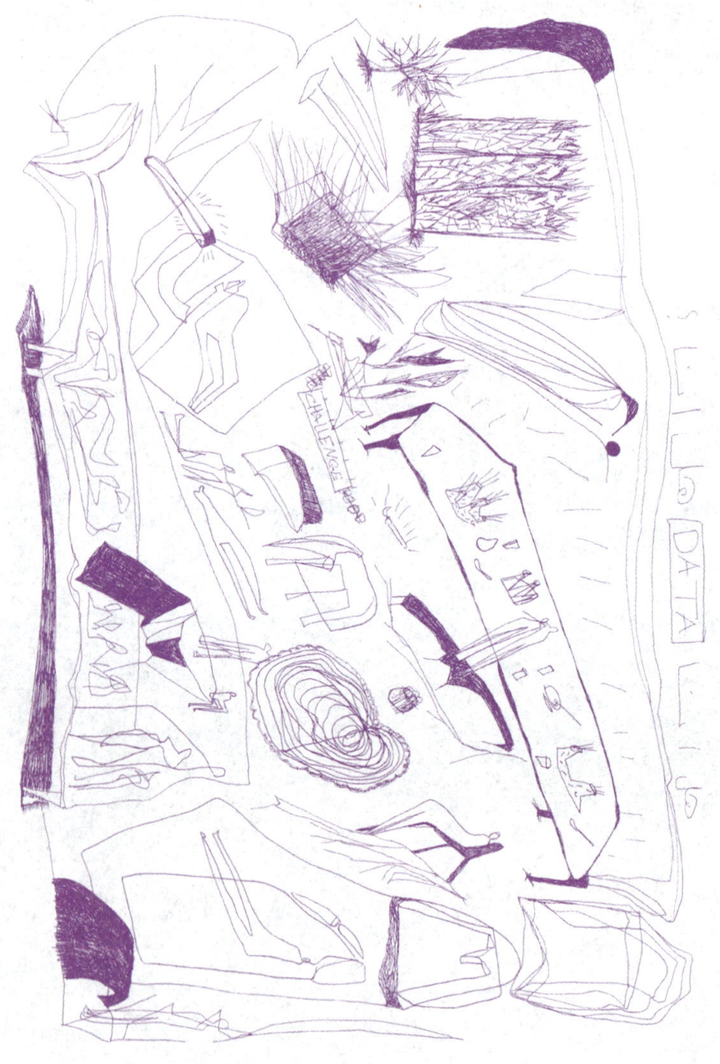
CHALLENGE
DATA

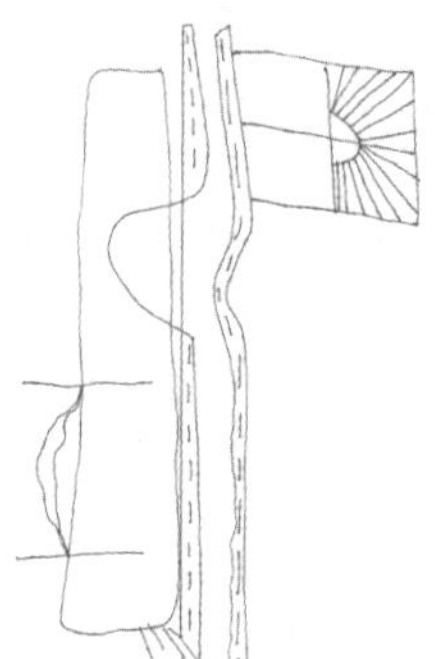

As the postgraduate programme of the Gerrit Rietveld Academie, Amsterdam, the Sandberg Instituut offers Master Programmes in Fine Arts, Interior Architecture, and Design. The five Main Departments aim to deepen the practices of artists, designers, and critics. In addition, the Temporary Programmes reflect on specific urgencies in society and the arts, and the Hosted Programmes focus on collaboration with other institutes.

The Temporary Programme Disarming Design, running from 2020 to 2022, is committed to cooking, making, weaving, screening, giving, talking, playing, mapping, workshopping, sensing, celebrating, tripping, documenting, witnessing, juxtaposing, translating, transposing, publishing, and unfolding. 'Disarming' positions design as a cultural tool to oppose authority, and to create knowledge with affection, desire, and imagination. The curriculum aims to question, challenge, and locate the emancipatory potential of design and other organisational art forms. We uphold artistic practices that deal with conditions of anti-coloniality, activism, and entangled histories, and operate at the intersection of crafts, language, architecture, community, politics, and translation.

Disarming Design is conceived as a studio-led programme where students receive feedback from peers and tutors on their research, projects, and practices. The programme focuses primarily on the artistic work of the participants, in which they find their own methods, language, and tools. In addition, collective and participatory projects are introduced by the department and its network. The structure of the curriculum is open, taking its final shape in response to the different initiatives, collaborations, and developments occurring across the two years.

Students
Lama Aloul, Saja Amro, Julina Vanille Bezold, Anna Celda, Rasha Dakkak, Farah Fayyad, Mohamed Gaber, Ayman Hassan, Siwar Kraitem, Ott Metusala, Naira Nigrelli, Karmel Sabri, Qusai Al Saify, Sarah Saleh, Mohammed Tatour, Jara van Teeffelen, Samira Vogel

Head of department
Annelys de Vet

Coordinator
Francisca Khamis Giacoman

Tutors
Hannes Bernard, Flavia Dzodan, Rana Ghavami, Lara Khaldi, Yazan Khalili, Sherida Kuffour, PING (Miquel Hérvas Gómez, Agustina Woodgate, Sascha Krischock), Huda Smitshuijzen-AbiFarès, Jonas Staal

Guests
Tunde Adefioye, Hazem Alqaddi, Anna Arov, Salim Bayri, Jurgen Bey, Lila Bullen Smith, Cara Crisler, Foundland (Lauren Alexander, Ghalia Elsrakbi), Loraine Furter, Anja Groten, Jeanne van Heeswijk, Brigitte Herremans, Aram Lee, Juliette Lizotte, Sekai Makoni, Liza Prins, Ana Teixeira Pinto, Helena Sanders, Bahia Shehab, Slavs & Tatars, Julien Thomas, Robin Vanbesien, Petra Van Brabandt, Daniel van der Velden

Sandberg Instituut
Master of Art and Design
Fred. Roeskestraat 98
1076 ED Amsterdam
The Netherlands

www.sandberg.nl/
temporaryprogramme-disarming-design

Durable Discussions
essays from the Disarming Design Department
Onomatopee 230, ISBN 978-94-93148-88-8

Authors
Lama Aloul, Saja Amro, Julina Vanille Bezold, Anna Celda, Rasha Dakkak, Farah Fayyad, Mohamed Gaber, Ayman Hassan, Siwar Kraitem, Ott Metusala, Naira Nigrelli, Karmel Sabri, Qusai Al Saify, Sarah Saleh, Mohammed Tatour, Jara van Teeffelen, Samira Vogel

Essay tutors
Rana Ghavami, Sherida Kuffour

Proof reading
Harriet Foyster

Editorial team
Rasha Dakkak, Rana Ghavami, Miquel Hervás Gómez, Annelys de Vet

Graphic Design team
Rasha Dakkak, Miquel Hervás Gómez, Siwar Kraitem, Ott Metusala, Mohammed Tatour

Illustations cover & index
Mohammed Tatour

Production
Ott Metusala

Fonts
KTF Rublena
Mizan ميزان
EB Garamond
Akkurat-Mono

Print & bound
Printon OÜ

Edition
1.000

Publisher
Onomatopee
onomatopee.net
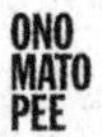

Generously supported by
Stichting Brave New Works

Acknowledgements
BB BookBinding Workshop (GRA/SI), Gemeente Amsterdam, Leonhard-Woltjer Stichting, Lutfia Rabbani Foundation

We want to thank the generous readers Anna Arov, Hannes Bernard, Lila Bullen Smith, Miquel Hérvas Gómez, Lara Khaldi, Yazan Khalili, Francisca Khamis Giacoman, Aram Lee, Liza Prins, Helena Sanders, Jonas Staal, Annelys de Vet, Agustina Woodgate, and you*

Creative commons
creative commons

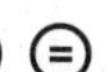
Based on the Creative Commons Attribution-Noncommercial-NoDerivatives 4.0 International license (CC BY-NC-ND 4.0) anyone may freely copy, distribute, and present 'Durable Discussions' and the works in it, under the following terms:
• Attribution — You must give appropriate credit, provide a link to the license, and indicate if changes were made. You may do so in any reasonable manner, but not in any way that suggests the licensor endorses you or your use.
• NonCommercial — You may not use the material for commercial purposes.
• NoDerivatives — If you remix, transform, or build upon the material, you may not distribute the modified material.
• No additional restrictions — You may not apply legal terms or technological measures that legally restrict others from doing anything the license permits.